TO LOOK LIKE AMERICA

TO LOOK LIKE AMERICA

---

*Dismantling Barriers for Women
and Minorities in Government*

Katherine C. Naff
San Francisco State University

Routledge
Taylor & Francis Group
New York London

First published 2001 by Westview Press

Published 2018 by Routledge
711 Third Avenue, New York, NY 10017, USA
2 Park Square, Milton Park, Abingdon, Oxon OX14 4RN

Routledge is an imprint of the Taylor & Francis Group, an informa business

Library of Congress Cataloging-in-Publication Data
Naff, Katherine C.
   To look like America : dismantling barriers for women and minorities in government / Katherine C. Naff.
      p.   cm.
   Includes bibliographical references and index.
   ISBN 0-8133-6763-8
   1. Women in the civil service—United States.   2. Civil service—Minority employment—United States.   I. Title.

JK721.N34 2001
352.6'5'080973—dc21

                                                            00-053178

ISBN 13: 978-0-8133-6763-7 (pbk)

Contents

Tables and Figures

Figures

Acknowledgments

Numerous people provided support, encouragement, and advice as I wrote this book. Thus I have decided to recognize these persons in loose order of appearance, like the character credits in a film. My list begins with a very talented group of analysts at the U.S. Merit Systems Protection Board, where I had the privilege of working for eight years shortly after coming into the federal government. They included Evangeline Swift, John Palguta, Bruce Mayor, Keith Bell, Jamie Carlyle, John Crum, Ligaya Fernandez, Lit Foley, Charles Friedman, Karen Gard, Carol Hayashida, Annette Johnson, Harry Redd, and Paul van Rijn. I can think of few greater professional opportunities than working with this exceptional group of very intelligent people who along with their insights provided me the opportunity to pursue much of the research described here. Another MSPB colleague, Dianne Clode, helped with the book proposal. I especially want to thank John Crum, with whom I have written several research papers and articles. John also coauthored an earlier version of Chapter 2.

Next are the faculty at Georgetown University who, in addition to giving me a fantastic grounding in my Ph.D. program, provided invaluable guidance and help, notably Sue Thomas, my adviser, William Gormley, Diana Owen, Mark Rom, and Clyde Wilcox. I would also like to mention John Samples, formerly of Georgetown University Press and now with the Cato Institute for his helpful advice and support. Also during my time in Washington, I want to acknowledge Linda Batts at the U.S. Customs Service, Wilett Bunton with the National Partnership for Reinventing Government, Frank Ferris of the National Treasury Employees Union, Robert Heim at the Office of Personnel Management, and Tim Clark of *Government Executive* magazine for their counsel and assistance.

I have also been fortunate in having many wonderful colleagues in academia. I am particularly indebted to David Rosenbloom at the American University, Mary Ellen Guy at Florida State University, J. Edward Kellough at the University of Georgia, Brian Pollins at Ohio State University, Carolyn Ban at the University of Pittsburgh, Audrey Mathews at Cal State University–San Bernardino, Matti Dobbs at San Diego State University,

Dennis Daley at North Carolina State University, Norma Riccucci at SUNY–Albany, Samantha Durst at the University of North Texas, Meredith Newman at the University of Washington–Vancouver, and Gregory Lewis at Georgia State. Many of these colleagues provided opportunities to write and collaborate on research; all of them have shared ideas and encouragement. I met many of these colleagues through my affiliation with the Conference of Minority Public Administrators and the Section on Women in Public Administration, two organizations within the American Society for Public Administration that I would like to single out for providing a continuing forum for dialogue and learning on the topics of race and gender and equal opportunity in the public sector.

Last in order of appearance are my colleagues at San Francisco State University—Genie Stowers, Joel Kassiola, Frank Scott, Richard DeLeon, Ray Pomerleau, Chris Bettinger, and Carol Edlund, and my other colleagues on the public administration faculty who have helped me both make the transition to full-time academic life and continue, as good colleagues often do, to provide an invaluable sounding board for new ideas and questions about an array of topics. I am deeply in their debt. I would be remiss if I did not mention my graduate students at SFSU, whose provocative questions have helped shape my thinking on the issues addressed in this book.

Other thanks are due. Leo Wiegman of Westview Press was a true pleasure to work with. Melissa Leavitt provided assistance with methodological and substantive issues. Finally, there is my family, and especially my husband, Al Hyde, whose confidence in me always seemed boundless. My deepest thanks to them for making it all worthwhile.

Katherine C. Naff

Introduction

———

The importance of a representative bureaucracy has long been emphasized in the scholarly literature analyzing the role of a bureaucracy in a democratic polity (e.g., Kingsley 1944; Levitan 1946; Long 1952; Krislov 1967, 1974; Krislov and Rosenbloom 1981). One of the many reasons articulated for a representative bureaucracy is the role that a diverse civil service plays in demonstrating that varied communities have input into decisions regarding policies and benefit allocation through these representatives. In recognition of the symbolic and substantive importance of this concept, President Bill Clinton took office in 1993 promising to create a government that "looks like America" (Weiner 1994).

He was not the first to recognize the value of diversity in government. Providing a "federal work force reflective of the nation's diversity" became the official policy of the U.S. government with the passage of the Civil Service Reform Act of 1978. The act also directed agencies to take steps to eliminate the underrepresentation of women and people of color in all federal occupations and at all grade levels (5 U.S.C. § 7201). Agencies now measure and report annually their progress toward achieving full representation of women and people of color in each grade level and occupational category.

This book begins with the assumption that if the government is to serve the goals envisioned by the theory of representative bureaucracy, analysis must go beyond simply looking at whether women and people of color hold an adequate number of government jobs. A more complete investigation requires examining whether the environments in which federal employees work are inclusive; that is, whether people of color and women are afforded the same authority and opportunities as their Euro-American male counterparts.

Previous research suggests that organizational dynamics sometimes tilt the playing field to the disadvantage of "nonmainstream" groups, often in subtle and even unintended ways. The question this book addresses is the extent to which such dynamics limit the inclusion of people of color and women within the federal bureaucracy. It asks what barriers, if any, stand

1

in the way of equal opportunities for the advancement and inclusion of women and people of color in federal agencies. It shows how empirical measures of the status, attitudes, perceptions, and experiences of federal employees can be employed to answer this question.

A primary audience for this book is researchers interested in investigating the extent to which the federal government is fulfilling its promise to be a "representative" institution. As discussed in greater depth in Chapter 1, this book adds a different dimension to the growing body of literature assessing the benefits of a representative bureaucracy. It does so by suggesting that such benefits can only be expected to emerge once women and people of color have the unfettered opportunity for full participation within the bureaucracy.

Another audience is executives and policy analysts charged with "managing diversity" in their organizations. A third is students enrolled in the growing number of public administration and human resource management programs that address workforce diversity as a stand-alone course or as part of a course on personnel policy. Current projections are that the U.S. workforce will become increasingly diverse over the next decade. As such, it is imperative that practitioners (or soon-to-be practitioners) learn how to respond to real or perceived barriers to the inclusion and advancement of women and people of color in their organizations. Although the analyses performed here are based on federal employment data, this book can also be of use to those concerned about representation and diversity in state and local governments, and even in private sector organizations. The methodology employed here, intended to identify and measure potential barriers to the full inclusion of women and people of color, can be replicated in any organization.

A Note on Terminology

The term *people of color* as used in this book refers to the four race/ethnic groups defined in the Office of Management and Budget's Directive 15, adopted May 12, 1977. They are African Americans, Latinos, Asian Pacific Islanders, and Native Americans (including Alaskan Natives). The term *minority* is generally not used because in some situations people of color may represent the majority. Although there may be others who consider themselves "of color," including people of biracial descent, this analysis is limited to these groups because the available data are limited in this respect.

Clearly, there are limitations to aggregating data in such a way. Even aggregating all Asian Pacific Americans or all Latinos together is not ideal because there is considerable variation within these groups. At times, small sample sizes make even that level of aggregation problematic, and so the four groups are combined into one category, people of color. Such aggregation is unfortunate but necessary to identify whether there are patterns suggesting barriers to the advancement and inclusion of members of these groups.

The term *Euro-American* is used to represent people of European descent who are often just referred to as "whites." The term *white* is not used, as many Latinos are also white. There are frequent references in this text to "women and people of color." *Women,* of course, includes both Euro-American women and women of color; the use of that term is not meant to imply mutually exclusive categories.

Why Women and People of Color?

Women and people of color are not the only nonmainstream groups in the federal workforce. People with disabilities, gays and lesbians, and older workers are examples of other groups that may confront barriers to inclusion or unequal opportunities. Indeed, in some situations Euro-American men believe they are at a disadvantage in organizations that prioritize the achievement of a diverse workforce. However, to give this book a manageable focus, only the disadvantages that women and people of color face are addressed here. This is in part because the well-documented history of discrimination based on race/ethnicity and gender in the government and in the nation as a whole (Fernandez 1999; King 1995) gives these characteristics particular political salience.

The fact that differences in treatment persist despite the numerous laws and regulations developed to combat sexism and racism is testament to the durability of these attributes in defining opportunities in the workplace (Fernandez 1999; Morrison 1992). Ann Morrison argues, "We need to pass through this lengthy, frustrating introductory course in diversity in order to make any meaningful headway in fostering a broader version of diversity" (Morrison 1992, 9). Moreover, the base of knowledge about these groups and the kinds of barriers they face is more developed, so the findings from previous research can be more readily applied (Cox 1994).

But if race/ethnicity and sex are the primary attributes to be addressed in this book, why not deal with differences in treatment experienced by Euro-American men? Indeed, the current administration's focus on achieving a government that "looks like America" has resulted in some Euro-American men charging that they are victims of "reverse discrimination" (Goshko 1994; Bridger 1994). It is certainly possible that the emphasis on correcting the underrepresentation of women and minorities has at times thwarted the aspirations of Euro-American men.

Considerable research, however, over the last few decades has revealed that their majority status in high-level positions in most organizations has accorded Euro-American men, in general, many advantages not available to people of color and women. For example, Euro-American men are much more likely than women and people of color to be given career-enhancing assignments, to be assigned to high-potential jobs, and to have access to networks that provide information, feedback, and contacts. Because they have held high-level positions in greater numbers for so long, they enjoy a presumption that they have the attributes required of successful managers, whereas people of color and women are assumed to lack these qualities (for a summary of this research, see Dugan et al. 1993).

The Euro-American male majority has been able to define the workplace culture to which women and people of color must adapt or be excluded (Rowe 1990; Fernandez 1999). Moreover, research has shown that unlike women, who face disadvantages when they form a minority in organizations or hold traditionally male jobs, similarly situated men are not disadvantaged, and sometimes even benefit from such a status (Ruble, Cohen, and Ruble 1984; Williams 1992; Crocker and McGraw 1984; Butler and Geis 1990). Research has further suggested that while reverse discrimination against Euro-American men does take place, it occurs much less frequently than discrimination against women and people of color (Burstein and Monaghan 1986; Burstein 1992; Merida 1995).

Overview of Contents

Chapter 1 provides the book's background and context. It begins with a brief history of the development of equal employment opportunity and affirmative action policies within government employment. It also describes the origin and development of the theory of representative bureaucracy and the definitional and measurement issues that have plagued efforts to assess whether the U.S. federal bureaucracy is representative. The chapter discusses the current status of research that focuses on the extent to which bureaucrats do represent their constituents, suggesting that such an assessment is premature until a more fundamental question can be addressed: Do representatives from all segments of society enjoy full participation in the bureaucracy, or are there are factors limiting their complete engagement?

Chapters 2 and 3 examine leadership barriers, or the extent to which those in positions to shape hiring and promotion decisions believe that a representative bureaucracy has value. An important question addressed in this section is whether support or lack of support for that concept has a measurable impact on the demographics of the workforce. Many women and people of color believe that their increasing representation in the federal workforce and at higher levels came to a halt under the administrations of Reagan and Bush, whereas many Euro-American men believe the

Clinton administration has dampened their prospects for advancement. Chapter 2 undertakes an empirical assessment of the extent to which the "macro-political environment," as defined by the president and his ideology, has actually affected the hiring and advancement of Euro-American men and women and men and women of color.

Although the president's ideology may be important, the representation of various racial/ethnic groups and men and women in the government is really the direct result of the thousands of individual hiring and promotion decisions made by supervisors and managers every year. Arguably, then, opportunities for women and people of color may also depend on the extent to which those supervisors and managers support the goal of achieving a diverse civil service at all levels, or the micro-internal climate. Chapter 3 undertakes an assessment of supervisors' attitudes and how they affect the likelihood of supervisors to attempt to recruit individuals from groups that are underrepresented in their work units.

Chapters 4 and 5 examine human resource management processes that affect the opportunities for the inclusion, advancement, and retention of women and people of color. Can we be assured that formal policies that bar discrimination in hiring, promotion, firing, and other personnel actions are enough to ensure that less formal policies or practices do not have an adverse impact on women or people of color? Chapter 4 addresses the "glass ceiling," the subtle barriers to the advancement of women and people of color in government. It uses data from two government-wide surveys to identify formal and informal criteria for advancement and suggests ways in which such criteria may limit promotion opportunities for women and people of color.

Advancement is not the only arena in which many people of color and women find themselves at a disadvantage. It is also the case that people of color—more specifically African Americans, Native Americans, and Latinos—are much more likely than Euro-Americans or Asian Pacific Americans to be subject to disciplinary action or be fired from their federal jobs. In Chapter 5, this apparent disparate impact of the disciplinary system provides a focus for a discussion of the ways in which race/ethnicity continues to affect relationships between supervisors and employees in the workplace.

Chapters 6 and 7 address the ways in which the work environment may indirectly affect employees' inclusivity and advancement potential by shaping their views of their own opportunities. Chapter 6 examines "subjective discrimination," the perceptions on the part of many women and people of color that their opportunities are limited because of their gender and/or race/ethnicity. It evaluates the circumstances under which such perceptions are likely to arise and their potentially adverse impact on the career-related decisions of those who experience them. Also of concern in this chapter is the extent to which men and women, and Euro-Americans and people of color, may hold sharply different perceptions of the impact of race/ethnicity and gender in the work environment. This perceptual divide is also examined in Chapter 7, which considers the prevalence and impact of sexual harassment of women in the government. This chapter explores the extent to which heightened attention to the issue in the early 1990s may have affected how men and women view sexual harassment. It further explores women's responses to harassment and the likelihood that they will be harmed by it. These two chapters suggest that even *perceptions* of disparate treatment or sexual harassment can undermine the goals envisioned by the theory of representative bureaucracy when people of color or women respond to such perceptions in a way that increases the likelihood they will leave their organizations and decreases their potential for advancement.

Chapters 8 and 9 shift the focus from barriers to the inclusion and advancement of women and people of color in government to prospects for eliminating those impediments. Chapter 8 examines the various strategies identified in the growing body of literature offering advice as to the best means for managing diversity. It employs a survey administered in the spring of 1999 to federal agencies to identify the efforts they are making in this regard, and their likely success. Chapter 9 concludes with a summary of lessons learned and a discussion of "emerging dimensions" that are likely to have an impact on the government's efforts to achieve a truly representative bureaucracy. These dimensions include the transition to team-based work structures, which some experts believe creates a better climate for diversity.

As the largest employer and enforcer of the nation's laws, the federal government plays a vital role in ensuring it serves as a model equal employment opportunity employer. Continuation of prejudice can undermine its effectiveness as well as its credibility in the eyes of citizens who believe they are denied full participation in the policy-making process (Krislov 1967). Previous research has been deficient in assuming that the government's success in achieving a representative bureaucracy can be evaluated simply based on an examination of the proportion of women and minorities at various grade levels. This book takes this evaluation to the next stage by examining the extent to which factors affecting employee inclusion in organizations are operative within the federal bureaucracy.

1

Why Look Like America?

The principal justification for policy determination by administrative officials in a democratic system is completely destroyed when its personnel are not representative of the heterogeneous American community.

David M. Levitan,
"The Responsibility of Administrative Officials in a Democratic Society,"
Political Science Quarterly *(December 1946)*

With the passage of the Civil Service Reform Act (CSRA) of 1978, Congress called for a "Federal workforce reflective of the nation's diversity" (5 U.S.C. § 2301[b][1]), officially acknowledging the importance of a "representative bureaucracy" for the first time. The theory of representative bureaucracy, explained in greater depth later in this chapter, assumes that by reflecting the demographic makeup of the nation, the government will manifest the values of the citizenry. Judgments made by government officials will be similar to those that would be made had the entire U.S. public been involved in the decision-making process. Representative public agencies also send an important message to citizens by demonstrating that all groups have occasion to participate in making policies that affect their lives. Ann Wexler, an official during the Carter administration who was critical of the inadequate representation of women in the Bush White House, put it this way: "It matters to women observing this Presidency from all over the country. It matters to women in colleges and universities who want to be in government working in public policy. It matters to little girls in the first, second, and third grade looking for role models" (Dowd 1991).

The purpose of this book is to examine policies and practices that may undermine the achievement of the goals envisioned by the theory of representative bureaucracy. This chapter is designed to lay the groundwork for that investigation. It does so first by examining changes in the workforce that have brought heightened attention to the demographic composition of organizations. It then describes the development of the theory of representative bureaucracy and the series of executive orders, statutes, and case law that has at times aided, and at others hindered, public organizations' efforts to achieve representative workforces. The chapter concludes with a discussion of the questions and problems that have engaged researchers interested in this subject and previews the way in which this book fills a void in the extant literature on representative bureaucracy.

The Changing Face of the American Workforce

A report written for the Department of Labor in 1987, *Workforce 2000*, has been described as a "wake up call" to employers across the country. The report, written by researchers with the Hudson Institute, forecasted the key trends that would shape the U.S. workforce and workplace at the end of the twentieth century (Johnston and Packer 1987). A year later, the Hudson Institute furnished a second report for the U.S. Office of Personnel Management, *Civil Service 2000*, which provided a similar analysis for the federal sector (Johnston et al. 1988).

Of particular importance were the Institute's warnings that more women would be entering the workforce, requiring employers to respond by offering new benefits such as day care and alternative work arrangements (e.g., part-time jobs, flexible schedules, work-at-home programs). Moreover, the Institute added, a greater proportion of new entrants into the job market would be people of color. These workers would be less likely to have the skills required for the jobs being created, and they could also have "language, attitude, and cultural problems that prevent them from taking advantage of the jobs that will exist" (Johnston and Packer 1987, xxvi). The federal government was in better shape than private sector corporations, noted the Institute in *Civil Service 2000*, because it was already a leader in the employment of women and people of color. But in both sectors, workplace policies that had been effective for a largely young, Euro-American, male workforce may no longer work as women and people of color become a larger share of the labor force and as the average age of employees rises.

Workforce 2000 was later assailed because it seemed to overstate the extent to which Euro-American men would shrink as a proportion of the labor force (Mishel and Teixera 1991; U.S. General Accounting Office 1992; U.S. Merit Systems Protection Board 1993a). Nevertheless, the two reports induced a flurry of activity and the development of an industry of consultants, books, and videos designed to sensitize employers and employees to the different perspectives and needs of a more diverse workforce.

A decade later, the Hudson Institute published a sequel to *Workforce 2000*, entitled *Workforce 2020*. This report predicts a gradual but continuing diversification of the workforce, suggesting a need for employers to continue to make efforts to "accommodate unconventional working arrangements" (Judy and D'Amico 1997, 8). The report predicts, for example, that by 2020, half of the nation's workforce will be women, up from 46 percent in 1994. It further forecasts that Euro-Americans' share of the workforce will decline from 76 percent to 68 percent in about the same span of time (Judy and D'Amico 1997).

To appreciate the impact of demographic changes in the workforce, it is important to recognize that many formal policies and informal norms in the workplace still in effect today evolved at a time when the workforce in general, and upper management positions in particular, were dominated by Euro-American men. In many workplaces there persists an image of the successful, career-oriented professional as a Euro-American man able and willing to work long hours, travel, and relocate geographically. He is able to do so because he has a wife at home who can manage the household and children.

The growing diversification of the workforce raises questions about the propriety of these policies and norms because they clearly work to the disadvantage of those who don't fit this traditional image. Any employer that is not equipped to tap the full potential of the workforce will likely pay a price in terms of lower motivation, lost productivity, and turnover. However, there are reasons that *public* sector agencies should be even more interested in ensuring that workplace policies do not present barriers to the inclusion and advancement of any segment of the workforce. Those reasons have to do with the notion of a "representative bureaucracy."

The Theory of Representative Bureaucracy

The theory of representative bureaucracy developed at a time when there was concern about the undemocratic nature of executive branch agencies where policy decisions were made by unelected civil servants. Since then, the importance of the theory has grown as the country has become more diverse. This section reviews the development of the concept of representative bureaucracy as an antidote to bureaucratic power in the United States, including its recent focus on the inclusion of women and people of color at all levels in the bureaucracy. It then attempts to sort out a number of conceptual and definitional issues that have plagued the literature on representative bureaucracy.

The Dilemma of Bureaucratic Power in a Democracy

The apparent contradiction between democratic principles and bureaucratic imperatives has troubled scholars since Max Weber described the inevitable "rationalization" of society in the early 1900s. In his essays on bureaucracy, Weber postulated that bureaucracies are a necessary corollary to a democratic society because of the regular, equal, and impersonal way in which they exercise authority. However, bureaucracies also in some ways undermine democratic principles. Bureaucrats exercise authority within a country through developing and implementing policies and yet are not elected by, nor directly accountable to, the citizens. The bureaucracy is powerful because it is a rational, efficient, and precise machine staffed by experts for whom elected representatives are no match (Weber 1968). Fifty years later, Samuel Krislov, writing about the U.S. bureaucracy, summarized the dilemma this way: "Why go through the elaborate razzle-dazzle of elections if the crucial element is the discretion of the bureau chief? More charades are not needed in our society, which is notoriously direct in attitude, but which has more than its share of empty formalism" (Krislov 1974, 35).

An early answer to this conundrum proposed in the United States was a doctrine known as the "politics-administration dichotomy." Promoted by progressive reformers, this doctrine stressed the necessity and desirability of bureaucratic agencies acting independently and free from political concerns. Civil servants would simply use their expertise and efficient methods to carry out the will of the people, according to laws enacted by elected representatives. Woodrow Wilson argued that "administration lies outside the proper sphere of *politics*" and confidently predicted that "this discrimination between administration and politics is now, happily, too obvious to need further discussion" (Wilson 1887, 210–211; see also Gulick 1937; Goodnow 1900; Willoughby 1927; and Hyneman 1950).

However, as the role of government, and consequently the discretion exercised by civil servants, continued to grow in the first half of the twentieth century, it became increasingly unrealistic to believe that civil servants did not have a significant role in the policy formulation and implementation processes. Congressional authorizations that create programs and specify agency power and procedures are generally vague, and most scholars now agree that Congress has neither the time nor the expertise (nor often the political will) to systematically oversee their implementation (Foreman 1988). Consequently, civil servants must exercise considerable discretion in applying these laws on a day-to-day basis. As Wallace Sayre put it: "Great power also belongs naturally to those who carry out the decisions of public policy. In this stage, the career staffs have had a paramount role. The choice of means, the pace, and tone of governmental performance reside largely in the hands of the federal service. Constraints are present, and most of these uses of discretion are subject to bargaining with other participants, but the civil servants have a position of distinct advantage in determining how public policies are executed" (Sayre 1965, 2).

Indeed, it has even been suggested that "government would come to a standstill if our 'closet statesmen' in the civil service suddenly started doing only what they were told" (Storing 1964, 152). Whether this is a positive development is not the issue. The point is that although in theory the public expresses its preferences to elected officials, who pass laws for the bureaucracy to implement, in practice unelected bureaucrats have considerable latitude within those broad mandates. Moreover, they are often the originators of policies that Congress reacts to through accepting, amending, or rejecting their proposals (Ogul 1976).

Once it became apparent that, as Don K. Price (1946, 96–97) put it, "The old proposition that policy and administration are mutually exclusive spheres of activity never fully applied anywhere," various proposals for ensuring that the bureaucracy would be responsive to the will of the people began to emerge. The Brownlow and Hoover commissions sought to ensure bureaucratic accountability by strengthening executive control, in part through appointment of a core of "political executives" by the president. Another proposal suggested that competition and negotiation among different groups within the bureaucracy, influenced by various outside interest groups and clienteles, would produce policies responsive to the people (Mosher 1982). Meanwhile, Congress sought to fortify its oversight of the executive branch agencies with the Legislative Reorganization Act of 1946 (Scher 1963).[1] By the 1970s, discontent with the bureaucracy as being unaccountable and unresponsive (as well as inefficient and ineffective) reached a peak, and a plethora of reforms were enacted designed to enhance the ability of legislators, chief executives, judges, and interest groups to check bureaucratic power (Gormley 1989).

"Representative Bureaucracy" Is Born

Alongside these other proposals for ensuring that the bureaucracy is responsive to the people arose the notion of *representative bureaucracy*. The term is generally attributed to J. Donald Kingsley (1944), who used it when describing his observations of the British civil service during World War II. Kingsley concluded that civil servants in that country had successfully carried out the wishes of the party in power because, due to various civil service reforms, they shared the party leadership's middle class origins. However, the rise to power of the Labour Party in the mid-twentieth century, based in the working class, would be "seriously handicapped in office by a middle-class Civil Service" (Kingsley 1944, 279) because "there are obviously points beyond which a man cannot go in carrying out the will of another" (Kingsley 1944, 278). For Kingsley, the experience of the Weimar Republic was evidence that formal checks and balances were not enough to ensure parliamentary control of the bureaucracy under modern conditions. Kingsley summed up his advocacy of representative bureaucracy as the most effective means for ensuring bureaucratic responsibility thus:

> As a matter of fact, of course, the essence of responsibility is psychological rather than mechanical. It is to be sought in an identity of aim and point of view, in a common background of social prejudice, which leads the agent to act as though he were the principal. . . . But if the essence of responsibility is psychological, the degree to which all democratic institutions are representative is a matter of prime significance. No group can safely be entrusted with power who do not themselves mirror the dominant forces in society; for they will then act in an irresponsible manner or will be liable to corruption at the hands of the dominant groups. (Kingsley 1944, 282–283)

Kingsley did not attempt to apply his theory to the U.S. scene. Nor was his argument particularly well articulated or convincing (Krislov 1974). Nevertheless, it has been said that his greatest contribution was in refocusing attention once again on the human composition of bureaucracies (Rosenbloom 1977). Other scholars then adopted his term, gave it greater clarity, and did so within the U.S. context.

Bureaucracy in the American Context

Although Kingsley has been credited with the articulation of the term *representative bureaucracy,* the idea that the bureaucracy is a political institution that should represent someone was not new. Thomas Jefferson sought to make his appointments to the civil service reflective of the partisan composition of the nation, and Andrew Jackson took steps toward making it more representative sociologically (Rosenbloom 1971). The Civil Service (Pendleton) Act of 1883 envisioned geographic representation, calling for civil service jobs to be "apportioned among the several States and Territories and the District of Columbia" (U.S. Civil Service Commission 1973). Moreover, David Rosenbloom (1977) argues that the introduction of the "merit system" into public personnel administration was also undertaken to accomplish political objectives. The reformers who called for merit-based hiring were mainly interested in displacing the "professional politicians" who were dominating the national political scene, in part through their appointments (Rosenbloom 1977, 32–33). Another example of a political purpose served by the civil service is the preference that veterans receive in appointment; a practice that has been attributed to the importance of veteran voting power as well as humanitarian objectives (Van Riper 1958, 271).

The first scholar to apply the concept of representative bureaucracy to the U.S. scene was David Levitan (Meier 1975). In his essay on administrative responsibility, Levitan (1946) contended that external controls on bureaucracies were ineffective in the service state and would likely "introduce a rigidity fatal to essential resiliency and flexibility" (Levitan 1946, 582). To make the bureaucracy more responsible, he argued, it is essential that it be representative of American society.

Norton Long (1952) went even further, suggesting that the bureaucracy has the capacity to be more broadly representative of the country and therefore more democratic than the Congress. Arguing that a representative bureaucracy contains a balance of social forces that ensures that it behaves responsibly and learns from its mistakes, he wrote, "Given the system of parties and primaries, rural overrepresentation, seniority rule, interest-dominated committees, and all the devices that give potent minorities a disproportionate say, it should occasion no surprise if Congress' claim exclusively to voice what the people want be taken with reservations. . . . The rich diversity that makes up the United States is better represented in its civil service than anywhere else" (Long 1952, 814–815).

Although Kenneth Meier (1975) suggests that Long's "extreme" theory of representative bureaucracy created a straw person for numerous critics, the theory continued to gain adherents among students of the American bureaucracy. Paul Van Riper, for example, suggested that "the concept of *representative bureaucracy* may be a most useful major addition to our arsenal of weapons bearing on the problem of administrative responsibility" (Van Riper 1958, 551). Defining a representative bureaucracy as "a body of officials which is broadly representative of the society in which it functions, and which in social ideals is as close as possible to the grass roots of the nation" (Van Riper 1958, 552), Van Riper, like Long, saw the U.S. federal bureaucracy as largely meeting this definition.

On the other hand, the concept was not without its critics. Some took issue with the underlying assumption that bureaucrats carry the values they have acquired from their social origins into the bureaucracy with them. If they don't, a representative bureaucracy may not, in fact, actively ensure that all interests in society are given due consideration (Subramanian 1967; Larson 1973; Meier 1975). Moreover, critics argued, it is unclear in a pluralist society whom the bureaucracy should represent (Larson 1973; Meier 1975). These critics also took issue with Van Riper's (1958) contention that the U.S. civil service fits the definition of a representative bureaucracy (Meier 1975; Larson 1973).

It is not surprising, then, that when Samuel Krislov reviewed the literature on representative bureaucracy (1967, 57–58), he concluded that it had not been adequately discussed nor justified. In summarizing the benefits of a representative civil service, however, he went beyond the notion that it simply serves as a means for checking bureaucratic power. Krislov suggested that a representative bureaucracy acts as a funnel for divergent points of view. It is also more likely to have diverse skills and talents, making it better able to deal with a wider variety of social problems. In addition, a representative bureaucracy ensures that social responsibility is shared, leading to a greater acceptance of governmental policies. It brings members of the segments of the society holding civil service positions a broader social point of view, which is in turn transmitted back to the group they represent.

Moreover, because governmental employment offers a coveted economic and social status, the extent to which that employment is shared provides an index of the concentration of power, the lack of access to which serves as an affront to unincluded groups (Krislov 1967, 57–58). The importance of a representative bureaucracy lies not just in its function as a mirror of the community. Rather, "bureaucracies by their very structure represent truths about the nature of the societies they administer and the values that dominate them" (Krislov 1967, 64).

Finally, Krislov argued, the composition of the bureaucracy has an impact on social conduct and future behavior in a society. If a particular community doesn't see its members represented among officeholders, its youth sees no point in investing financially or psychically in education or in gaining other prerequisites for those offices, and thus a cycle is perpetuated (Krislov 1967, 63–64). It is this self-generating cycle of signaling a lack of opportunity, in turn leading to reluctance to test that reality, that conscious efforts to achieve a representative bureaucracy can break.

To these reasons, Harry Kranz (1974) added others: A representative bureaucracy increases democracy internal to the organizations, reduces bureaucratic pathology through increased reliance on equity and individual human factors, provides a more efficient and just use of America's human resources, and increases stability by reducing alienation and apathy among people of color. Lois Wise (1990) further suggested that it allows a large portion of citizens to develop their political skills and to achieve the sense of public spirit that binds them to the political system. In one of the few studies that have examined clients' perspectives, Gregory Thielemann and Joseph Stewart (1996) found that persons living with AIDS cared if they received services from people of the same ethnic group. In other words, a representative bureaucracy, originally conceived as a means for ensuring bureaucratic accountability, has been extended to serve many other important purposes in a democratic polity as well.

Thus, for these scholars, many of the criticisms of the concept of representative bureaucracy were irrelevant, because its role extends beyond the purpose envisioned by early theorists: ensuring democratic accountability. A representative bureaucracy expands the participation of broad groups in society, thereby increasing the bureaucracy's effectiveness and legitimacy. The other way in which the theory of representative bureaucracy evolved was from suggesting that it mirror the population in terms of its many social attributes to focusing more narrowly on representation in terms of race/ethnicity and sex.

The Salience of Race and Sex in the American Bureaucracy

When J. Donald Kingsley espoused the importance of a representative bureaucracy in his now-classic work (1944), he was speaking of the importance of a civil service that reflects the class origins of the nation. Indeed, this same theme was carried through early analyses of the representativeness of the U.S. bureaucracy, which concluded that it was largely representative (see, for example, Long 1952; Van Riper 1958; Subramaniam 1967).

By the 1960s and 1970s, however, the bureaucracy's representativeness was being evaluated in terms of the extent to which women and people of color are represented in the civil service. Harry Krantz, for example, wrote, "By a 'representative' bureaucracy, I refer to one in which the ratio of each minority group in a government agency equals that group's percentage in the population in the area served by that office" (Krantz 1974, 435).

Given the importance of race in American society, an issue that reached its zenith and culminated in the passage of the Civil Rights Act of 1964 (Carmines and Stimson 1989), it is perhaps no wonder that an apparently seamless transition in the literature on representative bureaucracy occurred at this time. Representation in terms of social origins shifted to a focus on the representation of people of color (see also Krislov 1974; Rosenbloom 1977). Similarly, the entrance of substantial numbers of women into the labor force, coinciding with a decline in women's legal and social dependence on men, resulted in their demands for equal access to civil service positions (Hale and Kelly 1989). Even some critics of the concept of representative bureaucracy acknowledged that "correcting serious deficiencies in [the] pattern of representation—with respect to women and minority groups, for example," would make a "significant contribution to the responsiveness of the bureaucracy" (Larson 1973, 88).

In his history of federal equal employment opportunity, David H. Rosenbloom notes, "It is an interesting coincidence that the 1940s saw both the development of the first Federal Equal Employment Opportunity Program and the beginning of the formation of modern concepts of representative bureaucracy" (Rosenbloom 1977, 35). Indeed, the importance of a bureaucracy that is representative of the gender, racial, and ethnic composition of the nation can best be appreciated in light of the history of discrimination against women and people of color inside and outside the bureaucracy.

At one time, for example, Congress passed legislation providing that only "free White people" could be employed as mail carriers (Krislov 1967). Similarly, although women began entering bureaucratic employment in the late nineteenth century, they were not ensured equal pay for equal work until passage of the Classification Act of 1923. Steps were not taken to prohibit discrimination against women in other federal personnel policies until 1962 (Hellriegal and Short 1972). Until 1971, appointing officials had the right to request a list of qualified candidates for some kinds of jobs by sex (U.S. Civil Service Commission 1973).[2]

Discrimination in federal employment mirrored discrimination occurring in society as a whole. That historical discrimination has attached particular political salience to race and gender. Edward Carmines and James Stimson argue, "Race, with its deep symbolic meaning in American political history has touched a raw nerve in the body politic" (Carmines and Stimson 1989, 14). Others have argued that ethnicity and sex are similarly "lines of division" that have particular relevance to contemporary politics (Krislov 1974, Rosenbloom 1977).

Further underscoring the need for the federal bureaucracy to ensure its own house is in order with respect to the fair treatment of women and people of color is its own role in enforcing equal employment opportunity (EEO) in the nation as a whole. The Department of Labor, for example, is responsible for monitoring the compliance with equal employment opportunity laws of private sector companies of a certain size contracting with the government, an oversight responsibility it exercises through a yearly cycle of several thousand compliance reviews (U.S. Department of Labor 1991a). Failure of the government to hold itself to the same standards to which it holds non-government employers can, and has, brought it under severe criticism (see, for example, Borjas 1978).

In summary, the history of discrimination against women and people of color within and outside the federal government; the high political salience of race, ethnicity, and sex; and the role of the government as the enforcer of EEO laws and regulations are all factors that accent the importance of a bureaucracy that demonstrates its commitment to EEO by its representativeness. This notion was recognized by policy makers at least by 1970, when then-Civil Service Commission Chairman R. Hampton stated in a letter to an assistant secretary of defense: "We believe that to the extent practicable organizations of the Federal Government should, in their employment mix, broadly reflect, racially and otherwise, the varied characteristics of our population" (quoted in Grabosky and Rosenbloom 1975, 72).

As noted in the introduction to this chapter, Congress further reinforced this commitment by requiring that agencies make efforts to achieve representative workforces in its 1978 reform of the federal government's personnel system. More recently, the Federal Glass Ceiling Commission, created by Congress as part of the Civil Rights Act of 1991, recommended that government at all levels "lead by example" by ensuring that obstacles to the advancement of women and minorities are eliminated (Federal Glass Ceiling Commission 1995a).

Thus, the increasing demands of women and people of color for their share of political power gave a previously merely academic interest in representative bureaucracy a new impetus. Over the past several decades, executive orders, legislation, and decisions handed down by the courts have defined the means by which this goal can be accomplished.

Achieving a Representative Workforce

A retrospective view of the government's policies with respect to equal employment opportunity and affirmative action shows a gradual transition from merely ending discrimination in government employment to taking proactive steps to increase the representation of women and people of color in the civil service. Much of the early activity in this area took place within the executive branch through the issuance of executive orders. More recently, the courts have become involved in ruling on the constitutionality of affirmative action programs.

From Nondiscrimination to Affirmative Action

Discrimination against federal employees on the basis of race, creed, or color has been prohibited since the passage of the Ramspeck Act in 1940, which prohibited discrimination based on race with respect to hiring, promotions, transfers, salaries, or in other personnel actions. According to Rosenbloom (1977), the law was significant in that it served as a "catalyst" to further actions taken by the executive branch. For example, the following year, President Franklin Roosevelt issued Executive Order 8802 that, in addition to reinforcing the government's policy of nondiscrimination in government or in defense industries, established the Fair Employment Practice Committee (FEPC) to investigate complaints of discrimination. However, the FEPC had no enforcement powers. Five years later, Congress dissolved the FEPC in an amendment to an appropriations bill (Rosenbloom 1977).

Over the next two decades, responsibility for overseeing equal employment opportunity (EEO) policies was shifted several times as committees to do so were created and disbanded. In 1964, Congress finally passed a major piece of legislation outlawing discrimination, the Civil Rights Act. The act also established the Equal Employment Opportunity Commission (EEOC) with responsibility for preventing discrimination in private sector employment. A 1965 executive order, E.O. 11246, gave the Office of Federal Contract Compliance Programs (OFCCP) within the Department of Labor authority to monitor and sanction the EEO practices of companies contracting with the federal government. The same executive order transferred responsibility for federal EEO to the Civil Service Commission (CSC), where it remained until 1979. The CSC had been the federal government's central personnel agency since the merit system was established in 1883.

By the late 1960s it had become clear that a policy of nondiscrimination alone was not sufficient to ensure adequate representation of women and people of color, particularly in upper-level jobs (Rosenbloom 1977). The CSC drafted, for President Nixon's signature, a new executive order (11478) that was slightly stronger, emphasizing recruitment in addition to nondiscrimination. That executive order stated:

> It is the policy of the Government of the United States to provide equal opportunity in Federal employment for all persons, to prohibit discrimination in employment because of race, color, religion, sex, or national origin, and to promote the full realization of equal employment opportunity through a continuing affirmative program in each executive department and agency.

The executive order further required agencies to "maintain an affirmative program of equal employment opportunity." Agencies were to expand recruitment efforts to reach all sources of job candidates, provide training to enhance employees' skills and managers' understanding of the policy outlined in the executive order, and work to improve community conditions that affect employability. In 1971, the CSC took another step. Under pressure from the Commission on Civil Rights, the CSC issued a memo directing agencies to set goals and timetables "where minority employment is not what should be reasonably expected" (quoted in Rosenbloom 1975, 107).

An executive order, while binding on federal agencies, does not have the force of a statute because a subsequent president can revoke the order. The federal government's affirmative employment program was given a statutory basis when the Civil Rights Act of 1964 was extended to federal employment in 1972. The act also provided statutory authority for the CSC's oversight of EEO in the federal sector for the first time and required that agencies maintain affirmative action programs to ensure enforcement of EEO (U.S. Equal Employment Opportunity Commission 1983).

Several years later, in the Civil Service Reform Act (CSRA) of 1978, Congress took additional steps toward endorsing the importance of a representative bureaucracy. The preamble to the law (Pub. L. 95–454) called for a federal workforce "reflective of the nation's diversity." The act abolished the CSC and created in its place the Office of Personnel Management (OPM) and the Merit Systems Protection Board (MSPB). The OPM was given responsibility for establishing a Federal Equal Opportunity Recruitment Program (FEORP). The FEORP program required federal agencies to conduct affirmative recruitment activities aimed at correcting the underrepresentation of people of color and women in mid- and higher-grade levels. (5 U.S.C. § 7201). The CSRA further mandated that performance evaluation criteria for members of the then-newly established Senior Executive Service (SES) include their success in meeting affirmative action goals and achievement of EEO requirements (5 U.S.C. § 4313). At the same time, Reorganization Plan No. 1 of 1978 transferred responsibility for the federal government's EEO and affirmative action programs to the EEOC. Thus, although not explicitly mandating a specific affirmative action program, Congress nevertheless signaled its intent that full representation was a goal the government should strive to achieve, rather than simply to ensure nondiscrimination.

Thus, over four decades, employment policies in the federal government gradually shifted from prohibiting discrimination in federal employment to ensuring the full representation of women and people of color at all grade levels. This goal, espoused by the CSC as early as 1971, was endorsed by Congress and codified with the passage of the CSRA in 1978. From time to time members of Congress have introduced bills to derail this objective. For example, in 1995, Representative Charles Canady criticized the Civil Service Reform Act as "[causing] the federal government itself to seek proportionality for its own sake in the federal workforce" (Canady 1995, 2), and introduced a bill (HR 2128) to prohibit the consideration of race or sex in federal hiring and promotion decisions. To date, no such legislation has succeeded. Some argue that such legislation is no longer necessary, because of a 1995 decision of the Supreme Court.

The Role of the Courts

Not surprisingly, given the volatility of the issue, the legitimacy of the goal of achieving a representative bureaucracy has received mixed signals from the courts. In fact, very narrow majorities have handed down some of the most important decisions. The U.S. Supreme Court has clearly gone on record as upholding the imposition of race-conscious affirmative action plans to remedy past discrimination where such discrimination clearly has taken place. An example is *United States v. Paradise* (480 U.S. 150 [1987]), in which the Court upheld a one-black-for-one-white promotion requirement for Alabama state troopers as a result of finding that the Department of Public Safety engaged in a long-standing practice of excluding blacks from employment. Justice Brennan wrote in his opinion for the court that, "it is now well established that government bodies . . . may constitutionally employ classifications essential to remedy unlawful treatment of racial or ethnic groups subject to discrimination" (480 U.S. at 166). Only three other justices, however, joined that opinion.

The Court has also upheld, albeit narrowly, the use of *voluntary* affirmative action plans designed to increase the representation of women or people of color without a finding of past discrimination. For example, in *Steelworkers v. Weber* (443 U.S. 193 [1979]), the Court held that an employer seeking to adopt a voluntary affirmative action plan need not point to its own discriminatory practice, but could rather defend it on the basis of the existence of a "conspicuous imbalance in traditionally segregated job categories" (443 U.S. at 209). This reasoning was applied a decade later to a public sector jurisdiction in *Johnson v. Santa Clara County* (480 U.S. 616 [1987]), in which a six-justice majority upheld the county agency's decision to consider gender as one factor in evaluating candidates for promotion into a male-dominated job classification. However, in this decision Justice Brennan made it clear that such a voluntary plan was permissible only under certain conditions: (1) There is evidence of a manifest imbalance in traditionally segregated job categories; (2) the plan does not "unnecessarily trammel the rights of male employees or create an absolute bar to their advancement" by establishing a rigid quota system or earmarking of positions; and (3) the plan is temporary, intending only "to attain a balanced work force, not to maintain one" (480 U.S. at 616).

Nevertheless, the decision is significant because it upheld proactive affirmative action in the public sector. Indeed, Justice Stevens noted in his concurring opinion that it is perfectly legitimate for an employer, private or public, to implement an affirmative action program for any number of "forward looking reasons," including "improving services to Black constituencies, averting racial tension over allocation of jobs in a community, or increasing the diversity of a work force, to name a few examples" (Justice Stevens quoting from Sullivan, 100 *Harvard L. Rev.* 78, 96 at 480 U.S. at 647).

For purposes of this discussion of representative bureaucracy, it is also important to note that, until recently, the Court applied a more lenient standard to the federal government's race-conscious policies than to those undertaken by state or local jurisdictions. In *Metro Broadcasting v. Federal Communications Commission* (110 S. Ct. 2997 [1990]), the Court ruled that benign race-conscious measures mandated by Congress to serve governmental objectives—such as diversity—are constitutionally permissible, even if the measures are not designed to compensate victims of past discrimination.

In contrast, the Court invalidated a minority set-aside program employed by the city of Richmond, Virginia. In writing for the Court, Justice O'Connor stressed that state and local governments do not have the power Congress does to decide when such remedies are appropriate (*Richmond v. J.A. Croson Company,* 488 U.S. 489 [1989]). Where Congress finds that minority ownership policies are needed to promote diversity, and that such diversity is an important governmental objective, reasoned Justice O'Connor, such policies are constitutional. However, a local subdivision that wishes to enact such an affirmative action policy must "show that it had essentially become a 'passive participant' in a system of racial exclusion practices by elements of the local construction industry" (488 U.S. at 492).

More recently, however, the Supreme Court has taken a more conservative approach to affirmative action programs, applying a standard of "strict scrutiny" to any race-conscious policies regardless of whether they are promulgated at the federal, state, or local level. In the most recent decision—*Adarand v. Peña* 115 S. Ct. 2097 (1995)—a five-to-four majority of the Court ruled that any racial classification must serve a compelling governmental interest and be narrowly tailored to serve that interest. While explicitly overturning *Metro Broadcasting*, the Court, however, left *Johnson* unscathed. Moreover, Justice O'Connor, writing for the Court, noted that there remain circumstances under which governmental intervention may be required to ensure equal opportunities: "Finally, we wish to dispel the notion that strict scrutiny is 'strict in theory but fatal in fact.' . . . The unhappy persistence of both the practice and the lingering effects of racial discrimination against minority groups in this country is an unfortunate reality, and government is not disqualified from acting in response to it" (63 *Law Week* 4533).

Although its interpretation of the ambiguous decision is not the only possible one, the Justice Department (in the Clinton administration) has stated that the benefit to a federal agency of having a diverse workforce could meet the standard under *Adarand* requiring race-conscious programs to promote compelling governmental interests. Justice Department guidance to federal agencies explains:

> Some members of the Court and several lower courts, however, have suggested that, under appropriate circumstances, an agency's operational need for a diverse workforce could justify the use of racial considerations. This operational need may reflect an agency's interest in seeking internal diversity in order to bring a wider variety of perspectives to bear on the range of issues with which an agency deals. It also may reflect an interest in promoting community trust and confidence in the agency. . . It would, therefore, not necessarily be inconsistent with Adarand for race and ethnicity to be taken into account in em-

ployment decisions in order to ensure that decision makers will be exposed to the greatest possible diversity of perspectives. (Schmidt 1996)

Nevertheless, the *Adarand* decision turned up the heat on all affirmative action programs, especially federal ones. It is not surprising that in a 1997 speech, then-Acting Director of the Justice Department's Office of Civil Rights Isabelle Katz Pinzler urged federal agencies to "really scrutinize each of [their] affirmative action policies and practices to make absolutely sure each is in conformity with the law" (Katz Pinzler 1997, 5).

Executive orders and statutes have, therefore, required agencies to work to increase opportunities for women and people of color for many years. These requirements have been based on an understanding that it is important, for many reasons, for the government to mirror the demographic composition of the citizenry. Recently, the courts have stipulated that affirmative action programs designed to achieve this objective must meet a high standard of strict scrutiny if they are to pass constitutional muster.

Considerable progress has been made in recruiting people of color and women into the government; they now make up 42 and 31 percent of the federal civilian workforce, respectively (U.S. Equal Employment Opportunity Commission 1997a). According to some definitions of "full representation," these numbers suggest that the federal government is close to being a representative bureaucracy (U.S. Merit Systems Protection Board 1996). Just how one determines the extent to which the bureaucracy is representative, however, is an issue that has never been fully resolved.

Defining and Measuring Representation

Even those who believe in the merits of a representative bureaucracy won't necessarily agree as to how representation should be defined or measured. Most analyses have relied on the extent to which an agency reflects what Mosher (1968) called "passive representation" and Pitkin (1969) called "descriptive representation." In most cases, these analyses compare the proportion of members of the various race/ethnic groups and women in an agency to their proportion within the U.S. population.

By the early 1970s, it had become clear that just having proportional numbers of women and people of color in the government, or even in particular agencies, was not good enough if they remained concentrated at lower grade levels devoid of any real participation in the policy-making process. As one scholar noted, "A simple percentage of Hispanic employment in government, or in any agency, is not a valid statistic of the group's representation—or its lack therefore—in the policy-making process" (Pachon 1988, 309). The focus shifted from recruitment of people of color and women to ensuring their advancement into higher-level positions (Rosenbloom 1977). Indeed, Kenneth Meier was one of the first to take issue with many of his contemporaries who suggested that the U.S. federal bureaucracy was representative, arguing that, "Since most of the important decisions made by the civil service are concentrated at its higher levels, the unrepresentative nature of the elite of the civil service corps is cause for rejecting the notion that a representative bureaucracy exists in the United States" (Meier 1975, 541).

Thus, in the last two decades of the twentieth century, much of the research analyzing federal success in achieving a representative bureaucracy focused on the extent to which women and people of color are found at upper grade levels. These researchers have concluded that although women and people of color have made progress in moving into upper levels, they are still not found in numbers that could be considered representative.

It is not only academic researchers who have examined or expressed concern about this issue. Since the passage of the Civil Service Reform Act requiring full representation by grade level, OPM and the EEOC have conducted yearly reviews of federal employment data and have concluded that underrepresentation persists in high grade levels (U.S. Office of Personnel Management 1997; U.S. Equal Employment Opportunity Commission 1997a). Two other federal oversight agencies, the U.S. Merit Systems Protection Board (MSPB) and the U.S. General Accounting Office (GAO), have also examined the representation of women and people of color in federal employment and expressed concern about their paucity in top grades (U.S. Merit Systems Protection Board 1992, 1993a, 1996; U.S. General Accounting Office 1991a, 1993a). The GAO concluded in a 1991 report, for example, that "the representation of women and minorities in middle and upper levels is low enough on its face to warrant continued use of affirmative programs [for increasing their representation]" (U.S. General Accounting Office 1991a, 3).

One problem with these analyses of whether the federal bureaucracy has succeeded in becoming fully representative is that it has never been resolved as to what metric should be used to make this determination (Grabosky and Rosenbloom 1975; Dometrius and Sigelman 1984; Meier 1975; Nachmias and Rosenbloom 1973; Salzstein 1979). Many analysts have taken it for granted that a representative workforce would include people and women in the same proportion as their numbers in the population (Grabosky and Rosenbloom 1975; Pomerleau 1994; Van Riper 1958; Mosher 1982).

The EEOC and OPM, however, utilize a more limited benchmark, requiring agencies to compare the percentage of women and people of color in their own workforces with their proportions in the civilian labor force (CLF). The CLF includes all persons in the United States who are sixteen years of age or older and not employed by the U.S. military. Table 1.1 compares the representation of women and people of color in the general U.S. population, the CLF, the federal workforce, and federal senior-level positions.

Even direct comparisons between the CLF and the federal workforce can be problematic, however. To make this comparison, OPM relies on the Current Population Survey for identifying the proportion of women and each ethnic group in the CLF. This survey is administered by the Bureau of Labor Statistics and tabulated monthly. However, because these computations are based on only a sample of the population, separate counts cannot be provided for Asian Pacific Americans and Native Americans. These two groups represent very small segments of the overall workforce. Hence, OPM extrapolates those proportions using decennial census data (U.S. Office of Personnel Management 1997). Similarly, because the current population survey is only a sample, it cannot be used to make occupation-specific comparisons; hence OPM and the EEOC use decennial census data for this purpose as well (U.S. Office of Personnel Management 1997; U.S. Equal Employment Opportunity Commission 1997a). This means, however, that the analysis undertaken for 1999 will compare 1999 federal employment data with 1990 Census data, even though the national workforce has certainly changed during that nine-year period.

Moreover, OPM and EEOC use somewhat different numbers when computing representation in the federal workforce and the CLF. The EEOC includes the U.S. Postal Service and several other agencies that OPM does not. Hence, in 1997, OPM's analysis was based on a federal workforce comprising nearly 1 million fewer employees (1,595,089) than the federal workforce population on which EEOC's analysis was based (2,475,761). The OPM includes Puerto Rico in its computations, whereas the EEOC does not. As a result, the two agencies sometimes report slightly different percentages with respect to representation of Latinos in the civilian labor force and in federal agencies. For example, for fiscal year 1997, OPM reported that Latinos made up 6.2 percent of the federal workforce and 11 percent of the civilian labor force. The EEOC reported that Latinos represented 6.4 percent of the federal workforce and 8 percent of the civilian labor force (U.S. Office of Personnel Management 1997; U.S. Equal Employment Opportunity Commission 1997a).

The necessity of using outdated Census figures is only one problem with using the CLF as the standard for determining representation. Another criticism of the civilian labor force as a benchmark is that it includes people below the age of eighteen and noncitizens, who are generally ineligible for government employment. Hence, while Latinos are underrepresented in the federal workforce vis-à-vis their representation in the CLF, some have argued that this is an artifact based on the high number of Latino noncitizens

TABLE 1.1   Representation of Women and People of Color in the General
Population, Civilian Workforce, and Federal Workforces, 1997 (Percent)

	U.S. Population	Civilian Labor Force	Federal Workforce	Senior Federal Jobs
Women	51.2	46.4	42.8	22
People of color	27.3	26.3	29.6	12.4

NOTE: "People of color" includes African Americans, Asian and Pacific Islanders,
Latinos, and Native Americans.
SOURCES: U.S. population, U.S. Bureau of the Census (1999); other percentages,
U.S. Office of Personnel Management (1997).

in the CLF (Edwards, Thomas, and Burch 1992; U.S. Merit Systems
Protection Board 1997).

Even if agreement as to the appropriate benchmark could be secured, the
U.S. General Accounting Office (GAO) and some scholars have criticized
this method of comparing percentages as being too simplistic, and they
have attempted to devise other measures. In a 1993 report, GAO advocated
a "ratio-based approach" that compares the numbers of each EEO group
to a benchmark such as Euro-American men, arguing that such a measure
better states the extent to which each group makes progress relative to the
others (U.S. General Accounting Office 1993a).

For example, in 1984 there were 86,879 Euro-American women and
242,731 Euro-American men in key jobs in the largest twenty-five federal
agencies (key jobs are those that can lead to middle and upper management
positions). That is a ratio of .358 (86,879 divided by 242,731). A ratio of
less than 1.0 indicates that women are underrepresented in comparison to
Euro-American men in those jobs. That number can also be compared to
the same ratio computed based on the number of Euro-American women
and men in those jobs in 1990. That ratio turns out to be .438. Dividing
438 by 358 produces the number 1.22. That number means that Euro-
American women have increased their representation relative to Euro-
American men by a factor of 1.22, or 22 percent.

Despite GAO's insistence that this was a better approach to measuring
the relative standing of women and people of color in the federal workforce, the EEOC was unconvinced. Among other objections, then-EEOC
Chairman Evan Kemp protested that the appropriate benchmark for each
race/ethnic or gender group should be its representation in the same jobs in
the CLF, not a comparison to Euro-American men in those jobs in the federal workforce (U.S. General Accounting Office 1993a).

Similarly, David Nachmias and David Rosenbloom (1973) developed a
Measure of Variation (MV) that compares the total number of observed

differences within a group to the maximum number of possible differences. That is, it compares the total number of pairs of employees who are from different ethnic (or gender) groups to the total number of *possible* pairs of employees from different ethnic (or gender) groups, yielding a number between 0 and 1. The closer the number is to 1, the more equally represented the groups are. The number serves as a shorthand indicator of the degree of integration within a grade level, agency, occupation, or any other group, and can be used to show changes over time. In applying this measure to grade-level groupings, for example, Peter Grabosky and David Rosenbloom (1975) voiced concern about the lack of integration at the top policy-making levels (GS 16–18), where the index was only .09 in 1973. This measure continues to be used by scholars assessing the bureaucracy's representativeness, although not without evoking some questions and criticism (see Guajardo 1996).

Hence, even if one accepts that "passive" representation is the most legitimate means for assessing whether the government is the "representative bureaucracy" envisioned by Krislov and others, there is no one indisputable way to judge whether the federal government meets that test. Judgments must be made as to the most appropriate benchmark and the best means for assessing whether progress is being made.

The Relationship Between Active and Passive Representation

Even if the appropriate metric for measuring passive representation could be agreed upon, the theory of representative bureaucracy has been criticized from another standpoint. Some argue that the theory is meaningless if passive representation does not result in "substantive" (Pitkin 1969) or "active" (Mosher 1968) representation (Salzstein 1979; Thompson 1976). That is, unless a civil servant can be shown to "press for the interests and desires of those whom he is presumed to represent" (Mosher 1968, 12), there is little point in even being concerned with whether the bureaucracy is representative in the passive sense.

In the early days of this debate the focus was on administrators' attitudes and values. Researchers argued that a prerequisite for active representation is that bureaucrats share the values of those whom they are presumed to represent (Subramaniam 1967; Larson 1973; Meier 1975; Meier and Nigro 1976; Salzstein 1979). One could argue that what administrators *do* for the people they represent is more important than their attitudes. However, it is a lot easier to measure people's attitudes and values (e.g., with a survey instrument) than it is to measure their behavior.

Studies that looked for this attitude congruence found mixed results (Subramaniam 1967; Larson 1973; Meier 1975; Meier and Nigro 1976; Salzstein 1979; Rehfuss 1986; Rosenbloom and Featherstonhaugh 1977). In reviewing many of these studies, Frank Thompson concluded that, "Both pessimists and optimists concerning linkage [between passive and active representation] then, find some support for their conclusions in the existing theories and empirical findings of social science" (1976, 212).

One reason for the mixed findings may be that there has been little agreement as to how such attitude congruence should be measured. The problem, according to Salzstein (1979), is that these attempts to find empirical evidence of value congruence suffer from substantial methodological problems:

> The researcher must somehow decide which values should be congruent, and then measure the attitudes of the relevant group and the attitudes of the bureaucratic representatives. Further, what kind of values should be measured? Should the researcher select only those values felt most strongly by the group, generalized norms as to group goals and aspirations, values related to specific policy issues, or attitudes generally concerning the role of the bureaucracy? Should the researcher be concerned with the informational base underlying attitudes, variations in intensity, and the distribution of opinion within the group? In addition, how much value congruence is needed to demonstrate responsiveness? (1979, 469)

But even the debate about the extent of congruency between the attitudes of bureaucrats and of those whom they represent misses the point. The assumption that behavior necessarily follows from attitudes or values does not necessarily hold up to empirical scrutiny (Hindera 1993a). In fact, an accumulating body of research does provide evidence that where people of color hold decision-making positions in government agencies, greater benefits flow to those who share their race/ethnicity.

John Hindera's and Cheryl Young's analyses of decisions made by investigators in EEOC field offices are cases in point. The job of the investigators is to evaluate complaints brought to them by people who believe they have been discriminated against. The investigators determine whether there is probable cause to pursue the complaint. Hindera has found that the presence of African American and Latino investigators in field offices increases the likelihood that complaints brought by African American and Latino complainants, respectively, will be pursued (Hindera 1993a; Hindera and Young 1994, 1998).

Similarly, Kenneth Meier and colleagues have found that the greater the proportion of school teachers or school board members who are African American or Latino, the less "second generation discrimination"[3] occurs against African American or Latino students, respectively (Meier 1984; Meier and England 1984; Meier, Stewart, and England 1989; Meier and Stewart 1991; Meier 1993a). Sally Selden (1997a, 1997b) found that the presence of African American, Latino, and Asian American county supervisors in Farmers Home Administration Offices (a bureau within the U.S. Department of Agriculture) resulted in more favorable eligibility determinations for loan applications submitted by these three groups.

That at least some administrators perceive a link between passive and active representation is clear from a comment made by a Latino program analyst at the Small Business Administration: "The program benefits reflect the staff. An equitable level of Hispanic staff ensures [that] Hispanics get an equitable share of program benefits. As it stands now, we're getting short shrift any way you look at it" (quoted in Fernandez 1993, 54).

It should be noted, however, that this kind of representative role has not been found for every group. Sally Selden (1997b) found that neither the presence of women nor of Native Americans had an effect on Farmers Home Administration eligibility determinations for women and Native Americans. Hindera (1993b) similarly found that Euro-American female EEOC investigators filed *fewer* complaints on behalf of women and that there was no relationship between the presence of female African American investigators and complaints filed on behalf of African American women.

More recently, scholars have begun to ask whether active representation is facilitated in some situations more than others. After all, there are many reasons why administrators might not feel free to act on behalf of their "constituents" (Herbert 1974). One prerequisite is clearly that they exercise discretion over policies or programs where their actions can make a difference (Meier and Stewart 1991; Meier 1993a). Some researchers have suggested that active representation is also more likely to occur when there is external support for the advancement of minority interests (e.g., as during the civil rights era of the 1960s) or when there is political support within the agency (Thompson 1976; Henderson 1979). Administrators' comfort in acting as representatives may also increase when the decisions they make clearly have racial/ethnic ramifications (Thompson 1976; Meier and Stewart 1991; Meier 1993a). This would be the case with an EEOC investigator's decision as to whether to pursue a discrimination complaint. It is less clear that this was a factor in the Farmers Home Administration, whose mission does not focus on minority issues (Selden 1997a,b).

Meier (1993a) found that a critical mass was required for members of a group to act as active representatives of their group. Similarly, Sylvester Murray et al. (1994) speculated that their finding that minority administrators are more likely today to believe they should be active representatives than they were twenty years ago was a function of their increased numbers in administrative positions. The importance of proportions is consistent with a thesis proposed by Rosabeth Moss Kanter in her now-classic work, *Men and Women of the Corporation* (1977). She suggested that once groups that are in a minority in an organization reach a certain proportion, they become individuals distinguished from one another, and can form coalitions that affect the organization's culture (Kanter 1977, 209).

Hindera and Young (1998) similarly found that the number of positive decisions on behalf of African American complainants in EEOC field offices is at least partly a function of the proportion of African American investigators in those offices. The relationship they found was curvilinear. The number of charges filed on behalf of African Americans is greatest when African American investigators represent a plurality in an EEOC field office. Under those circumstances, even Euro-American investigators file more charges on behalf of African Americans. But where African Americans represent either a smaller proportion than a plurality or the majority of investigators, they pursue cases on behalf of African Americans, but at a lower rate than under a plurality model. In this situation Euro-Americans are neither more nor less likely to file charges on behalf of African Americans. These findings suggest that the social environment of the office, as influenced by its demographic composition, plays a role in inducing active representation in addition to demographic background of those in decision-making positions.

The research described thus far has focused on the demographic composition of "street-level bureaucrats," or those who are in a position to make discrete decisions affecting individual clients. But what about those at higher levels in the organization? It has been suggested that such administrators would be less likely to act on behalf of constituents because they have been subject to even greater socialization than those who are in lower-level jobs (Thompson 1976; Rehfuss 1986).

Henry Pachon (1988) alludes to the constraints administrators at these levels face in remarking that the percentage of people of color in significant policy-making levels within a department or within key agencies in a department only measures the *potential* for their representation in the policy process. Goodman (1993) similarly contends that there are still too few people of color in top policy positions to make it possible to identify their distinctive contribution to public policy. He suggests that, "If minorities were more numerous at the top, others aspiring to get there might feel that they could do so without giving up or changing the very attributes of culture and ways of thinking that make them distinctive" (Goodman 1993, 7).

Certainly, advancement can depend, in part, on the extent to which administrators have played the organization's game by its rules (Herbert 1974; Rehfuss 1986). Yet there is evidence that the demographics of those in top positions does matter, *at least* indirectly, because they are involved in the hiring of lower-level administrators (Meier 1993a; Meier and Smith 1994; Meier, Stewart, and England 1989; Selden 1997b). Little research has examined other ways in which administrators may directly or indirectly affect broader policy decisions or the allocation of benefits in ways that favor their constituents.

In sum, a growing body of research demonstrates that passive representation is important. The representation of at least some racial/ethnic groups has a positive impact on those groups' access to government benefits and services. There is also consensus that organizational factors can facilitate active representation. This occurs in situations where the administrator has discretion to make a decision regarding the allocation of benefits, where a group represents a plurality of administrators, and where there is a clear relationship between the program in question and the demographic characteristic (Meier 1993a).

This research is limited, however, in two ways. The first is that it focuses on only one piece of what government agencies do—providing direct services to citizens. Significant numbers of the nearly 2 million federal civil servants and 9 million state and local employees are in other important roles that affect the lives of Americans, including policy making, regulation, oversight, and contracting with third-sector service providers. The other limitation of this research is that it assumes that administrators who are disposed to act in the interests of their constituents will do so.

Yet considerable research in psychology, sociology, organizational behavior, and other fields suggests that women and people of color often face barriers that limit their opportunities to fully exercise discretion. As Charles Levine suggested more than two decades ago: "But, knowing the number and percentage of employees from minority groups has increased and that more minority group employees are being promoted to higher grades tell us little about their work experiences and the extent to which racism and sexism persist in public manpower management systems" (Levine 1974, 240).

People of color and women now hold an impressive proportion of federal jobs (see Table 1.1). But there is evidence that all is not equal. Women and people of color remain underrepresented in mid- and senior-level federal jobs (see Table 1.2). Moreover, people of color receive, on average, lower performance appraisal ratings and fewer opportunities to demonstrate their abilities, and are subject to discipline at a higher rate than Euro-American employees (U.S. Merit Systems Protection Board 1996).

That federal employees are aware of these differences is clear from the ongoing protests and lawsuits filed by women and people of color alleging disparate treatment (see, for example, Rivenbark 1994a,b; Harris 1994; Jennings 1993; Holland 1997; Love 1999; Fletcher 1999). This enmity has even received official recognition. The vice-president's government-wide re-

TABLE 1.2   Percentage of Positions Held in Each Grade Group by Gender and Race/Ethnicity

	GS 1–8	GS 9–12	GS 13–15	Senior Pay
Men	29.5	57.1	73.6	79.1
Women	70.5	42.9	26.4	20.9
African American	26.3	13.7	8.3	6.5
Asian Pacific American	3.6	4.1	4.0	1.8
Euro-American	59.9	74.6	83.2	88.4
Latino	7.4	6.0	3.6	2.6
Native American	2.7	1.6	0.9	0.7
Total	471,955	566,587	314,422	13,956

SOURCE: U.S. Equal Employment Opportunity Commission (1997a).

form effort, the National Performance Review, noted in its report on federal human resource management that the "federal government has not been successful at eradicating discriminatory barriers, and attracting, retaining, and advancing members of all segments of society at all grade levels" (Office of the Vice President 1993, 64).

Hence, before reaching any definitive conclusions about the relationship between passive and active representation, another question must be asked: Do people of color and women have the same opportunities as Euro-American men to make their voices heard, exercise influence, and advance into higher-level policy-making positions that can have an impact on broader communities? Or are there barriers that limit their full inclusion?

The remainder of this book sets about the task of evaluating the extent to which such barriers to inclusion may exist in the federal government. It does so through an analysis of government-wide data, including employment data, surveys, and focus groups. Previous research in a variety of disciplines, including public administration, psychology, sociology, and political science, suggests ways in which the opportunities and authority of women and people of color can be limited, albeit often unintentionally. In the chapters that follow, six factors are identified, and their nature and impact are evaluated empirically.

The list of potential limiting factors examined here is incomplete. Moreover, the means by which they and their consequences are measured is imperfect, limited by the data available. However, the analyses serve to illustrate the broader point: Even where administrators may want to serve the groups they represent, and even where it appears they have the discretion to do so, they may face constraints. Those constraints may not be obvious but rather take the form of subtle attitudes and perceptions. They may also take the form of practices and procedures that appear to be neutral but restrict the opportunities and authority that are required to act on behalf of constituents.

In summary, considerable support has emerged for the notion that the government should "look like America." This support, originally theoretical, has more recently taken the form of executive orders and statutes requiring that the federal government achieve this aim, albeit within a particular framework imposed by the Supreme Court. That a representative workforce directly benefits communities of color has been shown by research analyzing decisions made by street-level bureaucrats in specific agencies, such as the EEOC and Farmers Home Administration, as well as in school districts. But what has been missing has been research that investigates whether women and people of color enjoy the same opportunities and authority to participate in the policy-making process. Without those opportunities, their ability to exert influence is necessarily limited. This book contributes to filling that gap through an empirical investigation, based on government-wide data, of the nature and consequences of such limitations.

Notes

1. Among other provisions, the Act directed standing committees to exercise "continuous watchfulness" over the execution of laws by executive agencies under their jurisdiction (quoted in Galloway 1951, 59). In addition, following passage of the act, several "watchdog committees" were created in fields such as federal expenditures, atomic energy control, and defense production. For further discussion, see Galloway 1951.

2. Legislation extending equal rights to women and people of color in nonfederal employment has not always coincided with the extension of rights to federal employees. For example, the Equal Pay Act requiring equal pay for equal work was passed in 1963, forty years after the passage of the Classification Act of 1923. On the other hand, Title VII of the Civil Rights Act of 1964 prohibiting employment discrimination was not extended to cover federal employees until 1972.

3. Second generation discrimination refers to subtle inequities with respect to taking disciplinary actions against students of color and funneling into lower-quality programs and tracks; see Bullock and Stewart 1979 for more explanation.

2

The Macro-Political Environment

We've done quite well. . . . We are being sued by blacks charging discrimination [in a suit filed in the late 1980s], and now we are on the verge of being sued by a white male for reverse discrimination.

Richard Moose,
Undersecretary of State, in an interview with
The Washington Post *(April 1994).*

As should be evident from Chapter 1, efforts to achieve a representative workforce in the federal government have not taken place in a vacuum. Congress and the courts have established a basic, if unsettled, framework that acknowledges the importance of a representative bureaucracy and the need to take proactive steps to achieve that objective. There is a political dimension to that environment as well, however. Federal agencies are headed by secretaries and administrators who have been appointed by the president and so generally share his ideology and values. In recent history, that president's beliefs generally include support for or opposition to policies designed to increase the representation of women and people of color. There has been an understandable perception, then, that opportunities for the entry and advancement of men and women of various races/ethnicities have expanded or contracted depending on which president inhabits the White House.

The purpose of this chapter is to explore the extent to which this perception is justified. A major theme of this book is that such perceptions can be damaging if they have the effect of discouraging talented individuals from seeking employment with, or promotions within, the government because they believe their gender or ethnicity presents an obstacle. Hence, this chapter examines employment data across four presidential administrations to assess empirically whether there is a relationship between the ideology of the president in power and the demographic composition of the federal workforce, overall or in the top grade levels.

The President and EEO

Regardless of their personal preferences, presidents do not have complete latitude to impose their wills. Rather, presidential actions take place within a policy environment bounded by legislation and case law. With the exception of the added scrutiny with which affirmative action practices have to be viewed in light of the *Adarand* decision, the federal government's EEO program has remained intact for many years. That is, agencies are supposed to engage in efforts to achieve full representation of women and people of color at all grade levels, and in all occupational categories. They are required to have a plan for doing so and to report annually to the Office of Personnel Management (OPM) and the Equal Employment Opportunity Commission (EEOC) on their progress toward achieving these objectives. Nevertheless, within this policy framework, the president and his appointees do have some latitude to encourage or discourage proactive efforts to increase the representation of underrepresented groups.

For example, although affirmative action programs grew under the Nixon and Carter administrations, most analysts agree that these programs were no longer emphasized following the election of Ronald Reagan in 1980 (Mills 1994; Ewoh and Elliott 1998; Blum 1990; Collins 1983). Leonard (1994) analyzed the efforts of the Department of Labor's Office of Federal Contract Compliance Programs (OFCCP), which is responsible for ensuring that companies contracting with the government are complying with equal employment opportunity and affirmative action guidelines. The OFCCP can impose sanctions if it finds contractors are not complying with these laws. Leonard concluded from his analysis of the OFCCP during the 1980s that, "The 1980s then present an experiment on the effectiveness of affirmative-action with minimal threat of sanctions. The results of this experiment were to eliminate employment advancement for minorities and women as a result of the contractor compliance program" (Leonard 1994, 10).

Reagan signaled his position on racial issues in other ways. Among these was his appointment of Bradford Reynolds, who was openly hostile to affirmative action, to head the Civil Rights Division in the Department of Justice (Carnoy 1994). Reynolds vowed to "remove whatever race- or gender-conscious remedies exist in the regulatory framework." Reagan's chairman of the EEOC, Clarence Thomas, reinforced this view of an administration opposed to affirmative action when he expressed "serious reservations" about the employment guidelines he was to enforce ("From Action to Outreach" 1985, 16). Another ominous sign of Reagan's perspective, in the view of many, was his decision to downsize those federal departments where the representation of African Americans was higher than average, such as the departments of Education, Health and Human Services, and Labor (Edsall and Edsall 1992).

An example of the perceived impact of the Reagan presidency on the employment of people of color and women in the federal government can be found in the 1987 congressional testimony of then-President of Blacks in Government Rubye Fields. She said: "Affirmative action was in trouble well before 1980 when the Reagan Administration came into power. However, it may have been dealt a fatal blow over the past 6 years. We believe that affirmative action programs have come to a standstill in many agencies. Many managers no longer feel that they need to comply with EEO guidelines, and this is reflected in their personnel decisions" (quoted in Page 1994, 26). Similarly, Florence Perman concluded her review of reports issued by the House of Representatives and U.S. Commission on Civil Rights in 1987 by stating that, "It is clear that for federal enforcement of equal employment opportunity the rule of law was replaced in the 1980s by the rule of men for whom ideology was the criterion for actions. ... The net result . . . was that between 1981 and 1987 enforcement of the national policy on EEO [in both the federal and nonfederal arenas] came to a standstill" (Perman 1988, 832).

It has been suggested that President Bush continued Reagan's legacy of undermining civil rights enforcement (Shull 1993). In fact, Bush created such an uproar when a draft of his signing statement for the Civil Rights Act of 1991 resolutely rejected affirmative action that Congressman William Clay was quoted as saying, "There is about as much difference between David Duke and George Bush as there is between Tweedledee and Tweedledum" (Biskupic 1991, 3463).

Political scientist Steven Shull concluded from his analysis of the impact of the Reagan and Bush presidencies on civil rights that Reagan successfully manipulated appointments, executive orders, budgets, reorganizations, and programs to undermine aggressive agency enforcement of civil rights (Shull 1993). Burstein (1992), however, believes that Reagan did not attack the demands of women nearly as ferociously as those favoring the alleged preferential treatment of African Americans.

Clinton tried to send the opposite message through his appointment of more women and people of color to his cabinet than any previous president (Shull 1993) and his vow to fight to retain affirmative action following the announcement of a Supreme Court decision (*Adarand v. Peña*) that made such programs more difficult to defend (Savage and Dolan 1995).

Moreover, the National Performance Review (NPR), headed by Vice-President Al Gore, further acknowledged the importance of this objective, noting in its report on "reinventing" human resource management that the government has been "delaying attainment of an important goal of the Civil Service Reform Act of 1978 and other civil rights laws—full representation of all segments of society at all grade levels in government" (Office of the Vice President 1993, 64). In contrast to the Reagan Justice Department, which had defined affirmative action efforts as "intentional discrimination" (U.S. Department of Justice 1987), the Clinton Justice Department's guidance to federal agencies following the Supreme Court's *Adarand* decision stated that the federal government is firmly committed to employment practices that open opportunities to all Americans and draw on the full range of the nation's talent, and that "affirmative action efforts can advance those vital objectives" (Schmidt 1996).

The messages sent by all three presidents were not lost on federal civil servants. When the Labor Department finally settled a class action discrimination suit by African American employees who had been fired or laid off during the Reagan administration, their attorney praised the agreement as an end to the "unhappy legacy of the Bush-Reagan era" (Swoboda 1994). Neither have the Clinton administration's endeavors to encourage federal managers to increase the representation of people of color and women gone unnoticed. Among the efforts recorded in the press was a memo from Defense Secretary William Perry calling for a "vigorous, sustained effort to improve representation of women, minorities, and people with disabilities among the Department's civilian managers" (Bridger 1994). Another example was an article describing a system whereby directors within the Farmers Home Administration would be awarded points if the representation of people of color within their offices' workforce met or exceeded their representation in the state's rural population (Larson 1993).

Indeed, the Clinton administration's focus on achieving a government that "looks like America" has resulted in some Euro-American men charging that they are victims of "reverse discrimination" and so are, in fact, denied equal opportunity (see, for example, Larson 1993; Goshko 1994, Bridger 1994). A *Wall Street Journal* article criticized the Clinton administration as one that is "yet to see a racial preference it doesn't like" (Eastland 1994).

The divergent perspectives of various presidential administrations on EEO and affirmative action are also reflected in the shifting positions taken by the EEOC. During the Carter administration, for example, in 1980, the EEOC introduced a results-oriented approach to affirmative action with quantifiable goals and timetables. In its 1981 guidance to federal agencies (amended and reissued in 1983), the EEOC noted, "Federal agencies are obligated to undertake affirmative action under Section 717 of Title VII of the Civil Rights Act of 1964, as amended. Other public employers and many employers in the private sector may choose to undertake affirmative action voluntarily. Federal affirmative action, however, was mandated by Congress after specific findings of pervasive discrimination in Federal employment, not only at the national level, but at regional and local levels as well" (U.S. Equal Employment Opportunity Commission 1983, 5).

By 1987, the EEOC had backed off its affirmative action mandate and instead merely *permitted* agencies to set goals where there was a "manifest imbalance or conspicuous absence of minorities and women in the agency's work forces" (U.S. Equal Employment Opportunity Commission 1987, 2). It shifted major responsibility for EEO to agency heads, emphasized the development of flexible programs to identify and remove barriers to the advancement of people of color and women, and included no requirement that representation be analyzed by grade level (U.S. Equal Employment Opportunity Commission 1987, 13). Under the Bush administration's watch, the U.S. General Accounting Office (GAO) criticized the EEOC for its inconsistent and inadequate oversight of federal agencies (Ungar 1991), including allowing agencies to submit late and/or incomplete affirmative action plans (U.S. General Accounting Office 1991a).

In 1993, the EEOC circulated draft guidance that again prescribed affirmative employment programs for all agencies and required agencies to "establish viable and measurable affirmative employment objectives and action plans with specific target dates to eliminate identified under-utilization of minorities, women and people with disabilities" (U.S. Equal Employment Opportunity Commission undated, 8). Probably because of the renewed controversy that erupted over affirmative action at about that time, this draft guidance was never finalized, and the Commission recently announced the development of a task force to improve the federal government's EEO process (U.S. Equal Employment Opportunity Commission 1999a).

In short, there are many reasons to believe that if presidents do make a difference in federal employment practices, the change from the Reagan and Bush administrations of the 1980s and early 1990s to the Clinton administration that entered office in 1993, in particular, could have at least some impact on increasing the representation of women and people of color in the government and on their advancement into senior-level jobs. Clearly there are many environmental variables that affect progress toward achieving a bureaucracy that is representative at all grade levels, including demographic changes, congressional mandates, public opinion, and interest in public service careers. It is the ideology of the president, however, that has drawn the most scrutiny from supporters and opponents of affirmative action.

Yet little research has empirically addressed whether opportunities for women and people of color in the federal government have in fact changed as a result of changing administrations. One exception is Gregory Lewis (1988), who concluded that the rate of progress of women and people of color in terms of their overall representation and their movement into higher-level jobs remained consistent during the Carter and Reagan presidencies, despite these two presidents' opposing views on affirmative action. In a recent analysis of presidential influence on the appointment of women in the Foreign Service, James Scott and Elizabeth Rexford (1997) concluded that Clinton's commitment to women's rights explains at least part of the dramatic rise in the number of women holding authoritative foreign policy positions, although other factors have been involved as well. In the next section of this chapter these analyses are updated and extended, examining federal employment data spanning four administrations, from 1976 to 1996.

The President's Influence: An Empirical View

Data for this analysis come from the U.S. Office of Personnel Management (OPM), which maintains a database, the Central Personnel Data File (or CPDF), with information on nearly 2 million full-time, permanent, federal, civilian employees. (Excluded are employees in the U.S. Postal Service and other segments of the workforce exempt from personnel reporting requirements such as the intelligence agencies.) Employment data for white-collar employees are plotted by year to identify patterns associated with different presidential administrations. It is impractical to report the data for each underrepresented group separately by sex and ethnicity, and so African Americans, Asian Pacific Americans, Latinos, and Native Americans are combined into two groups: male people of color and female people of color. The objective is to discover whether the increase in the overall representation of women and people of color, their rates of advancement, and their representation in career and noncareer senior executive positions varied according to the administration in power, as has been the perception. Absent presidential influence, we would expect that the continued existence of EEO programs within federal departments and agencies during this twenty-year time period would result in a gradual but linear increase in the representation of women and people of color.

The Noncareer Senior Executive Service

The Civil Service Reform Act of 1978 created a special personnel system in the executive branch called the Senior Executive Service (SES). The SES includes about 8,000 employees who serve in key managerial, supervisory, and policy positions just below the top presidential appointees. Within this

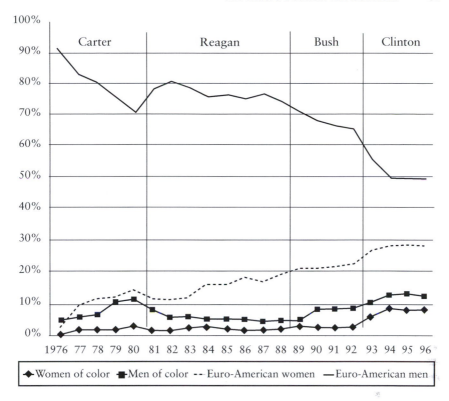

Figure 2.1   Representation Within Noncareer SES
SOURCE: U.S. Office of Personnel Management, Central Personnel Data File.

group, up to 10 percent are appointed by agency heads to support the president's goals and policies and are known as the "noncareer" SES. Because of delays in putting the administration's team in place, their numbers usually reach a high point during its second year and begin to decrease as the president's term ends (U.S. General Accounting Office 1993b). Thus, among the noncareer SES there is likely to be the greatest turnover and the president's priorities with regard to demographic composition of his government should be most readily visible. Figure 2.1 presents the representation of women, men, people of color, and Euro-Americans within the noncareer SES, by year.

As suggested in Figure 2.1, representation of each of the four groups within the noncareer SES has varied considerably among various presidential administrations.[1] The representation of Euro-American men dropped by about twenty percentage points during the Carter administration, from 91 percent in 1976 to 71 percent in 1980. Their representation increased after Reagan took office and remained at about 80 percent during most of the Reagan and Bush years. The proportion of the noncareer SES that were Euro-American men then started to decline again at the end of the Bush administration and dropped even more dramatically during Clinton's first term, to about 50 percent in 1996.

The representation of men of color shows the opposite pattern. Their proportion of noncareer SES positions had climbed to 11 percent by the time Carter left office and then dropped to about 5 percent, remaining there until about 1989. At that time, as Euro-American men were leaving their SES positions, the proportion of men of color increased to 8 percent and continued to increase to a high of nearly 14 percent in 1995.

The pattern for both groups of women is less erratic. With some variation, the proportion of noncareer SES jobs held by Euro-American women climbed steadily during the entire twenty-year period. These women, who held only 3 percent of noncareer SES positions in 1976, held nearly 30 percent by 1996. Women of color have consistently held a very small proportion of noncareer SES positions, hovering at about 2 percent until Clinton took office. For most of his first term, women of color held about 8 percent of noncareer SES positions.

Thus, there does appear to be a relationship between the views of the president and the appointment of people of color and women into politically appointed SES positions. This is particularly true with respect to men and women of color, who made little progress in gaining noncareer SES positions under the Reagan and Bush administrations and rather dramatic progress under the first Clinton term. Moreover, Euro-American men clearly held onto the lion's share of these positions under the Reagan and Bush administrations and lost ground during the Carter and Clinton years.

The Career Senior Executive Service

By law, the remaining 90 percent of SES positions are held by career employees (U.S. Office of Personnel Management 1994a). Individuals are selected into the career SES through a merit staffing process and can be removed only for misconduct or inadequate performance. The president and his appointees clearly have less potential for directly deciding who will hold these positions than they have with respect to noncareer appointments. However, presidential appointees can become involved when they have the opportunity to recruit and hire for the career SES positions under their supervision that become vacant. It should be noted, however, that the representation of women and people of color in these jobs also reflects the extent to which they are present in the "pipeline" of jobs from which promotion to SES positions is possible. As shown in Table 2.1, the representation of the three groups in the GS 13–15 "feeder" jobs has increased gradually and steadily over the two decades, suggesting that all else being equal, there should be a gradual and steady increase in career SES jobs as well.

TABLE 2.1   Representation of Men and Women of Color and Euro-American Women in GS 13–15 Jobs

Fiscal Year	Euro-American Women (Percent)	Women of Color (Percent)	Men of Color (Percent)	Total Employment GS 13–15
1976	4.34	0.82	5.65	182,734
1977	4.67	0.93	5.72	187,750
1978	4.96	1.01	5.83	190,494
1979	5.39	1.21	6.26	193,098
1980	6.12	1.49	6.72	195,775
1981	6.77	1.78	7.20	194,679
1982	7.08	1.87	7.41	196,015
1983	7.58	2.02	7.51	197,867
1984	8.14	2.14	7.62	203,285
1985	8.79	2.31	7.69	209,344
1986	9.48	2.47	7.70	212,842
1987	10.35	2.74	7.79	221,678
1988	11.27	2.99	7.88	230,786
1989	12.18	3.30	8.01	242,198
1990	13.06	3.61	8.06	256,675
1991	14.00	3.95	8.14	271,882
1992	14.67	4.27	8.31	284,245
1993	15.28	4.56	8.48	289,151
1994	15.89	4.87	8.67	288,021
1995	16.52	5.24	8.84	289,574
1996	16.77	5.40	8.94	288,914

SOURCE: U.S. Office of Personnel Management, Central Personnel Data File.

The president inherits the career senior executives already in place when he steps into the White House. What we are concerned about, then, is how the composition of the SES changes at the margins under his watch. Figure 2.2 is designed to address both of these issues. The bar chart shows the representation of Euro-American men and women and men and women of color in the career SES at the time the president took office. The line chart shows the marginal change in representation from one year to the next.

The bar chart shows that from administration to administration, there has been a gradual decrease in the proportion of SES jobs held by Euro-American men, and a gradual increase in the proportion held by every other group. However, at the margins the change has been much more erratic. Of course, the increases and decreases in the representation of each group are small, seldom varying more than plus or minus two percent. Nevertheless, there was a significant drop in the rate at which men of color increased their representation in the SES after Reagan took office in 1981. In fact, the overall result was a net drop of one-tenth of a percentage point

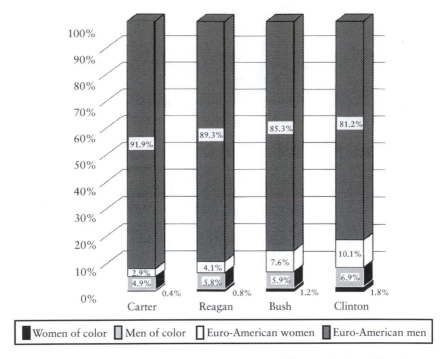

Figure 2.2a   Representation in Career SES at Time of Entry of New Administration
SOURCE: U.S. Office of Personnel Management, Central Personnel Data File.

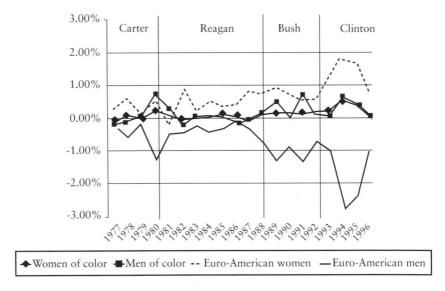

Figure 2.2b   Change in Representation in Career SES
SOURCE: U.S. Office of Personnel Management, Central Personnel Data File.

by the end of Reagan's term. Similarly, the increase in representation of women of color, which had improved slightly during the Carter years, remained under 1 percent during the Reagan administration. The rate of increase began to rise under Bush, but improved more markedly under Clinton. By 1996 women of color held 3 percent of career senior executive positions.

In contrast, the rate at which Euro-American women have gained SES jobs has generally grown fairly steadily throughout every administration. Perhaps Paul Burstein was correct when he stated that "the Reagan administration did not attack the demands of . . . women with anything like the intensity directed at those favoring what they saw as preferential policies favoring blacks" (Burstein 1992, 918). However, it is under the Clinton administration that the increase in the representation of Euro-American women has been most dramatic. By 1996 they held 14 percent of senior executive jobs, more than double the share they held ten years earlier. This change occurred largely at the expense of Euro-American men. In contrast to the other three administrations presented, Euro-American male representation in the SES remained fairly constant during the Reagan administration, declining at less than 0.5 percent per year. However, their share of senior jobs fell from about 86 to 82 percent during the Bush years, and then to 75 percent in 1996.

Much of this decline, however, can probably be accounted for by the higher than usual turnover rate within the SES in 1994 (15 percent turnover versus a normal rate of 8 percent, U.S. Office of Personnel Management 1994a). It was in this year that many of the older senior executives (who were largely Euro-American men) took advantage of early retirement incentives and buyouts, offered as part of the Clinton administration's effort to reduce the size of government. Another incentive to retire in 1994 was a 1991 pay increase that raised retirement incomes for those who retired after January 1, 1994. This elevated turnover had the effect of creating greater opportunities to improve the representation of women and people of color. Figure 2.2 suggests that Euro-American women have benefited the most.

Overall, then, there does seem to be some support for the contention that a presidential administration is in a position to influence the composition of the career senior executive core, at least at the margins. Men and women of color did not increase their share of these jobs under Reagan, despite their steady advancement into GS 13–15 "feeder" positions. The representation of Euro-American women increased less under Reagan than the other administrations, while the representation of Euro-American men increased the most during that period. Clinton's aim to achieve greater diversity under his administration is clearly apparent in the composition of the career SES.

The Rank and File Workforce

Representation in the SES is certainly significant because, as Kenneth Meier (1975) has argued, this is where major policy decisions are made. However, diversity among rank and file civil servants is also important. At least one study has shown that clientele care about who delivers government services to them (Thielemann and Stewart 1996). Moreover, the government's affirmative action programs are really intended to increase opportunities for women and people of color to enter and to move up within the rank and file workforce. Thus, if various presidents' differing attitudes toward affirmative action were to have an impact on the operation of EEO programs, as many have suggested, we would expect to see this impact at grade levels below the senior executive level. This section examines how the overall representation of women and people of color changed over the twenty-year time frame. The next section looks at whether promotion opportunities for people of color and women were, in fact, restricted during the Reagan/Bush years and whether promotion opportunities for Euro-American males were restricted during the Clinton administration.

Figure 2.3 shows the overall representation of Euro-American women and men and women of color in the federal white-collar workforce at the beginning of each administration and the marginal changes that have occurred from one year to the next. The bar chart shows what one would expect if the federal EEO and affirmative actions were operating as intended, with no intervention to either speed them up or slow them down. There is a gradual increase in the proportion of federal jobs held by men and women of color and a concomitant decrease in the proportion of jobs held by Euro-American men. For the most part, this pattern is consistent with the civilian labor force, where the participation of men has decreased as a percentage of the overall workforce, and the participation of women and people of color has increased over the past few decades (U.S. General Accounting Office 1992). The representation of Euro-American women in federal white-collar jobs does not show a significant change, remaining at about 31 percent for the entire two decades.

It is not clear why the representation of Euro-American women has not continued to grow in concert with their increased participation in the civilian labor force. The OPM (1997) reports that Euro-American women remain underrepresented vis-à-vis the civilian labor force. One possible explanation is that while women are increasing their share of professional and administrative jobs, the large number of clerical jobs, held disproportionately by women, is decreasing. For example, from the end of 1994 to the end of 1997, the number of women holding clerical jobs in the federal government was reduced by more than 43,000 (U.S. Office of Personnel Management 1994b, 1997).

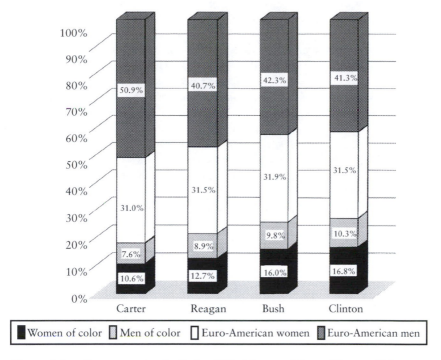

Figure 2.3a   Representation in Federal Workforce at Time of Entry of New
Administration
SOURCE: U.S. Office of Personnel Management, Central Personnel Data File.

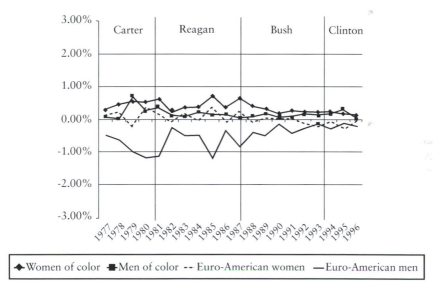

Figure 2.3b   Change in Overall Representation in Federal Workforce
SOURCE: U.S. Office of Personnel Management, Central Personnel Data File.

The line graph shows some differences among administrations at the margins, but they are very small. For the most part, the representation of men and women of color has increased at between 0 and 1 percent per year. This increase was at the expense of Euro-American men, whose share of jobs declined by as much as 1.1 percent in the early and mid-1980s and at a slower rate during all other years. In general, however, the graph presents little evidence that fears that the intake of people of color and women was cut short during the Reagan and Bush years were justified.

This aggregate figure masks the fact that one ethnic group—Latinos—continues to be underrepresented in the federal workforce (U.S. Merit Systems Protection Board 1997). However, an analysis of changes in representation by ethnic group (not shown) shows that Latino participation in the federal workforce has increased at the rate of 0.1 or 0.2 of a percentage point each year, regardless of who is in the White House. The increase of Latinos in federal employment has not kept pace with the growth of Latino participation in the civilian labor force (CLF), which jumped from under 6 percent in 1980 to just over 9 percent in 1995 (U.S. Bureau of the Census 1996, 393). There are many reasons for this, which were discussed in an MSPB report (1997), but the ideology of the president does not appear to be among them.

In summary, the representation of people of color, both male and female, continued to increase under each presidential administration, while the representation of Euro-American women remained stable. Although the rate of change has varied, there is no discernible pattern. This suggests that the concern that the president's attitudes toward affirmative action affects opportunities for women and people of color to enter and remain in the federal civil service is probably overstated. The fact that Euro-American women have not increased their representation at all over this long period is puzzling, but analysis of that issue will have to be pursued separately. Thus, it seems that at least with respect to overall intake into the federal government, employment trends have proceeded independent of presidential administrations.

Advancement Opportunities

Finally, it is important to address the issue of promotion rates. The steady increase in the proportion of women and people of color in federal employment, regardless of whether affirmative action policies were being emphasized, does not mean that they and their Euro-American male counterparts have enjoyed the same opportunities for advancement into higher-graded positions. For many years, there has been a perception among people of color and women that a "glass ceiling" inhibits their opportunities for promotion (see Chapter 4), and more recently Euro-American men have claimed that Clinton administration policies have resulted in reverse discrimination (U.S. Merit Systems Protection Board 1992, 1996).

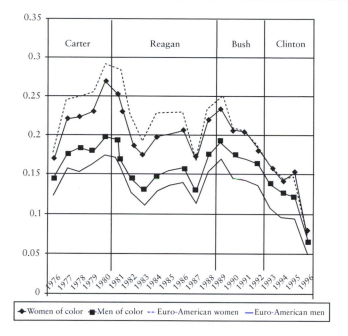

FIGURE 2.4   Promotion Rates
SOURCE: U.S. Office of Personnel Management, Central
Personnel Data File.

Figure 2.4 shows the promotion rates for Euro-American men and women and men and women of color from 1976 to 1996.[2] Promotion rates for each group were calculated by dividing the number of promotions received by each group by the total number of employees in that group.

These data suggest that although there has been considerable variation in opportunities for promotion across administrations, the overall pattern of changes in promotion rates is the same across all four subgroups. When Reagan took office, he initiated a large downsizing effort that reduced promotion rates for white-collar employees considerably (from 22 percent to 14 percent; see Table 2.2). But Figure 2.4 indicates that people of color and women were no more likely to have been adversely affected by this reduction than were Euro-American men. This supports J. Edward Kellough (1989) and Kellough and David Rosenbloom's (1992) analysis of the decrease in the rate of gain in African American, Latino, and female employment in mid-level and higher grades that occurred during the Reagan administration. They speculated that the decrease might have been at least partly a function of federal budget reductions and lower personnel ceilings, rather than simply Reagan's aversion to affirmative action. Indeed, promotion rates declined for Euro-American men as well as for Euro-American women and people of color.

TABLE 2.2   Total Employment in Noncareer SES, Career SES, and Federal
Workforce and Total Promotions, 1976–1996 (Numbers for figures 2.1–2.5)

Fiscal Year	Total Employment			Total Promotions
	Noncareer SES	Career SES	Federal Workforce	
1976	338	4898	1,276,835	184,504
1977	343	5029	1,298,765	249,043
1978	413	4498	1,306,274	252,679
1979	600	5991	1,301,784	260,030
1980	725	5979	1,303,073	291,699
1981	647	5802	1,299,087	281,448
1982	822	6162	1,323,939	219,853
1983	841	5963	1,330,525	193,590
1984	641	7020	1,354,136	229,217
1985	737	6513	1,409,146	246,965
1986	891	6080	1,339,332	248,323
1987	898	5533	1,440,688	204,589
1988	967	6132	1,451,526	275,455
1989	845	6617	1,474,866	305,011
1990	1138	7054	1,497,033	267,131
1991	1175	7222	1,520,273	265,606
1992	1165	7420	1,529,011	248,387
1993	688	7378	1,492,608	203,085
1994	1160	6681	1,442,303	174,590
1995	1217	6488	1,397,547	172,007
1996	1199	6346	1,381,666	84,916

SOURCE: U.S. Office of Personnel Management, Central Personnel Data File.

The data presented in Figure 2.4 also suggest that although the difference is small, women, and particularly Euro-American women, have been promoted at higher rates than the other three groups. Women's apparent advantage is deceptive, however, because these aggregate data mask differences in promotion rates among grade level groups. For example, in lower-graded positions (GS 1–8) where women hold the majority of jobs, their rates of promotion are lower than those of Euro-American men (not shown). This is consistent with a previous analysis conducted by the U.S. Merit Systems Protection Board (1996).

Another important point illustrated by Figure 2.4 is that the concerns expressed by many Euro-American men about their promotion opportunities during the Clinton administration are unfounded. Their promotion rates did not decline at a higher rate than those of people of color or Euro-American women after Clinton took office in 1993. Rather, promotion rates, which began to drop toward the end of the Bush years, took a steep decline across the board in the wake of the Clinton administration's efforts to reduce the size of government. Whereas in 1992 about one in every six white-collar employees could expect to be promoted, by 1996 the number had dropped to about one in sixteen.

These data on promotion rates by group support the finding with respect to employment in the rank and file workforce discussed in the previous section. Changes in presidential administrations have not benefited one group at the expense of another. There has been a gradual increase in the proportion of rank and file jobs held by Euro-American women and people of color over the last two decades of the twentieth century, mirroring the increase that has occurred in the nonfederal workforce. Although promotion rates have varied in response to policy changes among administrations, these have not been directed at any particular group, but rather have affected all about equally.

Conclusion

This chapter has shown that perceptions of the impact of presidential administrations on opportunities for hiring and promotion in the federal civil service are justified, but only in part. Reagan's apparent lack of interest in ensuring adequate representation of women and people of color in his administration does appear to be reflected in the poor representation of these groups among noncareer SES positions in particular, throughout his two terms in office. He also appears to have had some impact on the composition of the career SES as well. The representation of people of color within these ranks did not increase at all during his watch. Since the men and women in these jobs are in positions to make important policy decisions, those who believe the elite corps should be diverse (see Meier 1975) may be justified in their concern about the views of the president toward the importance of diversity.

By the same token, Clinton's avowed effort to deliver a government that "looks like America" is clearly reflected in the increase in the number of people of color, and especially Euro-American women, who were appointed to noncareer SES positions during his administration. The same is true for career SES positions, although progress in this regard was facilitated by circumstances that led to an unusually high turnover in the career SES in 1994.

That having been said, the ideology of the president does not appear to make a difference with respect to the hiring and promotion of rank and file federal employees in white-collar jobs. As would be expected given the changing demographics of the country and the existence of EEO and affirmative action policies within government, Euro-American women and people of color increased their representation in the federal civil service at a steady rate over the last two decades of the twentieth century. Moreover, perceptions that women and people of color had fewer opportunities for promotion under Reagan and that prospects for Euro-American men languished under the Clinton administration are correct, but incomplete. Promotion rates did indeed decline sharply in the first Reagan and Clinton terms, but all groups were affected about equally. This suggests that EEO and targeted recruitment programs put in place in the early 1970s have continued to function. They have done so regardless of the extent to which the president, his cabinet, and his appointees to the oversight agencies (EEOC and OPM) have believed in or actively enforced efforts to increase workforce diversity. By the same token, however, the retrogression in promotion rates also means that it will take longer for women and people of color to reach full representation in higher-level jobs. One could argue that more aggressive affirmative action practices are needed.

From that standpoint, recent actions taken by the other two branches of government are alarming. Such actions include, in particular, the recent *Adarand* decision, which requires federal affirmative action programs to meet a heightened standard of strict scrutiny. Moreover, certain members of Congress, also apparently not satisfied with the clarity of *Adarand's* ban on preferential treatment, have introduced legislation to end affirmative action in federal employment, contracting, and other actions (see Chapter 1).

Thus, it is not clear whether the steady progress made by people of color and women in increasing their representation would continue if such affirmative action strategies were unequivocally forbidden by the courts or Congress rather than simply being discouraged by presidential rhetoric. Moreover, as the size of government is expected to be reduced by an additional 140,000 employees by 2006 (Franklin 1997, 49), promotion rates will continue to be restricted, and it will take a long time for women and people of color to find themselves on an equal footing with Euro-American men in top positions.

There are two lessons to be learned here. One is that presidential and congressional policies with respect to the size and shape of the federal bureaucracy will ultimately make some difference in whether a bureaucracy, representative of America at all grade levels, can be achieved. Presidents will likely continue to influence the composition of the senior executive corps, at least at the margins. Congress and the courts will have an effect on the rank and file to the extent that affirmative action and EEO programs continue to have a statutory basis.

The other lesson is that employees' perceptions of the influence of the political environment on their own prospects for advancement may at times be overstated. As will become clear later in this book, such perceptions can have consequences to the extent that they affect civil servants' views of the fairness of their employer and their own prospects for advancement. Before turning to that issue, however, two more leadership questions must be addressed: Do individual supervisors within government support efforts to achieve a representative bureaucracy? Does their perspective affect their hiring decisions? These are the issues addressed in Chapter 4.

Notes

1. Numbers reported for the period prior to the establishment of the SES refer to SES equivalent positions.

2. Because data on the number of promotions awarded were available only for the first two quarters of FY 1996, I imputed an overall rate for FY 1996 by doubling the number of promotions awarded for the first two quarters.

3

The Micro-Internal Climate

In some cases, the most significant barriers to advancement of women and minorities exist in the minds of the officials who select candidates for promotions or developmental assignments. These barriers are often difficult to confront because they tend to be subtle and hard to identify.

Constance Newman,
former director of the U.S. Office of Personnel Management (OPM),
in her testimony before the Senate Committee on Governmental Affairs,
October 1991

The previous chapter opened with a discussion of how cues from the political leadership have influenced perceptions among some federal employees that their opportunities for advancement are limited because of their race, ethnicity, or gender. As it turned out, at least on a government-wide basis, there did not appear to be a relationship between the president's views on affirmative action and EEO and the employment of Euro-Americans, people of color, or women. However, as Ms. Newman's remarks above confirm, the perspectives of individual supervisors may indeed matter. It is they who make the thousands of individual hiring and promotion decisions that ultimately determine how representative the federal workforce is. This chapter analyzes the extent to which federal supervisors support the concept of representative bureaucracy, and perhaps more important, the impact of their attitudes on their hiring decisions. These are important issues because if few supervisors subscribe to the concept, and particularly if such attitudes do have an impact on their hiring decisions, the general lack of endorsement among federal supervisors may indeed constitute a barrier to the achievement of a fully representative bureaucracy.

Supervisors' Attitudes Toward Achieving a Representative Workforce

Research conducted during the 1970s and 1980s suggested that federal supervisors and managers did not wholeheartedly support programs designed to achieve a representative bureaucracy (Rosenbloom 1981, 1984a; Slack 1987; Milward and Swanson 1979; Daley 1984; Davis and West 1984; Huckle 1983). About one-third of federal managers responding to a survey by the U.S. Office of Personnel Management in 1979 believed that "compared to other employees hired into or promoted into Senior Executive positions, minorities in this agency are *less* qualified" (Rosenbloom 1981, 68–69). Those scholars who focused on the federal sector noted that affirmative employment policies designed to increase the representation of women and minorities were being subverted in many agencies. Many of those who opposed such policies deliberately limited employees of color to minor roles and nonessential tasks, or promised to fill 100 percent of clerical jobs with women to increase female representation (Levine 1974; Rosenbloom 1977; Milward and Swanson 1979).[1]

H. Brinton Milward and Cheryl Swanson (1979) theorize that such a response is explained by organizational behavior that is naturally resistant to externally imposed demands. In the case of affirmative action, they suggest, organizations will minimize the effect of such requirements through shuttling women and people of color into functions external to their technological core. Employees who lack experience in jobs that are fundamental to their organization's mission are much less likely to have an impact on organizational outputs or to be promoted into senior-level positions. Indeed, the Department of Labor, in its study of the glass ceiling in corporate America, found that people of color and women are often steered into staff positions, such as human resources, research, or administration, rather than those jobs that affect the bottom line. Without experience in bottom line–related functions, they are derailed from "the fast track to the executive suite" (U.S. Department of Labor 1991b, 16).

Some aspects of the environment have changed, however, since resistance to increasing the representation of women and people of color was reported (Rosenbloom 1981, 1984a). The publication by the Hudson Institute of *Workforce 2000* (Johnston and Packer 1987) and *Civil Service 2000* (Johnston et al. 1988) focused attention on the increasing proportion of women and minorities in the labor force and the need for employers to respond to these changes in the nature of the labor force (Robinson, Allen, and Abraham 1992; U.S. Merit Systems Protection Board 1993a). Indeed, although noting that the Hudson Institute's projections about the severity of the change in demographics were probably overstated, the U.S. Merit Systems Protection Board (MSPB) nevertheless emphasized that "the

Federal Government needs to give unfaltering attention to programs that foster minority intake and advancement and promote good human relations" (U.S. Merit Systems Protection Board 1993a, 21). The Clinton administration has, of course, gone on record as encouraging agencies to achieve representative workforces. Indeed, the Farmers Home Administration within the Department of Agriculture, the Federal Aviation Administration, and the Office of the Secretary of Defense were some of the agencies that were criticized in the press for directives that were issued to managers encouraging them to set goals to achieve representative workforces (Bridger 1994; Larson 1993, 1995).

Table 3.1 presents responses to a survey of supervisors (hereafter referred to as Supervisor Survey) administered by the MSPB in late 1994 to a government-wide sample of about 10,000 federal supervisors, stratified by race/national origin, grade level, and occupational group. About 5,700 of deliverable surveys were returned, for a response rate of 61 percent. As considerable research has suggested that women and people of color tend to be more supportive than men and Euro-Americans of policies designed to increase the representation of underrepresented groups (Clayton and Crosby 1992; Jacobson 1983), the responses of these groups are broken out separately in Table 3.1.[2]

These questions more directly assess supervisors' perspectives on the goals of the theory of representative bureaucracy than those regarding affirmative action that were asked of supervisors in the 1970s and 1980s. Although Dennis Daley (1984) argues that the concepts of affirmative action and representative bureaucracy are merely different sides of the same coin, it is not at all clear that those who oppose or support one would necessarily have the same attitude toward the other.

As expected, there is considerably more support for the notion that supervisors should be held accountable for achieving a diverse workforce among people of color than among Euro-Americans, and somewhat greater support among women than men. More than two-thirds of people of color (68.6 percent) but only about one-third of Euro-Americans (35.3 percent) agreed or strongly agreed with that statement (see Table 3.1). About half of women (49.1 percent) compared to 39.2 percent of men were in agreement with the statement.

People of color are also more likely than Euro-Americans to agree that their work units would be more productive if they reflected the demographic makeup of the local labor force, although only about one-fifth (20.2 percent) of supervisors of color expressed agreement with this concept. Although about the same percentage of women (10.9 percent) and men (11.7 percent) expressed agreement that their work unit's productivity would be increased if it were representative, more men (43.5 percent) than women (35.8 percent) disagreed with the statement. Women were also

TABLE 3.1   Federal Supervisors' Attitudes Toward Achieving Representative Workforce (Percent)

	Euro-Americans	People of Color	Men	Women
Selecting officials should be held accountable for achieving a workforce that is as diverse as the available civilian labor force.				
Strongly agree/agree	35.3**	68.6	39.2**	49.1
Neither	17.4	14.2	16.1	18.8
Strongly disagree/disagree	45.3	13.9	42.7	29.2
N	4,540	1,094	4,170	1,467
My work unit would be more productive if it reflected the demographic makeup of the local labor force				
Strongly agree/agree	9.4*	20.2	11.7**	10.9
Neither	36.9	32.4	35.0	39.0
Strongly disagree/disagree	43.4	33.1	43.5	35.8
N	4,517	1,072	4,134	1,455
When I am choosing among qualified candidates to hire, I take into consideration whether a candidate is a member of a group that is underrepresented in my work unit(s).				
Strongly agree/agree	45.9*	46.1	45.8	46.2
Neither	19.6	18.8	19.6	19.0
Strongly disagree/disagree	31.9	30.3	31.8	31.0
N	4,509	1,073	4,134	1,453

*p<.01
**p<.001
NOTE: Not shown are those responding "don't know."
SOURCE: U.S. Merit Systems Protection Board, *Supervisor Survey* (1994).

more likely than men to express neither agreement nor disagreement with the statement (39 percent of women and 35 percent of men), or to respond that they did not know how representation would affect their work unit's productivity (14.4 percent of women and 9.8 percent of men, not shown).

With respect to whether they take underrepresentation into account in choosing among qualified candidates, the differences between the groups are not meaningful. In the case of men and women, the difference does not even reach statistical significance. Nevertheless, nearly half of all supervisors did report that they take underrepresentation into account when choosing among qualified applicants. That suggests that many supervisors consider underrepresentation for reasons unrelated to any potential improvement of work output.

Factors Affecting Likelihood to Support Representative Bureaucracy

It would be useful to know what, other than race/ethnicity or sex distinguishes those supervisors who support representative bureaucracy from those who don't. In order to do so, a multiple regression model was estimated. The dependent variable is an index (scaled 2 to 10) that combines the first and second items reported in Table 3.1.[3] Independent variables are included that previous research or logic suggests would predict support for a representative workforce. The most obvious of these are race/ethnicity (Euro-American or person of color) and gender.

Because supervisors are accountable to their own supervisors, variables representing the race/ethnicity and sex of respondents' supervisors were included in the model. Variables were also included representing whether the respondent's own work unit consists of primarily women and/or primarily people of color. It seems logical that a supervisor who already has a diverse work group would be more likely to support the importance of achieving representation than one whose work group is more homogeneous. Whether the workforce supervised is primarily professional and administrative rather than blue collar, clerical, or technical was also taken into account because previous research has indicated that there is at least a slight tendency for professionalism to generate support for employing people of color (Thompson 1976).

In addition to these organizational factors, individual attributes are also included in the model. These include years of supervisory experience, years in current supervisory position, grade level, supervisory level (first line, second line, etc.), and amount of education. Previous research has suggested that education and grade level are positively correlated with support for affirmative action (Kluegel and Smith 1983; Slack 1987; Clayton and Crosby 1992), and a case could be made that the same relationship would hold with attitudes toward the importance of achieving a representative workforce. However, research that has examined the circumstances under which administrators are more likely to serve as "active" representatives has found that tenure, rank in an organization, and education are inversely related to an advocacy role. These researchers have speculated that tenure and education contribute to a socialization process that influences employees' attitudes (Thompson 1976; Meier 1993a; Selden 1997b). In this case it was expected that such socialization would lead supervisors to emphasize hiring according to a strict merit system over representativeness.

Table 3.2 presents this analysis of support for a representative workforce. The model is significant, explaining 12 percent of the variance in supervisors' support for a representative workforce. As predicted, women and people of color are more supportive of the notion of a representative workforce, even controlling for all else. However, neither the sex nor the race/ethnicity of their own supervisors, nor whether their work units are already dominated by women or people of color, appears to have an impact. Those who supervise primarily women are slightly less likely to support the notion that a representative workforce is important. It may be that these respondents supervise largely clerical staff among whom the value of representativeness would be less obvious. Note that those who supervise professional or administrative workforces are more supportive, as anticipated, than those who supervise primarily technical, clerical, and/or manual work.

The suggestion that education and experience in the workforce would provide socialization in favor of the merit system over representation was only partially supported. Those with less education show more support for a representative workforce, while tenure as a supervisor has no bearing, controlling for all else. Of course, the survey did not ask how much of this experience took place in the federal government and how much may have been outside the government.

In terms of grade levels, senior executives and supervisors in grade GS 13–15 jobs are less supportive than lower-graded supervisors (GS 12 and below). Bivariate analysis (not shown) confirms this linear, inverse relationship between grade level group and support for representation. In contrast, there is no such linear relationship when comparing the views of supervisors holding different levels of managerial responsibility. Those who describe themselves as executives in charge of major programs and those who are second-line supervisors are more supportive than first-line supervisors (the reference group). The level of support among managers, who wield greater responsibility than those in second-line jobs but less than executives, is not distinguishable from that of first-line supervisors.

TABLE 3.2 Factors Predicting Support for Representative Workforce

Variable	B	SE B	Beta	Sig. T
Person of color	1.254	.071	.256	.000
Gender (female)	.343	.067	.081	.000
Has supervisor of color	−.013	.078	−.003	.864
Has female supervisor	−.070	.073	−.014	.341
Supervises primarily people of color	−.083	.080	−.015	.302
Supervises primarily women	−.151	.076	−.032	.047
Professional/Administrative	.197	.060	.053	.001
Education	−.301	.033	−.149	.000
Tenure as supervisor	.039	.021	.028	.065
Pay grade				
Senior executive	−.805	.224	−.058	.000
GS 13–15	−.362	.059	−.097	.000
Supervisory level				
Executive	.525	.153	.056	.001
Manager	−.014	.081	−.003	.859
Second-level	.192	.065	.045	.003
Knows how representative workforce is	.224	.030	.105	.000
(Constant)	5.152	.199		

$R^2 = 12.3$
$p < .001$
$n = 4526$
NOTE: See Appendix 1 for item coding.
SOURCE: Merit Systems Protection Board, *Survey of Supervisors,* 1994.

At first blush it may appear contradictory that while those with executive-level responsibilities tend to be *more* in agreement with the importance of a representative workforce than lower-level managers, members of the SES show *less* agreement than employees who hold jobs at the GS 12 level or below. However, there is less overlap between those who describe themselves as executives and those who report their grade level as SES than one might think. Only 24 percent of those who described their jobs as executive level also reported that they were members of the SES, and only about half (58 percent) of members of the SES described their jobs as executive.[4] Finally, as expected, those who know how representative their work units are show more support for the concept of representation as important.

Thus, among federal supervisors and managers, those who believe in the importance of having a representative workforce are most likely to be less educated and female—supervisors of color supervising professional and administrative workforces. Although those in lower graded positions are more likely to be supportive, there is no such linear relationship between level of managerial responsibility and endorsement of the concept. The factor having the greatest impact, however, is the supervisor's own race/ethnicity. Because supervisors of color (and women) represent a minority of federal supervisors,[5] they are less likely to have an impact on the demographic makeup of the overall federal workforce. The more important issue, to be addressed next, is whether supervisors' attitudes have an impact on their hiring decisions, or whether these decisions are made independently of their personal beliefs. If supervisors antagonistic to the concept of a representative bureaucracy are less likely to make an effort to recruit or hire members of groups that are underrepresented in their work unit regardless of official policy, then such attitudes may indeed constitute a barrier to the achievement of a fully representative bureaucracy.

Supervisors' Recruitment Efforts

To examine the relationship between supervisors' attitudes about representation and their actual recruitment efforts, a subsample of the supervisors responding to the MSPB Supervisor Survey was employed. The survey was designed, in part, to address the issue of the persistent underrepresentation of Latinos in the federal workforce (see U.S. Merit Systems Protection Board 1997). Therefore, it asked supervisors several questions of interest here:

- Do you have final authority to select candidates for vacant jobs under your supervision? [If not] do you recommend selection to a supervisor? (5,141 supervisors responded affirmatively.)
- How many candidates have you recommended or selected in the past three years for vacant positions under your supervision? (4,512 supervisors recommended or selected at least one.)
- Do you believe Hispanics are underrepresented in your work unit? (2,125 supervisors responded yes.)

Only the 1,294 supervisors who responded positively to all three questions (and for whom there was complete information) were included in this analysis. The dependent variable is an item that is coded 1 if supervisors reported that either they had been personally involved in recruiting Latinos, or they had actively considered Latino applicants in the past three years. The item was coded 0 if they answered no to both of these questions. The dependent variable is dichotomous (has recruited or considered Latino applicants or not), so logistic regression is used to evaluate the effect of supervisors' attitudes on their actions. The primary independent variable is the index measuring "support" that was the dependent variable in Table 3.2.

TABLE 3.3   Effect of Support for Representative Bureaucracy on Efforts to Recruit Latinos (Logistic Regression Coefficients)

Variable	B	S.E.	Sig	Odds Ratio
Support for representative workforce	.065	.031	.038	1.067
Latino	1.545	.304	.000	4.689
Education	.317	.067	.000	1.372
Pay grade: GS 13–15	.408	.127	.001	1.503
Responsibility: Executive level	1.117	.246	.000	3.055
Constant		-2.243	.339	.000

Chi sq. = 98.93, adjusted R^2 = .094, N = 1294
NOTE: See Appendix 1 for item coding.
SOURCE: Merit Systems Protection Board, *Survey of Supervisors*, 1994.

Initially, all the factors that affect supervisors' attitudes toward the value of a representative workforce from Table 3.2 were included in the model (not shown). However, because in this case the dependent variable specifically addresses the recruitment of Latinos, variables were included to indicate whether the respondent was specifically Latino or not, or a non-Latino supervisor of color. The model was respecified to find the best fitting, most parsimonious one, and that is presented in Table 3.3.

The results show that, even controlling for other factors, support for a representative workforce increases the likelihood that a supervisor will recruit Latinos. The effect is small, however. What turns out to be of even greater significance is whether the supervisor himself or herself is Latino. This is consistent with research on the employment of people of color in cities, which has found that the presence of a chief executive of color contributes significantly to the proportion of minorities employed by the city government (Eisinger 1982; Stein 1986; Dye and Renick 1981; Cole 1976). More highly educated, executive-level supervisors in GS 13–15 jobs are also more likely to make the effort than those with lower-level responsibilities. In fact, an executive is more than three times as likely as a non-executive to make an effort to recruit or consider Latinos.

Whether these findings can be generalized to other hires of people of color is difficult to say. As Fernandez (1981) argues, people of color have been subject to different stereotypes and unique experiences with respect to discrimination (see also Federal Glass Ceiling Commission 1995b). Latinos were classified as Euro-Americans until 1970 and at times have been viewed very positively, whereas attitudes toward African Americans have been consistently negative (Fernandez 1981). These differences in experi-

TABLE 3.4   Probability of Recruiting or Considering Latinos (Percent)

	Level of Agreement with Value of Representative Workforce		
	Strong Disagreement	*Neither*	*Strong Agreement*
Non-Latino	49	56	62
Latino	82	85	88

SOURCE: Merit Systems Protection Board, *Survey of Supervisors*, 1994.

ences more than likely have an impact on the consciousness of members of the various groups and the relative importance they give to the need to recruit others from their group when they have the opportunity.

The relative weight that support for a representative workforce holds in supervisors' decisions to engage in recruitment or consideration of Latinos is demonstrated in another way in Table 3.4. In this table, covariates are held constant using the characteristics of the "average" supervisor responding to the survey (i.e., the modal response) and varying the level of the score on the Support index. (Recall that the index is coded from 2 for strong disagreement to 10 for strong agreement with the value of a representative workforce.) The plurality of supervisors is in GS 13–15, non-executive jobs, and has a college degree.

As shown in Table 3.4, there is a 62 percent probability that a typical supervisor who believes in the value of a representative workforce and knows that Latinos are underrepresented in his or her work unit will make an effort to recruit or consider Latino candidates. For supervisors who disagree with the importance of a representative workforce, there is only a 49 percent probability that they will make an effort to correct Latino underrepresentation in their work units.

However, the results also suggest that the hypothetical average supervisor who is Latino is even more likely to try to recruit Latinos than are non-Latino supervisors, whether or not that supervisor believes diversity is important. Even a Latino supervisor who *disagrees* that representation is important has an 82 percent probability of taking steps to hire additional Latinos. A Latino who believes representativeness is important has an 88 percent chance of making such efforts.

Thus, it seems that if an agency is concerned about correcting Latino underrepresentation, its efforts are best spent on recruiting or promoting Latinos into supervisory positions, who will, in turn, likely make an effort to ensure their work units reflect adequate Latino representation. An additional, though somewhat less effective strategy, would be to educate supervisors about the value of a representative workforce, because such a belief does have at least a small impact on their recruitment efforts.

Limitations and Future Research

This analysis has shown that despite efforts by the Clinton administration to promote the value of workforce diversity, fewer than half of federal managers and supervisors who make actual hiring and promotion decisions take underrepresentation into account when choosing among applicants. Only about one-tenth believe diversity contributes to their work units' productivity. While we know that minorities, and to a lesser extent women, are more committed to ensuring that they have representative workforces, we have not learned much more about the factors that influence such support. Whether that supervisor's own supervisor is a woman or person of color does not seem to affect his or her views, nor does the composition of his or her work unit. Tenure in the workforce also apparently has little influence. Those in grades above GS 12 are more supportive, as are executives and second-level managers. Supervisors of professional and administrative or blue-collar workforces appear to be more likely to support efforts to achieve full representation.

Research on attitudes toward affirmative action programs has demonstrated the importance of perceptions of fairness of the procedures used to distribute opportunities and awards (Clayton and Crosby 1992; Nacoste and Hummels 1994; Peterson 1994). How supervisors evaluate the fairness of the procedures they are expected to follow to achieve representative workforces, and perhaps also the means by which they are held accountable for their efforts, may better explain their support or opposition to the policy than any of the variables used in this analysis. It is possible that if this survey had included items measuring supervisors' evaluations of procedural fairness in their organizations, a model could have been estimated that would have explained a greater proportion of the variance in support for a representative workforce.

This chapter began by suggesting that what is most important for this analysis of the barriers to achieving a representative federal bureaucracy is whether supervisors' lack of support has a discernible impact on their efforts to correct underrepresentation in their workforces. An index measuring beliefs that their workforces would be more productive if diverse and whether supervisors should be held accountable for diversity did register a small impact on the likelihood that they would make an effort to recruit an underrepresented group (in this case, Latinos). What is of more consequence, however, appears to be supervisors' own race/national origin.

Whether such strong commitment to hiring members of their group would be found among African Americans, Asian Pacific Americans or Native Americans, or Euro-American women is not known; this survey did not include questions about hiring members of those other groups. Mexican Americans, who make up the largest share of Latinos in this country, share a sense of community and common values that may bind them more than other groups (Rubaii-Barrett and Beck 1993) and influence their hiring decisions. At the same time, prior research has found that women do benefit when women are in political decision-making positions (Warner, Steel, and Lovrich 1989). The employment of people of color has been found to increase with the presence of a mayor of color, as well (Stein 1986; Cole 1976; Dye and Renick 1981).

Research on the treatment of people of color in organizations suggests reasons to believe that other groups may *not* exhibit the same behaviors as Latinos. The greater discrimination perceived by African Americans has led to their more critical views as to how they are treated in organizations (Fernandez 1981; see also Naff 1995). Thus, they may well be as likely to hire African Americans as Latinos are to hire Latinos. On the other hand, although Asian Americans are not well represented in supervisory positions, they face little discrimination in achieving high grades and salaries (Kim and Lewis 1994). Thus, Asian Pacific Americans may not feel equally compelled to recruit other Asian Pacific Americans to follow in their footsteps. Although Fernandez finds that Native Americans have less sympathy for other people of color than members of those other groups (Fernandez 1981), their numbers are so few within the federal workforce that it is probably not possible to conduct an analysis like the one carried out for Latinos in this chapter. Still, it is clear that future research examining whether non-Latino supervisors of color are equally likely to make an effort to recruit members who share their race/ethnicity would have value for understanding catalysts that could be engaged to achieve a representative bureaucracy.

Conclusion

This analysis has shed light on another potential barrier to the achievement of a representative bureaucracy, and that is insufficient support for the concept among federal supervisors and managers. There is not overwhelming support for this notion among federal supervisors. However, supervisors who believe in the importance of achieving a representative workforce do appear to be more likely to engage in efforts to recruit from groups that are underrepresented in their work units. This suggests that educational efforts aimed at convincing supervisors of the value of representation could be effective in amplifying their efforts to eliminate underrepresentation through targeted recruitment or other strategies consistent with the current legal framework (see Chapter 1).

The findings presented in this chapter indicate that the best means for increasing the representation of people of color in the workforce may be to ensure that people of color are adequately represented in the supervisory ranks. Latinos, at least, show a much greater willingness to attempt to correct Latino underrepresentation in their work units than do non-Latinos. However, Latinos hold fewer than 10 percent of supervisory jobs in the government (U.S. Office of Personnel Management 1999). Moreover, the Clinton administration has been engaged in a successful effort to downsize and "flatten" government by eliminating supervisory positions (National Performance Review 1993). Relying on Latino supervisors or other supervisors of color to correct underrepresentation may have limited utility. A better approach may be to ensure that nonsupervisory people of color are included on panels that engage in the recruitment and evaluation of candidates for jobs.

The next issue to be addressed, however, is what happens to women and employees of color who are hired into government jobs. Will the goals envisioned by the theory of representative bureaucracy be met simply by making efforts to hire those who are underrepresented in federal agencies? Or are there policies and practices that limit the authority and opportunities available to those employees who are already on board? That question is the focus of Chapter 4.

Notes

1. Research has shown that support for affirmative action varies depending on how the question is worded (Fine 1992; Kravitz and Platania 1993). S. M. Lipset and W. Schneider (1978) explain the apparent contradiction in responses to various opinion polls as evidence of the conflict between two values at the core of the American creed: individualism and egalitarianism. Americans believe minorities and women should have equal opportunities, but their success in achieving employment should depend on their individual initiative. In light of the many benefits of a representative bureaucracy described in Chapter 1, it is not clear whether affirmative employment policies in government would be equated with ensuring equal access to bureaucratic positions or unwarranted preferential treatment.

2. There were too few supervisors in each of the race/ethnic categories to break them out separately.

3. A factor analysis showed that the question concerning the supervisor's own behavior represents a different construct and so was not included in this scale.

4. Another possible explanation for these apparently contradictory results is that they could reflect multicolinearity among the grade level and job level categories. However, multicolinearity diagnostics showed no evidence of this problem.

5. According to data from the Central Personnel Data File for September 1995, 61 percent of supervisors are Euro-American men. They are also higher graded, on average, than supervisors from other groups.

4

Glass Ceilings

There is a level to which the majority will allow minorities to proceed up the ladder. Once you hit that level, you are not going to go any further.

A Latino man participating in a focus group assembled by
the Federal Glass Ceiling Commission, circa 1994

Since first used in a *Wall Street Journal* article in 1986 (Hymowitz and Schellhardt 1986), the term *glass ceiling* has been used to describe subtle, almost invisible barriers that hinder the advancement of women and people of color as they try to climb career ladders in organizations. The metaphor suggests that the underrepresentation of women and people of color in top-level positions cannot be entirely explained by a lack of qualifications, disinclination to hold such positions, or even because of overt discrimination. Rather, the obstacles that impede them are elusive, and nearly imperceptible.

Research in both the private and public sectors has found evidence of such a glass ceiling (U.S. Department of Labor 1991b, U.S. Merit Systems Protection Board 1992, Federal Glass Ceiling Commission 1995b). The Federal Glass Ceiling Commission, created by Title II of the Civil Rights Act of 1991, noted in its fact-finding report that "equally qualified and similarly situated citizens are being denied equal access to advancement into senior-level management on the basis of gender, race, or ethnicity" (Federal Glass Ceiling Commission 1995b, 10).

Federal employment data suggest a similar pattern. Women held 43 percent of federal jobs in 1997, but only 21 percent of senior-level jobs. At the same time, people of color held 29 percent of federal jobs, but only 12 percent of senior-level jobs (U.S. Office of Personnel Management 1997).

Is there, then, a glass ceiling in the federal government, or are there other reasons, having nothing to do with race/ethnicity or sex, for the poor representation of people of color and women in top jobs? If there is a glass ceiling, then what does it look like? What are the "invisible" barriers that women and people of color face that the current Equal Employment Opportunity (EEO) programs fail to address? If women and people of color are stymied in their efforts to move up into senior-level positions by a glass ceiling, that ceiling clearly represents a barrier to the achievement of a representative bureaucracy. This chapter uses government-wide survey data, complemented with observations made by federal participants in focus groups, to identify the existence and nature of a glass ceiling in the federal government. It begins with a brief discussion of the glass ceiling's ascension as a national policy issue.

The Glass Ceiling Unveiled

An effort to systematically understand the nature of the glass ceiling in the private sector was initiated in 1989 by the Office of Federal Contract Compliance Programs (OFCCP), under the leadership of then-Secretary of Labor Elizabeth Dole. Housed in the Department of Labor (DOL), OFCCP has the responsibility to ensure that private sector companies (of a certain size) that do business with the federal government comply with EEO and affirmative action requirements. To do so, it conducts several thousand compliance reviews each year (U.S. Department of Labor 1991a). In the fall of 1989, OFCCP announced that it would undertake a "glass ceiling initiative" to discover where and why there was poor representation of women and people of color within the executive ranks. The results of the pilot study of nine unnamed corporations were released in 1991 (U.S. Department of Labor 1991b). The study found that people of color and women faced "attitudinal and organizational barriers" including incommensurate access to developmental practices and credential-building experiences and narrow recruitment practices (U.S. Department of Labor 1991b, 4–5). The OFCCP ultimately institutionalized glass ceiling analyses as part of its regular compliance reviews.

Meanwhile, the labor secretary's husband, Senator Robert Dole, introduced legislation to create a "Federal Glass Ceiling Commission" charged with "examining the reasons behind the existence of the glass ceiling and making recommendations with respect to policies which would eliminate any impediments to the advancement of women and people of color" (*Congressional Record*, U.S. Senate, February 21, 1991). This legislation was then incorporated as Title II of the Civil Rights Act of 1991 (Pub. L. 102–166, 105 Stat. 1071), and signed into law in November 1991.

The bipartisan commission issued two reports in 1995. The first was a "fact-finding report" that confirmed that "significant barriers continue to exist ... [that] impede the advancement of qualified people of color and women" (Federal Glass Ceiling Commission 1995b, 9). This was followed by a second report that made recommendations directed toward businesses and government. Among its recommendations to government was that it should "lead by example" by making an effort to eliminate internal glass ceilings in its own agencies (Federal Glass Ceiling Commission 1995a).

Senator John Glenn, then-Chairman of the Senate Committee on Governmental Affairs, the U.S. Merit Systems Protection Board (MSPB), and the U.S. Office of Personnel Management (OPM) addressed the possible existence of a glass ceiling in federal employment. In May and October 1991, Senator Glenn held hearings to address the underrepresentation of women and people of color in federal agencies. Called to testify, then-Chairman of the Equal Employment Opportunity Commission (EEOC) Evan J. Kemp admitted that the agency had not fully enforced affirmative action requirements among federal agencies and so was partly at fault for the glass ceiling (Newlin 1991). In response to requests from Senator Glenn and others, the U.S. General Accounting Office (GAO) conducted several analyses of the representation of women and people of color in federal agencies (see, for example, U.S. General Accounting Office 1991a, 1991b, 1991c).

At the same time, and partly in response to the heightened attention given to the glass ceiling by the Department of Labor, MSPB undertook its own examination of the phenomenon with respect to women in 1990. The MSPB report, issued in 1992, reported that "a glass ceiling does exist in the Federal Government [that] consists, in part, of factors that women can control, such as their education, experience, and mobility. It also consists of factors outside of women's control such as unfounded judgments about their lack of job commitment and their ability to do their jobs well" (U.S. Merit Systems Protection Board 1992, 37). The MSPB undertook a subsequent study of the glass ceiling as it affects federal employees of color, later broadened to focus on a wider range of employment practices, and released it in 1996 (U.S. Merit Systems Protection Board 1996). Following on the heels of the Department of Labor, GAO, and MSPB, OPM established an interagency glass ceiling planning group that met for the first time in October 1992. That group, however, was disbanded shortly after James King took over the directorship of the agency in 1993.

The Center for Women in Government at the State University of New York, Albany, drew attention to the glass ceiling in state and local agencies. The Center's newsletter, issued in the winter of 1991–1992, reported that women and people of color only held about one-third of top-level state and local jobs, compared to 58 percent of other jobs (Center for Women in Government, 1991/1992). A later issue of the newsletter coined another metaphor—the "sticky floor"—to suggest that many women are also found in low-paying jobs in state and local governments, which offer little mobility (Center for Women in Government 1992).

In summary, the glass ceiling is an important issue in the federal government because it describes one set of obstacles that women and people of color face in organizations. These obstacles limit their opportunities for advancement into positions of greater authority. However, it is also an issue that has received national attention and therefore has gained more notoriety and perhaps legitimacy than some of the other barriers described in this book. What, then, does the glass ceiling really entail?

Factors Affecting Advancement

Most discussions of the glass ceiling start by describing the poor representation of women and/or people of color in senior jobs in organizations. The 1986 *Wall Street Journal* article in which the term *glass ceiling* was coined reported, for example, that only 2 percent of top executives surveyed in 1985 were women. Nearly a decade later, Secretary of Labor Robert Reich made a similar observation in his preface to the Federal Glass Ceiling Commission's fact-finding report: "The [Commission's] fact finding report . . . confirms the enduring aptness of the 'glass ceiling' metaphor. At the highest levels of business, there is indeed a barrier only rarely penetrated by women or persons of color. Consider: 97% of the senior managers of Fortune 1000 industrial and Fortune 500 companies are white; 95 to 97% are male" (1995b, iii).

However, the objection can be raised (and often is) that concluding that there is a glass ceiling from these statistics doesn't take into account differences in qualifications or aspirations to hold top-level positions on the part of women and people of color. Any individual's advancement potential depends, at least in part, on the investments that person has made in himself or herself, that is, his or her "human capital." Such investments generally include education, professional experience, and occupational choice.

This is certainly true in the federal government, where those who are in higher graded jobs tend to have more education and experience than those in lower graded jobs (Grandjean 1981; Lewis 1988; Hale and Kelly 1989; Powell and Butterfield 1994). Data from the Office of Executive Resources at OPM confirms that on average, federal career senior executives have twenty-three years of service, and the majority (69 percent) have advanced degrees. About half are in professional jobs (49 percent) and the other half in administrative or technical jobs (51 percent).

In many organizations, advancement is also tied to other labor market experiences, such as working in more than one part of the country or in more than one agency (Markham et al. 1983; Rosenbaum 1979; Stroh,

Brett, and Reilly 1992). For many employers, these kinds of experiences and accomplishments demonstrate a desirable breadth of experience as well as commitment to one's career that are justifiably considered in promotion decisions (Markham et al. 1983). Taking leaves of absence, regardless of the reasons, can result in fewer promotions (Judiesch and Lyness 1999). Federal employees will have an easier time advancing into higher grades if they work in Washington, D.C., where most agency headquarters are located and grade levels tend to be higher (Lewis 1995). According to OPM, 73 percent of federal senior executives work in the Washington, D.C. area. In the federal government, senior managers are generally expected to put in long hours (Bayes 1991).

There are other factors that affect advancement as well. These factors, however, are less a matter of individuals investing in their own career advancement than work-related opportunities that they may or may not have access to. For example, in its report on the glass ceiling in corporate America, the Department of Labor noted that many corporations identify key employees early and then ensure they are given credential-building experiences such as rotational assignments, mentoring, and highly visible projects. Networks also play an important role in recruiting, and those who have access to them are much more likely to have a shot at a good job. The DOL noted that women and people of color are less likely to be identified for key assignments or to be part of such networks (U.S. Department of Labor 1991b). The same is often true in public sector agencies (Kelly et al. 1991; Hale 1992; Moore 1992).

Finally, it should be noted that previous research has found that, although representing neither human capital nor opportunities, one's family can affect career prospects. There is evidence that successful women are more likely to be unmarried and childless. Having a family does not appear to have such an impact on the advancement of men, however (Hale and Kelly 1989; Johnson and Duerst-Lahti 1992; Kelly et al. 1991; Newman 1993; Guy 1993).

Considerable research has examined advancement patterns and income inequality in the federal government and concluded that some, but by no means all, of the gaps between men and women, and Euro-Americans and civil servants of color, can be explained by differences in human capital (Long 1976; Borjas 1978; Taylor 1979; Lewis 1986a, 1986b, 1986c, 1987, 1992, 1995, 1998). A study of salary attainment in one Navy installation concluded: "No matter what their education, females started at lower salaries and stayed lower than their male counterparts" (U.S. Naval Air Warfare Center Weapons Division 1994, 3). A study by an OPM analyst found that women were 19 percent less likely than men to be promoted during the first five years of their careers, but 11 percent more likely than men to be promoted after that point. He also found that African Americans were less likely to be promoted than other racial/ethnic groups (Heim 1997). However, most of these analyses have relied on data available in the government's employment database: the Central Personnel Data File (CPDF). In doing so, they have not been able to take into account all of the variables that affect career advancement.

This chapter employs government-wide survey data to examine reasons for the poor representation of women and people of color in high-level federal jobs. Because the surveys asked respondents about career-related experiences in addition to their human capital, we can do a more comprehensive analysis to discern whether it is gender or race/ethnicity alone that explains the lower career attainment of women and people of color, or whether it is explained by these other factors. The next two sections of this chapter examine the career advancement experiences of women and people of color, respectively.

Women and Career Advancement in the Federal Government

Women's career advancement is assessed primarily using responses of federal mid- and senior-level employees to a Survey on Career Development administered by MSPB in 1991 as part of its study of the glass ceiling as it affects women (U.S. Merit Systems Protection Board 1992). The survey (hereafter referred to as the Career Development Survey) was mailed to a government-wide, stratified, random sample of 13,000 mid- and senior-level employees in white-collar jobs. The sample was designed to be representative of men and women in three grade groups (GS 9–12, GS 13–15, and the SES) and by major department or agency. A total of 8,400 employees responded, for a response rate of 65 percent. For this analysis, only the responses of the approximately 6,600 men and women in professional and administrative jobs are used because it is only these jobs that have advancement potential to senior levels. When weighted to correct for oversampling, the dataset includes 4,500 men and 2,141 women. These survey data are supplemented with information obtained from focus groups of men and women in GS 13–15 and SES jobs, convened by MSPB as part of the same study.

Responses to the Career Development Survey, which asked respondents to report their current grade, show that women on average have not advanced as far as men. The average grade level for women is 11.39, compared to 12.26 for men. This difference would likely have been even greater if employees in lower-level jobs had also been included in the survey, because women are found disproportionately in those jobs.[1] What accounts for the difference?

Explaining Differences in Grade Attainment

If there are differences in human capital or work-related opportunities, these might account for the difference in average grade. Table 4.1 provides the responses of male and female survey respondents when asked about these factors.

The data in Table 4.1 suggest that there are differences between men and women with respect to human capital. For example, considerably more men than women have over twenty years of experience. More than twice as many women lack college degrees. Survey data confirm the important relationship between education and advancement. A comparison of the average grade attained by survey respondents with various levels of education shows that there is more than a two-grade difference between those with no college degree (average grade of 11.1) and those with a doctorate or professional degree (average grades of 13.4 and 13.6 respectively).

It is important to note that the education differential between women and men is changing—the same proportion of both groups who reported that they had been working for the government for ten or fewer years have at least a bachelor's degree. But advancement depends on experience as well as education. Only 48 percent of women, compared to 71 percent of men, who reported having ten to twenty years of federal experience have at least a college degree. Similarly, only 23 percent of women with more than twenty years of experience have at least a college degree, compared to 68 percent of men with comparable experience.

Women are also less likely to have had work experience in their current profession outside of government. They are slightly more likely than men to work at headquarters where there are a greater number of higher-level jobs. Twice as many men have relocated three or more times during their careers. The survey also asked respondents about any leaves of absence of six or more weeks they may have taken, as these would presumably detract from their career advancement. Women are more likely to have taken leaves of absences, although only a minority of either group has done so. Women tend to work fewer hours per week, on average, than men, although the difference isn't marked. About half of each group works between forty-one and fifty hours per week; 10 percent more men than women work more than that.

Multiple regression analysis is used to examine whether women are less likely than men to advance into higher-grade levels once all of these factors

TABLE 4.1   Comparison Between Men and Women of Factors Affecting Career
Advancement (Percent)

	Women	Men
Human Capital Factors		
Education		
No college degree	35.7	15.8
Bachelor's degree	34.7	40.5
Graduate degree	28.7	43.7
Federal service		
Up to 5 years	12.0	9.8
5 to 10 years	13.7	9.9
10 to 20 years	41.0	31.3
20 to 30 years	28.6	35.8
More than 30 years	4.7	13.2
Experience outside government		
None	50.1	39.5
Up to 5 years	31.9	32.5
More than 5 years	18.0	28.0
Number of geographic relocations		
None	68.4	49.9
One	14.2	15.4
Two	7.2	11.7
Three or more	10.3	23.1
Work location		
Headquarters	43.4	35.9
Regional office	17.6	17.0
Field office	33.9	41.3
Average hours of work per week		
Less than 40	1.9	1.1
40	34.7	27.5
41 to 45	32.1	26.4
46 to 50	21.2	25.2
51 or more	10.1	19.7
Number of leaves of absences		
None	61.1	88.4
One	21.5	8.2
Two	12.0	2.1
Three or more	4.5	1.0
Work-Related Opportunities		
Mentor		
Had	77.1	69.1
Did not have	22.9	30.9

(continues)

(continued)

Average days of travel per month		
0 to 5 days	43.6	56.4
6 to 10 days	32.4	67.6
10 or more days	4.9	6.5
Family circumstances		
Spouse		
Yes	68.7	88.4
No	31.3	11.6
Children during career		
Yes	62.0	80.4
No	38.0	19.6

NOTE: All relationships significant at the .05 level
SOURCE: U.S. Merit Systems Protection Board, *Career Development Survey*, 1991.

have been taken into account. The dependent variable is the current grade level of respondents.[2] The results are presented in Table 4.2.

The model predicts 24 percent of the variance in advancement. As would be expected, more education and experience, as well as the ability to work long hours and travel, are important characteristics shared by those who have successfully moved into high-level jobs. However, even controlling for these factors, women are less likely to advance into higher grade levels. These results do lend support to the notion that a glass ceiling is inhibiting the advancement of women into senior-level jobs.

The next step is to examine the impact of family-related variables on career advancement. Because previous research has suggested that having a family affects men's and women's careers in different ways, we specify separate models for each. These results appear in Table 4.3.

The results show that, even controlling for all other career-related factors, family is important. Having a spouse or partner has a positive effect on men's career advancement, but does not affect women's. The presence of young children in the household has a negative impact on women's careers, but has a positive impact on men's careers. This finding is consistent with research in the private and public sectors, which has found a similar dichotomy in the impact of children on men's and women's careers (Brett and Stroh 1999; Guy 1992, 1993; Hale and Kelly 1989). Another look at the Career Development Survey shows this effect in a different way. Although 86 percent of male respondents who successfully reached the senior executive ranks had children living with them during their careers, only 54 percent of women did. We shall discuss these findings in more detail shortly.

TABLE 4.2   Impact of Factors on Career Advancement

Variable	B	S.E.B.	Beta	Sig. T
Gender (female)	−.413	.072	−.115	.000
Federal experience	.221	.017	.242	.000
Nonfederal professional experience	−.007	.018	−.007	.695
Education	.208	.019	.198	.000
Number of geographic relocations	.031	.020	.028	.129
Number of absences of more than six weeks	−.078	.044	−.034	.073
Work at headquarters	.185	.087	.044	.032
Work in field office	−.386	.064	−.125	.000
Average hours of work per week	.338	.026	.239	.000
Average days of travel per month	.039	.037	.019	.287
Has/had mentor	−.122	.065	−.034	.061
(Constant)	9.702	.210		.000

$R^2 = .24$ $p < .001$ $n = 6600$

NOTE: See Appendix 2 for item coding.

SOURCE: U.S. Merit Systems Protection Board, *Career Development Survey*, 1991.

First, it is important to address the possibility, as yet unaccounted for in the models, that women are less career-oriented than men.

The MSPB Career Development Survey asked respondents about the extent to which various statements applied to themselves. Nearly all men and women (95 percent of women and 93 percent of men) reported that they were very committed to their jobs to some or a great extent. An equal proportion of both groups also indicated that they were always enthusiastic about their jobs (about 90 percent). Slightly more women (78 percent) than men (74 percent) reported that they were willing to devote whatever time is necessary to their jobs to advance their careers.

There is no evidence, then, that women are less career oriented than men. Nor is there reason to believe women don't do their jobs as well as men. Lewis (1997) analyzed data from the CPDF for the years 1990 to 1995 and found that higher percentages of women receive outstanding performance ratings at every grade level. He notes, "If these ratings were unbiased, they suggest that women were more productive than white men at the same grade levels and that women were being held to levels below their abilities" (Lewis 1997, 488). There is every indication, then, that women are equally committed to, and capable of doing, their jobs as men. What is the nature of the glass ceiling, then, that is limiting their advancement? And what are we to make of the differential impact of family on men's and women's careers?

TABLE 4.3 Effect of Family on Women's and Men's Career Advancement
(Regression Coefficients)

	Women	Men
Federal experience	.168***	.210***
	(.040)	(.020)
Nonfederal professional experience	−.132***	.015
	(.041)	(.021)
Education	.208***	.206***
	(.040)	(.022)
Number of geographic relocations	.016	.038
	(.049)	(.023)
Number of absences of more than six weeks	−.022	−.091
	(.060)	(.069)
Work at headquarters	.055	.272**
	(.175)	(.101)
Work in field office	−.659***	−.331***
	(.138)	(.073)
Average hours of work per week	.341***	.329***
	(.060)	(.029)
Average days of travel per month	.088	.043
	(.071)	(.045)
Has/had mentor	−.018	−.091
	(.116)	(.082)
Had spouse/partner during federal career	.170	.254**
	(.120)	(.098)
Had young children during federal career	−.250*	.250**
	(.123)	(.084)
(Constant)	9.40***6	8.879***
	(.384)	(.218)
R²	.21	.22
N	572	1848

*p<.05 **p<.01 ***p<.001
NOTE: See Appendix 2 for item coding.
SOURCE: U.S. Merit Systems Protection Board, *Career Development Survey*, 1991.

At this point, it is useful to look at qualitative data collected by MSPB as part of its study of the glass ceiling. In the summer of 1991, MSPB analysts conducted nineteen focus groups at nine different federal departments. The focus groups consisted of segregated groups of men and women in high-level jobs (GS 13–15 and senior executives). Some of the comments made by focus group participants may help shed some light on the nature of the potential glass ceiling.

For example, note that in Table 4.2 one of the factors that has the greatest impact on advancement is the number of hours, on average, that respondents devote to the job each week. This item does not attempt to differentiate between part-time and full-time work; only 2 percent of survey respondents reported working less than forty hours per week, on average. The question was designed to examine the relationship between working considerably more than forty hours per week and career advancement. The following comments made by focus group participants illustrate this association. One noted:

> In my division [the boss] would come through and he would say, "I expect to see all your faces when I come here in the morning, and I expect to see you here when I leave at night. And only the people who do that will be promoted."

Another said:

> . . . and I have worked in organizations . . . where the leadership tended to be there until 6:30, 7:00, 7:30 in the evening. And to the extent that you wanted to become part of the management team, you didn't leave at 5:30. You simply didn't.

And still another:

> I think that there's the ethic in this department, if you're in the SES, you really better be available from seven to seven. It's strong in some places.

As discussed previously, women are just as willing to work the necessary hours to advance their careers. However, at times they may not be able to do so because, although more women than ever are in the workforce, there has not been a concomitant reduction in their responsibility for childrearing and household duties (Duxbury and Higgins 1991; Newell 1992). Table 4.3 showed that having young children does hinder women's career advancement. The following comment from another focus group participant may help to put that finding in perspective:

> There is this business that as a successful senior executive you come in at 7:00 and you stay longer and work harder than anybody else and you really don't

start your rumination about really important things until 10:00 or so at night. And the effect of this was that the only people who [they] wanted to discuss the job [vacancy with] were men of any age, single women and older women with no kids. I mean there were 2 or 3 names in the hat and they said "I don't want to talk to her because she has children who are still home in these hours." Now they don't pose that thing about men on the list, many of whom also have children in that age group.

Another focus group participant, responding to a question about the above comment, suggested that women are also at a disadvantage when applying for jobs that may require travel.

I've seen that [kind of thinking] added to how [assignments/promotion decisions are made] in the workplace with some frequency and I would even have to admit to being guilty of thinking it myself. I mean, we're sitting around this table and saying, "I don't know how that woman can travel and raise a family, too." And it's hard to not let it factor into your thinking.

Another said:

I had two children at the time. . . . I remember being told once that, "You can't go on any trips. Who's going to take care of your children?" Well, that's my concern and I would like to pick and make that decision myself.

Similarly, women may not be encouraged to apply for jobs where relocation is required:

Relocations have always been a problem in many agencies, the concept of career advancement being associated with taking different geographical relocations. . . . And there's been an assumption that wives will follow husbands but husbands will not follow wives, and I don't know if it's changing.

Moreover, assumptions may be made about women even when they are single and childless. Another participant observed:

I think the assumptions are that women are going to marry and have families. And then the further assumption is that if you do that, you're not very career oriented. And that perhaps you're not mobile.

Responses to the Career Development Survey show that women may, on average, be less willing to relocate than men. Only 48 percent of women (compared to 58 percent of men) said they would be willing to relocate to advance their careers. But almost no women (4 percent) or men

(7 percent) indicated that they had ever refused to relocate as a federal employee.

It seems that women, then, may face an "image" problem over and above any difficulties they have in meeting advancement requirements. Regardless of whether they are able to put in long hours at work, travel, or relocate, there is a *perception* that women, especially those with young children or of childbearing age, are not going to be able to do so, and so they are sometimes passed over for promotions. This phenomenon is not unique to the federal government (Kennelly 1999). A study of Harvard University professional school graduates found that nearly all of those that are mothers reported experiencing discrimination after announcing their pregnancy; 25 percent felt forced to leave their jobs (Lewis 1993). The next section looks at this issue in greater depth.

Work Schedules, Women, and Families

The nature of work and the workforce has changed. The "Ozzie and Harriet" model of a two-parent family where men are focused on their jobs and women on the family is out of date. The proportion of families where women are the sole breadwinners or co-breadwinners with their spouses continues to increase. Whereas in 1960 only 19 percent of women with children under six were working, 64 percent are today (Judy and D'Amico 1997, 53). As a result, many employers are developing "family-friendly" policies. The federal government has been described as a "trendsetter" in the use of flexible work arrangements (Bruce and Reed 1994). Nearly all federal agencies now offer flexible work schedules and part-time work. More than half of the agencies offer on- or near-site child care. Three-quarters of agencies allow telecommuting from home or a satellite office (Daniel 1999).

What has been much slower to change is the persistent view that work is of central importance to men and the family of central importance to women (Duxbury and Higgins 1991; Newell 1992; Kennelly 1999). This stereotype becomes the basis for supervisors' decisions about who should be hired, promoted, and given career-enhancing work assignments or training. For this reason, women are often reluctant to take advantage of family-friendly work arrangements because to do so would reinforce the stereotype. In many women's view, there is an unwritten rule that women who make use of such programs will not be able to advance (Schwartz 1994; Lewis 1993; Sharpe 1994; "Averting Career Damage" 1992). Perhaps it is not surprising, then, that only 17 percent of federal employees have taken advantage of the opportunity to have flexible schedules, and less than 2 percent telecommute (Daniel 1999).

This comment by a manager participating in an MSPB focus group is illustrative:

Well, actually, I've got a technical person I'm looking at right now, who wants to go out on maternity leave starting in October and for some health reasons, she's going to have an extended period. . . . It makes a big difference and unfortunately it makes a big difference in my boss' perception of her. She's clearly made a priority decision . . . there's nothing irrational about the decision . . . but it's much less likely that she'll get a managerial shot or critical deadline driven assignment shot. That's much less likely.

When pressed on whether he would be holding this woman's extended maternity leave against her for the rest of her career, the participant shifted responsibility to his boss:

I'm going to have an interesting time [convincing my boss] that in the spring, when this person comes back and is working fully, that he can trust her to take serious, intense projects, time driven, and finish them.

A woman participating in a different focus group noted:

I was going on job interviews. . . . Men as well as women that were interviewing me asked, "Will the children hinder [you] from coming to work on time? . . . How much leave do you have?" . . . I went [with a man] on the interview. . . . He had two kids also, but he was not asked that question.

Another commented:

In the last month I was in a meeting . . . and a [high level official] said . . . "I'm not going to hire that [woman] because she just had a baby, and I just hired one of those and she had to take a lot of time off from work with her pregnancy." They all nodded . . . crossed her off the list and went on.

A decade ago, the term *mommy track* was coined in response to an article by Felice Schwartz in the *Harvard Business Review* (1989). She proposed that companies would make better use of women's talent if they distinguished between those who were "career primary" and those who were "career-and-family." The latter category would comprise women who would be "willing to trade some career growth and compensation for freedom from the constant pressure to work long hours and weekends" (Schwartz 1989, 70).

The problem with this kind of thinking is that although the intention is to reduce the stress that working mothers often face, it accepts the premise that women with children are less worthy of promotion without asking whether their performance really is inferior to that of men or women without children. It assumes that there is a connection between the amount of time devoted to the job and the quality of the work product that isn't necessarily there. Working long hours, relocations, and availability to travel can be a convenient, though rigid, "litmus test" for advancement. It is clearly one which women with children have an especially difficult time passing. The difficulty arises not just because they often have less flexibility with their time, but also because it is *assumed* that they cannot perform on these measures. Consider the following comment made by a female focus group participant reflecting on her career at the time she was raising her children:

> *I tended to work much harder during the working day and my attention was more focused on what I was doing than some of my male colleagues' was. This was in part because they would stay later than I did, or they tended to have much more in the way of informal interactions that I didn't have time to do in anything other than a focused way.*

In other words, although she may not have worked as many hours, she was able to accomplish just as much as her male colleagues because she used her time more efficiently while she was at work. But in many federal and nonfederal organizations, an underlying presumption persists that women with children (and especially those who visibly take advantage of flexible work schedules or other family-friendly options) don't have what it takes to be a manager. As long as this axiom endures, women will bump up against this glass ceiling. Debra Meyerson and Joyce Fletcher (2000), describing a company whose culture included the practice of calling spontaneous meetings at all times of the day, put the problem this way:

> The company's norms made it extraordinarily difficult for everyone—women and men—to work effectively. But they were particularly pernicious for women for two reasons. First, women typically bear a disproportionate amount of responsibility for home and family and thus have more demands on their time outside the office. Women who worked set hours—even if they spanned ten hours a day—ended up missing essential conversations and important plans for new products. Their circumscribed schedules also made them appear less committed than their male counterparts. In most instances, that was not the case, but the way the company operated day to day—its very system—made it impossible to prove otherwise.

Some private sector companies, in recognition of how this culture of presumed work-family conflict may continue to limit women's career advancement, are looking for ways to eliminate the stigma. A *Wall Street Journal* article reported that Xerox "urges managers to stress results rather than time spent in the office, numbers of transfers or other corporate 'rituals' when considering whom to promote." The article quoted Xerox's director of benefits: "We don't assume someone has to put in a 60-hour workweek just because a predecessor took 60 hours to do the job" ("Averting Career Damage" 1992). Companies now are realizing that they are losing many of their top female employees, not to raise their families as many suspected, but because those women are not getting the opportunities for advancement they require (Trost 1990; Wick and Company 1990). More recently, with unemployment at a thirty-year low, some companies are going even further. Hewlett-Packard requires employees to set annual goals for leisure as well as productivity (Kaufman 1999).

Men, Families, and Careers

The findings presented in Table 4.3 suggest that children have just the opposite effect on the careers of men in the federal government. Fathers and married men have advanced farther than single and childless men, even controlling for all else.

The *New York Times* recently reported on studies showing that men in "traditional families," that is, with wives who are full-time homemakers, receive more promotions and salary increases than men whose wives work. Those interviewed for the article offered several possible reasons. One was that those in top positions who are in traditional families are more comfortable with people who seem like themselves, and therefore offer greater opportunities to similarly situated men. Another suggestion was that men benefit from having a wife who can help them in their career rather than concentrating on her own. A third reason was related to the relationship between working long hours and advancement: Men whose wives work may put in less "face time" because they sometimes have to leave to pick up the children (Lewin 1994). Indeed, it is possible that men who take advantage of family-friendly policies may also find their career advancement threatened (Newman and Mathews 1999).

Participants in the MSPB focus groups made the following observations:

Where people's bonuses, grades, salaries were being discussed and it was literally mentioned by the other men that "Look, he's a male, and he has a family to support; if anybody should get the promotion it should be him. Or if anybody should get the extra money it should be him." They always feel like women, if they are married, then let their husbands take care of them—that their salary doesn't make any difference.

When it comes to [a senior executive's salary] . . . they say, "Well. She doesn't really need the money . . . she just works because she wants to, and she is such a dedicated, loyal, wonderful human being. But the men need the [senior executive salary] because . . . look what they've done. And they have kids to put through college."

They will push males because they say he's got to take care of his family. So they are going to do everything they possibly can to get him to the next step [on the career ladder].

These comments attest to the intractability of an organizational culture that may have made sense for many middle class families of the 1950s and 1960s, but clearly has no place in today's work world, which demands as much from women as from men.

Summing Up: Women and the Glass Ceiling

There is substantial evidence that women do face a glass ceiling in federal employment. As shown in Table 4.2, women have not progressed as far as men, even controlling for myriad other factors associated with successful advancement. It is also clear that many of those factors in and of themselves, while seeming to be gender-neutral, have had a disproportionate adverse effect on women. These include having children and being unable to work long hours, travel, or relocate (or even having a perceived inability to do so). A barrier that women face, particularly those with children or of childbearing age, is a stereotype of women as more committed to their families than their careers. It is a stereotype that runs headlong into an organizational climate that associates working long hours, geographic relocations, and an ability to travel with promotability. This chapter will return to the issue of stereotypes and how they can be addressed in its final section.

For now, it should at least be clear that it is necessary, but not sufficient, for federal agencies to expand their family-friendly work options including child care, flexible work schedules, and telecommuting. The existence of these programs contributes to the job satisfaction of those who use them, especially mothers (Ezra and Deckman 1996; Durst 1999). But to shatter the glass ceiling that limits the advancement of women in the government, agencies also must work actively to change an organizational culture that penalizes employees who make use of family-friendly options. The next question to be addressed in this chapter is whether there is evidence that people of color also face a glass ceiling, one that might pose a double impediment to women of color.

Civil Servants of Color

The government is often considered to be the employer of choice for many people of color. Indeed, with the exception of Latinos, people of color hold proportionately more jobs in the federal civil service than they do in the civilian labor force (U.S. Equal Employment Opportunity Commission 1997a). Moreover, as shown in Chapter 2, more people of color hold senior-level positions than ever before. However, they remain underrepresented in the upper grades. Chapter 1 included a table showing representation, by race/ethnicity, in each grade level grouping in the federal white-collar workforce. Table 4.4 shows distribution of each race/ethnic group by grade level grouping.

This table shows, for example, that although 1.2 percent of Euro-Americans can be found in senior pay jobs, only about one-half of 1 percent of African Americans, Asian Pacific Americans, Latinos, or Native Americans can be found at that level. On the other hand, nearly 12 percent of Native Americans are in the lowest-level jobs (GS 1–4), compared to only 4 percent of Euro-Americans.

As with women, concluding that there is a glass ceiling limiting the advancement of people of color requires first accounting for any differences in qualifications between them and their Euro-American colleagues. We will undertake this analysis based on responses to the Survey on Workforce Diversity administered by MSPB in 1993 as part of its study of minority employment (U.S. Merit Systems Protection Board 1996). This survey, hereafter referred to as the Workforce Diversity Survey, was mailed to a government-wide, stratified random sample of nearly 22,000 employees at all grade levels, in white- and blue-collar jobs. The survey was designed to be representative of employees by race/ethnicity (i.e., African American, Asian Pacific Americans, Latinos, Native Americans, and Euro-Americans), grade grouping, and major department or agency. Responses were received from 13,328 employees, for a response rate of 61 percent. For this analysis only employees in professional and administrative positions are included. After weighting to correct for oversampling, this leaves 5,821 employees, of which 655 are African American, 204 are Asian Pacific Americans, 249 are Latino, 74 are Native American, and 4,634 are Euro-American (the remaining 6 either marked "other" or did not designate their race/ethnicity).

Differences Among Groups with Respect to Career-Related Factors

The Survey on Workforce Diversity did not replicate all of the items regarding career-related factors that were included in MSPB's Career Development Survey (see Table 4.1). It did not ask respondents about their professional experience outside of government, whether they had partners or children living with them during their careers, or for their current work locations. In other cases, it asked questions a little differently than the Career Development Survey did. For example, respondents were asked to report the exact number of hours of uncompensated overtime they work each

TABLE 4.4 Distribution of Federal Employees in White-Collar Jobs by Grade
Level Grouping and Race/Ethnicity (Percent)

	Euro-American	African American	Asian Pacific	Latino	Native American
GS 1–4	4.0	9.6	5.9	6.4	11.6
GS 5–8	23.6	42.9	23.8	35.4	39.1
GS 9–12	41.2	32.9	40.6	40.4	35.9
GS 13–15	25.5	11.0	21.9	13.5	11.8
Senior pay	1.2	0.4	0.5	0.4	0.4
Other white collar	4.5	3.2	7.4	3.8	1.2
	100.0	100.0	100.0	100.0	100.0
Total white collar	1,025,717	236,754	57,471	83,999	24,781

SOURCE: Equal Employment Opportunity Commission (1997a, 118–119).

week in the office and at home, and the number of years of federal experience they have, rather than being presented with grouped response categories (e.g., one to five years). The Workforce Diversity Survey also included some additional factors that MSPB analysts had reason to believe contribute to advancement that were not asked in the Career Development survey. These include other measures of mobility such as the number of lateral transfers respondents had made during their careers.[3] In addition to educational achievement, survey respondents were asked to report their class ranking. Table 4.5 shows how each race/ethnic group compares with respect to these career-related factors.

The table shows that although there are differences among groups with respect to most of the human capital and work-related opportunity factors, there is no group that appears to be the most "qualified" in every respect. Asian Pacific Americans bring to their federal jobs more education than many of the other groups and are least likely to have taken a leave of absence. However, as a group they appear to have had fewer opportunities such as temporary promotions or the benefit of mentors. Native Americans, although less well-educated on average, bring considerable experience, more mobility in terms of travel, geographic relocations, and lateral transfers and have benefited from temporary promotions.

African Americans are less well educated and have less experience than Euro-Americans and are not as likely to relocate. They are more likely to have taken a downgrade than Euro-Americans. African Americans have made as many lateral transfers as other groups, but a smaller proportion than Euro-Americans have had the benefit of mentors or assignments involving travel.

TABLE 4.5 Comparison Among Racial/Ethnic Groups with Respect to Career
Advancement–Related Factors

	African American	Asian Pacific American	Euro- American	Latino	Native American
Human Capital Factors					
Years of federal service (mean)*	14.5	10.7	15.4	13.6	16.2
Education (percent)*					
No college degree	41.2	13.9	29.6	41.1	47.5
Bachelor's degree	41.8	57.0	47.0	39.5	35.6
Graduate degree	17.0	29.1	23.4	19.5	16.9
Class standing (percent of those who know their class standing)					
Top 10%	38.1	42.0	42.5	32.8	27.8
Top 25%	38.6	44.9	37.2	40.3	44.4
Top 50%	23.3	13.0	20.3	26.9	27.8
Number of geographic relocations (percent)*					
None	71.3	75.6	62.0	62.1	47.8
One	14.8	12.2	18.4	16.3	17.9
Two or more	14.0	12.2	19.6	21.7	34.3
Took a leave of absence (percent answering yes)*	18.5	10.7	18.3	15.1	25.4
Took a downgrade to advance career (percent answering yes)*	24.1	13.3	19.9	25.5	23.5
Number of lateral transfers*					
None	42.4	53.3	39.5	44.6	39.7
One	27.6	29.9	28.5	31.3	25.0
Two	14.9	11.7	16.9	12.1	20.6
Three or more	15.1	5.1	15.1	12.1	14.7
Hours of uncompensated overtime worked each week (mean)					
In current job	4.3	4.1	4.5	4.9	5.7
In last job at lower grade level	4.7	3.8	4.6	4.8	5.9

(continues)

(continued)

	African American	Asian Pacific American	Euro-American	Latino	Native American
Work Opportunities					
Was promoted or detailed temporarily (percent answering yes)	33.8	25.9	35.2	36.3	40.3
Had a mentor (percent answering yes)*	43.0	41.9	50.4	45.6	47.1
Weeks of travel per year (percent)*					
None	38.2	36.4	22.2	31.0	14.9
Less than one	17.2	18.7	14.2	11.6	17.9
One to two	19.9	17.7	20.6	18.6	22.4
Three or more	23.2	26.8	43.0	38.4	44.8

*Differences significant at .05 level. N = 2263–5710
SOURCE: U.S. Merit Systems Protection Board, *Workforce Diversity Survey,* 1993.

Latinos have less education than Euro-Americans and Asian Pacific Americans and less federal work experience than most other groups. They are in the middle range with respect to geographic locations and lateral transfers but are the most likely to have taken a downgrade. The same proportion of Latinos as Euro-Americans has had the benefit of a temporary promotion, but a slightly smaller proportion has had a mentor.

The Survey on Workforce Diversity, as did the Career Development Survey, asked respondents to report their current grade. Not surprisingly, responses show that it is Euro-Americans who have advanced farther than the others in professional and administrative jobs. The average grade for Euro-Americans was 11.7, compared to 10.9 for African Americans, 11.4 for Asian Pacific Americans, and 10.8 for Latinos and Native Americans. A multivariate analysis is required to determine whether these differences can be explained by differences in human capital or work-related opportunities, or whether a gap persists once all career-related factors are controlled.

Evidence of a Glass Ceiling

The dependent variable is the current grade of respondents. Independent variables consist of the human capital and opportunity-related variables presented in Table 4.5.[4] In this analysis, separate variables are entered representing men and women from each race/ethnic group. The exception is Native Americans, where the sample size is too small to separate by gender. In addition, Euro-American women are included, leaving only Euro-American men as the reference category.

It is important to look at women of color separately because they tend to be the poorest segment of society, disproportionately represented in single-parent households, on welfare roles, and in low-paying occupations (Thomas and Alderfer 1989). Even studies that conclude that Asian Pacific American men earn salaries nearly equal to Euro-American men in the federal sector have found that Asian Pacific American women do not (Kim and Lewis 1994; U.S. Naval Air Warfare Center Weapons Division 1994). Some research has found that African American women do not advance as far as comparably qualified Euro-American women (Bell and Nkomo 1994), while another study found that Latina women did not do as well as Latino men or other women (Mauricio Gaston Institute 1994).

The results of the multiple regression analysis are presented in Table 4.6. The model explains 40 percent of the variance in advancement. In this model the coefficients for all groups except Asian Pacific American men and women are significant and negative. That suggests that African Americans, Latinos, and Native American men and women face a glass ceiling unrelated to differences in human capital.[5] The results confirm that Euro-American women have also not advanced as far as Euro-American men, controlling for all else. The table suggests that Asian Pacific Americans do not face a glass ceiling.

Of course, aggregating all Asian Pacific Americans does mask some of the differences among them. Pan Suk Kim and Gregory Lewis (1994) report, for example, that in 1979, the median annual family income for Asian Americans ranged from about $5,000 for Laotians to over $27,000 for Japanese Americans. Nevertheless, data presented in Table 4.6 do suggest that Asian Pacific Americans are doing better in the federal government than in the private sector, where they earn less than similarly educated Euro-Americans of the same age (Federal Glass Ceiling Commission 1995b).

Many Asian Pacific Americans express a concern that despite achieving relatively high grade levels, they are perceived as too technically or research-oriented to be effective supervisors. In fact, research undertaken by the Federal Glass Ceiling Commission shows that although Asian Pacific American professionals "are held in high regard in private employment and in employment with state, local, and federal government agencies . . . [they] are not selected to become members of management teams" (Federal Glass Ceiling Commission 1995b, 111). Whether Asian Pacific Americans are as likely to advance into management positions as comparable Euro-

TABLE 4.6   Multivariate Analysis of Impact of Race/Ethnicity and Gender on
Career Advancement (Regression Coefficients)

Variables	B	SE B	Beta	Sig. T
African American men	−.285	.117	−.028	.015
African American women	−.454	.109	−.049	.000
Asian Pacific American men	.141	.166	.010	.396
Asian Pacific American women	−.289	.234	−.014	.218
Latino men	−.321	.154	−.024	.037
Latina women	−.978	.197	−.057	.000
Native American	−.906	.217	−.047	.000
Euro-American women	−.519	.058	−.114	.000
Total years of federal service	.082	.003	.355	.000
Education	.408	.015	.336	.000
Number of geographic relocations	.019	.022	.011	.394
Has taken at least one leave of absence	−.242	.063	−.045	.000
Took downgrade	−.377	.060	−.074	.000
Number of lateral transfers	.067	.020	.042	.001
Average hours of uncompensated overtime per week	.029	.005	.079	.000
Has been temporarily promoted to higher level job	.063	.052	.015	.225
Has or had a mentor	.228	.047	.055	.000
Average weeks of travel per year	.300	.019	.199	.000
(Constant)	7.388	.117		.000

$R^2 = .40$ $p<.001$ N = 4788
NOTE: See Appendix 2 for item coding.
SOURCE: U.S. Merit Systems Protection Board, *Workforce Diversity Survey*, 1993.

Americans in the government is a question that will be returned to later in this chapter.

Advancement is certainly also affected by factors not measured by this survey, including the specific previous experience and training one has on one's record when being considered for promotion. It is possible that had other factors been included, the apparent disadvantage faced by most racial/ethnic groups would disappear. Nevertheless, the fact that with 40 percent of the variance in advancement explained, there is still a negative effect for being Native American, Latino, or African American is compelling support for the suggestion that a glass ceiling limits their advancement in the federal government.

As with women, there is no evidence that a lack of interest in advancement or willingness to do what it takes to get ahead explains the disadvantage faced by people of color. Responses to items related to work attitudes on the Workforce Diversity Survey show that at least three-quarters of each race/ethnic group is committed to their job "to a great extent." Nearly half of each group indicated that they were willing to spend whatever time on the job is necessary to advance their careers; the exception was Euro-Americans, where only about one-quarter responded that this was true to "a great extent."

This analysis is consistent with findings of researchers examining career advancement within and outside the government. People of color continue to face obstacles to advancement, often subtle, indirect, and complex (Greenhaus and Parasuraman 1993; Thomas and Alderfer 1989; Ilgen and Youtz 1986). Exactly how race/ethnicity affects one's prospects for securing work-related opportunities requires further discussion. It is in part a function of stereotypes and even self-limiting behavior, and these are discussed more at the end of this chapter and in other chapters of this book. First, however, it is important to examine more closely the finding that Asian Pacific Americans face no glass ceiling in the federal government.

Asian Pacific Americans and Management

Asian Pacific Americans have been called the "model minority" because of their impressive educational and occupational attainment. Table 4.6 indicates that Asian Pacific Americans have achieved the same grade levels, on average, as Euro-Americans, taking into account all the career-related factors included in that model. Table 4.4 shows that in addition to high levels of education, Asian Pacific Americans have been less likely to take a leave of absence or downgrade, both of which are career-limiting.

Nevertheless, this finding of comparable grade attainment between Asian Pacific Americans and Euro-Americans stands in contrast to widely held perceptions on the part of Asian Pacific Americans, that they, too, confront a glass ceiling (Federal Glass Ceiling Commission 1995b; Wong 1994;

Asian Americans for Community Involvement 1993). Moreover, considerable research in the nonfederal sector has shown that Asian Pacific Americans earn less than comparably educated Euro-Americans (Friedman and Krackhardt 1997; Duleep and Sanders 1992; Woo 1994; Federal Glass Ceiling Commission 1995b). Even Kim and Lewis (1994), who examined federal employment data, determined that the grades and salaries of Asian Pacific Americans in the federal service were, on average, slightly lower than Euro-Americans with comparable education and experience. They relied on data from the government's Central Personnel Data File (CPDF), however, and so were not able to control for the range of career-related factors that are included in the analysis presented in Table 4.6.

Kim and Lewis (1994) also found a dramatic difference in the proportion of Asian Pacific Americans in supervisory and management positions compared to Euro-Americans with the same qualifications. According to their analysis, nearly twice as many Euro-Americans held supervisory jobs as Asian Pacific Americans. Again, similar patterns are found in other sectors (Woo 1994; Xin 1997; Duleep and Sanders 1992; Friedman and Krackhardt 1997). Based on data from the EEOC, the *San Jose Mercury News* found that Asian Americans were the least represented in San Francisco Bay Area government in proportion to their representation in the population (cited in Asian Americans for Community Involvement 1993, 5).

Moreover, the same pattern has been documented within many different job categories, including journalism, academia, science, and engineering (Woo 1994), suggesting that the difference is not attributable purely to occupational choice. Former EEOC member Joy Cherian put it this way: "Virtually across the board, in private employment, in employment with state, local, and federal government agencies ... Asian Americans enjoy the distinction of being represented very highly as professionals. But for some strange reason, the same data show that when it comes to being part of the management team, those same professionals—a category of workers from which most managers come—do a disappearing act" (quoted in Woo 1994, 64).

Responses to the Diversity Survey confirm a perception by many Asian Pacific Americans that their race limits their ability to advance into supervisory positions. Of those Asian Pacific American respondents in professional and administrative positions who recently applied for a promotion into a supervisory position and were turned down, 38 percent indicated that their race/national origin was of "major importance." Thirty-six percent of Asian Pacific Americans agreed with the statement, "My organization is reluctant to promote people of color to supervisory or managerial positions."

Raymond Friedman and David Krackhardt (1997) suggest that Asian Americans are less able to translate their high levels of human capital into "social capital," defined as the capability to turn their standing in the organization into an ability to influence others. In a similar vein, Katherine Xin (1997) suggests that Asian Americans tend to not use the kinds of "impression management" techniques that would convince their superiors of their leadership abilities. Based on her exhaustive review of studies in this area, Deborah Woo (1994, 98) concluded that, "For Asian Americans, the issue of a glass ceiling represented a shifting or highly uncertain context, in which subjective biases intersected with informal criteria to impede or block mobility." In other words, as with African Americans, barriers faced by Asian Pacific Americans in pursuit of management positions are subtle and intertwined.

It is significant that much of this research has found that Asian Pacific Americans have not advanced as far as Euro-Americans, even when they have more education and experience (Woo 1994). In a survey of Asian Pacific American employees at the U.S. Department of Agriculture, nearly two-thirds (63 percent) responded that they (and other employees of color) have to be better performers than Euro-American employees to get ahead (Wong 1994). Evidence from the MSPB Diversity Survey shows a mixed assessment of whether greater credentials are expected from Asian Pacific Americans than from Euro-Americans who aspire to be supervisors. Asian Pacific American supervisors have, on average, more education than Euro-American supervisors, and tend to be found at slightly higher grade levels (13.0 compared to 12.8). However, Asian Pacific American supervisors tend to have fewer years of service (15.9 years) than Euro-American supervisors (18.4 years).

There are many factors that have an impact on the likelihood that one will successfully enter the managerial ranks besides education, experience, and grade level attainment. These include the structure of the "career track" in which one finds oneself and norms that have been established in any given organization (Rosenbaum 1979). Most federal agencies emphasize technical competence when they evaluate candidates for supervisory positions (U.S. Merit Systems Protection Board 1989). Neither the CPDF nor the Workforce Diversity Survey provides information on these variables. They cannot, therefore, be "controlled for" in comparing the relative prospects of Euro-Americans and Asian Pacific Americans to be promoted into supervisory positions.

However, it is possible to determine at least whether Asian Pacific Americans are less likely to be supervisors than Euro-Americans, members of the other racial/ethnic groups, or women with comparable education and experience, and who have reached the same grade levels. We address this question by estimating a logistic regression model in which the dependent variable is supervisor/nonsupervisor. The results are presented in Table 4.7.

The findings displayed in Table 4.7 suggest that even Asian Pacific Americans with the same education and the same years of federal experience

TABLE 4.7   Impact of Race/Ethnicity on Likelihood to Be Supervisor (Logistic Regression Coefficients)

Variable	B	S.E.	Sig	Odds Ratio
Education	.085	.023	.000	1.088
Years of federal experience	.038	.004	.000	1.039
Current grade level	.397	.024	.000	1.487
Asian Pacific American	−.429	.216	.047	.651
African American	−.587	.136	.000	.556
Latino	.026	.182	.888	1.026
Native American	.585	.303	.054	1.795
Gender (female)	−.240	.077	.002	.786
Constant	−6.158	.312	.000	

Chi sq. = 888.51   p < .001   n = 5436
Percent of cases in modal category = 65%
Percent predicted correctly = 73.5%
Proportional reduction in error = 19.4%
NOTE: See Appendix 2 for item coding.
SOURCE: U.S. Merit Systems Protection Board, *Workforce Diversity Survey*, 1993.

as Euro-Americans, and who have reached the same grade levels, are less likely to hold supervisory positions within the federal professional and administrative workforce. The effect is very small, however, barely achieving significance at the .05 level. It appears that comparably qualified African Americans and women are also less likely to be in supervisory positions, whereas Latinos and Native Americans are not, controlling for experience, education, and grade level. This is consistent with David Maume's (1999) longitudinal study of promotions in the American workforce, which also found African Americans less likely to be promoted than Euro-Americans.

Nevertheless, these results do add some credence to the notion that Asian Pacific Americans face obstacles unrelated to their qualifications in pursuing promotions to supervisory positions. Prior research has suggested that such obstacles may take the form of stereotypes of Asian Pacific Americans that tag them as better suited to technical positions than leadership ones (Woo 1994; Federal Glass Ceiling Commission 1995b). Stereotypes also affect prospects for the advancement of women and non-Asian people of color. The next section of this chapter discusses the role that stereotypes play in the work environment.

The Power of Stereotypes

This chapter has shown that in small but significant ways, women and people of color face barriers to their advancement in the federal government unrelated to their ambitions or qualifications. All factors that affect people's prospects for promotion could not be accounted for, and so the claim cannot be made that discrimination must have occurred. However, it is significant that many factors related to career advancement, including the two most important—education and experience—were controlled for and, in most cases, direct negative effects of gender and race/ethnicity persisted. Moreover, there was evidence that certain career-related factors have an indirect, adverse effect on certain groups. An example is the expectation that those on management tracks will work longer hours, which runs headlong into the perception that women with children cannot meet that requirement. In Chapter 5, evidence of other differences in the treatment of members of some groups of color is discussed as well. The purpose of this section is to offer some explanations for the disadvantages that women and people of color continue to face.

First, of course, it should be kept in mind that discrimination and prejudice do continue to exist in this country. A plethora of research attests to this fact (see, for example, Edley 1996; Burstein 1998; Stetson 1997; Sniderman and Piazza 1993; Swim, Cohen, and Hyers 1998). Gallup polling data show that Euro-American views on whether "blacks have as good a chance as white people in your community to get any kind of job for which they are qualified" have remained the same since the late 1970s; one-quarter believe they do not (Gallup and Hugick 1990). Although these studies do not directly address federal employment, it is unrealistic to think that the federal government, an employer of more than 2 million (including the Postal Service), is immune from the attitudes and values that exist in the rest of the country.

More important, however, is one manifestation, albeit subtle, of lingering racism and sexism in our society. That is the tendency to judge people based on stereotypes. Stereotyping is a normal part of the process in which people organize information about the world they live in, simplifying its complexity. As such, stereotypes are not necessarily biased or wrong. The problem is that people often associate particular characteristics with groups of people that are inaccurate or that may not apply to any given member of that group. That thought process then can lead to distorted expectations and judgments of people's behavior and form the basis for discriminatory treatment.

For example, considerable research on sex stereotypes has shown that traits that are desirable in highly valued and influential jobs—competence, independence, self-confidence, and achievement orientation—are consistent with stereotypes about men and inconsistent with stereotypes about women. As a result, women face an uphill battle even being selected for such jobs, let alone getting good reviews for performing them. Moreover, when a woman is successful, her performance is often attributed to luck rather than her abilities, as it would be for a man (American Psychological

Association 1991). The same has been found to be true for people of color, who are also sometimes assumed to be less competent than Euro-American men (Greenhaus and Parasuraman 1993; Braddock and McPartland 1987).

The use of negative stereotypes in hiring or promotion decisions is sometimes called "statistical discrimination" (Braddock and McPartland 1987). Even where an employer makes an effort to hire according to a set of explicit, predetermined qualification requirements (as is the case for most government jobs), the selection decision always requires some subjective judgments. It is not uncommon for selecting officials, anxious to get someone on board quickly, to rely on race/ethnicity or gender as shorthand means for predicting the candidate's potential performance on the job (Braddock and McPartland 1987; Russell Sage Foundation 1999; Rosen and Jerdee 1974). For example, Ivy Kennelly (1999) found that employers in Atlanta associated African American women with being single mothers, and therefore likely to be late or absent from work.

Such stereotyping is most likely to occur when the individual is one or few-of-a-kind in an otherwise relatively homogenous organization (Kanter 1977; Fiske et al. 1991). Race/ethnicity and/or gender stand out in such an environment, and the heterogeneity of the group that would belie a stereotype is more obscure. Moreover, mistakes made by that person are more visible and are used to confirm the stereotype (e.g., "we never should have hired a woman for this job"). "Tokenism," as this phenomenon is sometimes called, can take a heavy emotional toll. It can impair the confidence and self-esteem of "token" individuals and force them to work to outperform their colleagues to legitimize their place in the organization (Bell and Nkomo 1994).

Stereotyping is also more likely to occur when individuals are in jobs that are not typically associated with that group. In that case, the group stereotype doesn't match the characteristics associated with the job. For example, management has typically been viewed as a male job. Managers are expected to be aggressive, masterly, and competitive. Women (and Asian Pacific Americans) are assumed to be unassertive, unavailing, and noncompetitive. When the stereotype of the person doesn't match the stereotype associated with the job, the person is seen as more likely to fail, both by themselves and others (Fiske et al. 1991; Heilman 1983). (Even worse, a woman who is assertive may be labeled as aggressive and so be marginalized as "unwomanly.")

People who internalize their own "lack of fit" with jobs may engage in self-limiting behavior, performing far below their capacity. The same lack of fit often results in biased appraisals of their performance by others (Heilman 1983). A view that someone cannot succeed in a job then becomes a reason for not giving him or her high-profile, career-enhancing work assignments. Jeffrey Greenhaus, Saroj Parasuraman, and Wayne

Wormley (1990) found in their study of employment settings that African American managers were given less-challenging work. This resulted in lower skills development and less feedback on their performance, which in turn stunted their prospects for long-term career development.

Underrepresentation in higher status jobs and media images of particular groups can also reinforce stereotypes and even self-stereotypes. Keith James et al. (undated) suggest that Native Americans may come to believe they are not suited to assert authority over Euro-Americans because of their scarcity in high-level jobs. Further reinforcing the notion that they are best suited for lower-level work, according to James and his colleagues, is a tendency by the media to portray Native Americans only in stereotypical work such as rug weaving or "rain making."

Stereotyping is also more likely to occur when evaluative criteria are unclear or information about the individual is scant or ambiguous (Rosen and Jerdee 1974; Fiske et al. 1991). Unclear assessment standards are often present when deciding whom to select for a supervisory job, for which such indistinct competencies as "interpersonal skills" or "leadership abilities" are often preferred. Even in the federal government, which has emphasized selection decisions based strictly on merit, as measured by predetermined, "objective" qualification requirements, subjective judgments inevitably come into play.

In summary, stereotyping can have a powerful, if surreptitious, impact on the employment of women and people of color, including their prospects for advancement. The power lies in the fact that the effects of stereotyping, although small, are often mutually reinforcing. Women and people of color are often presumed to lack the traits associated with influential positions. Even if that presumption is overcome and they are hired or promoted into that position, their successes are often attributed to something other than their abilities (e.g., luck) and their failings serve to confirm the stereotype. They are less likely to be given skill-building assignments or feedback, further limiting their development. They may then begin to doubt their own competence and perform according to expectations, rather than their potential. Needless to say, prospects for further promotions are dimmed.

Can the Glass Ceiling Be Shattered?

Title VII of the Civil Rights Act of 1964 prohibits employment discrimination, and the Equal Employment Opportunity Commission adjudicates thousands of cases every year to ensure that employees' rights in this regard are respected. But the barriers described in this chapter don't necessarily constitute the kind of overt discrimination the EEOC was set up to exorcise. Rather, these barriers often take the form of formal or informal criteria for advancement that seem to be gender- or race-neutral, but that often have an adverse impact on women and people of color. A claim of disparate impact certainly can be made within the rubric of Title VII. But substantiating such a claim in a situation where the disparate impact results from the seemingly innocuous expectation that all employees conform to norms that traditionally have been taken for granted is a daunting task (see Flagg 1995 for further explanation).

Moreover, the effects of glass ceiling barriers can be indirect. An African American whose performance is judged more harshly because of her "token" status within the organization may be given a lower performance rating. She would then probably be less likely to be given a high-visibility assignment. Some research has shown that men are more likely to be sought out for such assignments, whereas the burden falls on women to identify and obtain them (Brett and Stroh 1999). If she is passed over for promotion by someone who appears to be better qualified because that person has received higher performance ratings and has demonstrated his abilities in high-profile assignments, it appears that no discrimination occurred with respect to this particular personnel action. The tendency for people to internalize self-stereotypes also makes it less likely that they will file a claim of discrimination.

Existing law and redress procedures are not sufficient, then, to overcome glass ceiling barriers. This is, in part, the rationale for affirmative action (Clayton and Crosby 1992). Such policies were designed to counteract the disadvantages faced by women and people of color who face the hurdle of presumed lesser suitability for certain jobs and more limited opportunities to gain credential-building experiences. Of course, in some cases affirmative action can backfire. This can occur when the program is implemented in such a way as to cause the individuals or their coworkers to believe they were hired only to meet affirmative action goals and not because of their qualifications. Nevertheless, there is sufficient evidence of the value of affirmative action programs to warrant regret that they are increasingly being dismantled (Crum and Naff 1997). However, there are other steps that employers and employees can take to reduce glass ceiling barriers.

Organizations can take affirmative steps to ensure they have diversity within their applicant pools. One of the first barriers people of color often face in employment is learning about job opportunities that are available because they often have less access to the networks that provide this information (Braddock and McPartland 1987). Moreover, by definition, members of minority groups are often few in number and so there is a lower probability that they will be among the applicants for jobs, especially higher-level ones. Agencies that wish to increase the representation of underrepresented groups in nontraditional or higher-level jobs can engage in broad outreach efforts to increase the number of high-quality applications received. For example, to ensure Native Americans are among the pool of applicants, employers may need to deliberately reach out to tribal and other Native American organizations (James et al. undated).

Criteria for advancement should be evaluated to determine whether particular experiences or qualifications really are valid predictors of future job performance. Is the employee who has made several geographic relocations or lateral transfers really likely to be better suited for this particular job than one who hasn't? Or are we assuming such experiences are important because that is what we were expected to do when we were climbing the career ladder? Is the fact that an employee puts many hours of overtime into his job really evidence that he is more productive or even more committed to his job, or is the one who must leave at 5:00 P.M. to pick up the children just as likely to be a stellar performer? In relying on criteria that may be traditional, but not necessarily job-related, an organization risks excluding members of particular groups. Perhaps more important, it risks overlooking employees who in fact may have been the best qualified for the job.

It is clear that efforts must be made to reduce the likelihood that stereotypes will distort the evaluation of an individual's abilities and competence. Stereotypes are extremely tenacious (Heilman 1983), and dismantling them can be difficult. But there are steps that can be taken to reduce their impact.

Stereotypes are more likely to come into play when an individual's qualifications are ambiguous or unknown. It is important, then, that supervisors provide such information in as specific a form as possible when making decisions regarding assignments or promotions (Heilman 1983). Selecting officials as well as employees should be made aware of the tendency to stereotype and the subjectivity inherent in most employment-related decisions. Women and people of color should also be warned against engaging in self-limiting behavior (Ilgen and Youtz 1986).

Conscious efforts should be made to ensure women and people of color have access to mentors and career-enhancing assignments, rather than leaving this up to chance. Such assignments and other developmental activities help build skills and self-confidence. They also give individuals the opportunity to demonstrate their competence, undermining negative stereotypes. Of course, it is also incumbent on women and people of color to seek out and take advantage of such opportunities as they arise. Supervisors must also take care to avoid giving stereotype-reinforcing assignments, such as assigning a woman to organize the office Christmas party.

There is also evidence that peer relationships can be as important to one's career prospects as mentors. Peers in one's workplace can provide valuable information, advice on career strategies, and feedback (Ilgen and Youtz 1986). Such peer relationships, which also include otherwise isolated employees, should also be actively encouraged.

Some recommend hiring in "batches" to reduce tokenism and the isolation of women and people of color in jobs in which they are few in number. This would provide evidence of the diversity among them. Evident differences among people reduce the basis for stereotypes and make gender and race/ethnicity less salient (Heilman 1983). Others, however, caution that this solution can backfire. Ella Bell and Stella Nkomo (1994) cite studies showing that Euro-Americans feel threatened with the increased representation of a minority group in their work unit. Further research will be required to understand the best means for reducing the ill effects of tokenism.

Conclusion

The survey and focus group data discussed in this chapter provide evidence to support the notion that a glass ceiling is inhibiting the advancement of women and people of color in the federal government. Of course, everything that affects advancement was not measured by the surveys and so could not be included in the models predicting advancement. But controlling for experience and education, and many other factors that contribute to advancement, people of color and women have not reached the same grade levels as Euro-American men. The exception is Asian Pacific Americans, although it does seem as though they are somewhat less likely than Euro-American men to achieve supervisory positions.

It is unlikely that the differences reflect outright discrimination in very many cases. Rather, they reflect differences in treatment that are often subtle and indirect. Bell and Nkomo (1994, 52) write that the "dynamics of [race and race relations] operate on the subconscious, conscious, interpersonal, and structural levels in organizations, survey methods can never fully provide an accurate picture of the barriers African-American managers experience and their consequences."

This chapter began by describing the emergence of the notion of the glass ceiling as a national policy issue. The metaphor's incorporation into the American lexicon means that more people than ever before recognize that differences in treatment don't need to be blatant to have a powerful effect. Women and people of color are increasing their numbers in senior-level jobs in government as elsewhere, suggesting that such barriers are slowly being dissolved. But it is clear that proactive measures must be taken to facilitate this process. Stereotypes in particular are slow to change, while their effects are deep and pernicious. The government cannot achieve the goals envisioned by the theory of representative bureaucracy if people of color and women are prevented from exercising their full potential by moving into influential senior-level positions.

Notes

1. Although the objection could be raised that this gap may have narrowed since this survey was administered in 1991, the EEOC reported in 1997 that the difference in the average grade for men and women in professional and administrative positions remained between one and one and one-half grades for the previous nine years (U.S. Equal Employment Opportunity Commission 1997a).

2. Models were also estimated using the number of promotions employees received over the course of their careers. This was to see whether more men or women entering government at higher grade levels may account for the difference in grade attainment. However, the results were virtually the same.

3. Another measure of mobility, the number of different agencies respondents worked for, was dropped from this analysis since it showed no clear relationship with career advancement.

4. Class standing was not included in the model because of the high number of missing cases. Amount of overtime in previous job was excluded because it is highly correlated with amount of overtime worked in present job.

5. Although small sample sizes prevented us from breaking out Native Americans into males and females in this model, separate analyses suggest that Native American men have not been as limited in their advancement as Native American women.

5

Disparate Impact

You may have conduct where, when a white guy does it, you tell him that if he
does it again, you'll kick his . . . , whereas you end up firing the black guy. That
kind of bias will be impossible to show, because there is no record of your con-
versation with the white guy.

Arthur Cizek,
a top civil rights official at the Department of Commerce,
in an interview with Frank Greve of
Knight Ridder newspapers, October 1994

In December 1993, newspapers around the country reported findings from
federal workforce data obtained from the U.S. Office of Personnel
Management (e.g., Pierce 1993; Greve 1993a, 1993b; Barr 1993; "Racial
Disparity Found" 1993; "Racial Disparity Seen" 1993). The data showed
that during the previous year, the federal government had fired workers of
color at more than three times the rate of Euro-American employees.

The disparity in discharge rates is significant not so much because of the
number of employees involved; only about one-half of 1 percent of federal
employees are dismissed from their jobs each year (U.S. Office of Personnel
Management 1995). Rather, the disparity may be a symptom of a larger
problem. Oscar Eason, former president of Blacks in Government, an advocacy group representing African American federal employees, put it this
way: "In fact, disparate decisions based on race are being made across the
board—in appraisals, promotions, assignments and disciplinary actions.
Thus, to view the disparate rate of terminations as a separate issue is to
miss the real problem" (Rivenbark 1994c).

This chapter examines the apparent disparate impact of the federal disciplinary process as a vehicle for understanding the extent to which race/eth-
nicity may continue to affect the relationships between supervisors and sub-

ordinates within the bureaucracy. Employees subject to disciplinary action will clearly find their authority and potential for advancement to be severely restricted, even if they keep their jobs. Thus, such disparate impact has adverse consequences for the extent to which people of color are able to act in the interests of the communities they represent. Yet this powerful disparity remains unexplained. The OPM concluded its fourteen-month investigation of the disparity by noting, "There is no other shown quantitative factor or combination of factors, excluding race, that entirely accounts for the disparity in discharge rates for African Americans and Native Americans" (U.S. Office of Personnel Management 1995, 17). Whatever dynamic is in play here—discrimination, miscommunication, a mismatch in cultural expectations, or anything else—would clearly represent a barrier to achieving a truly representative federal bureaucracy.

In 1994, while the OPM study was still in progress, the U.S. Merit Systems Protection Board (MSPB) undertook its own analysis of the disparity in an attempt to identify its causes. That study addressed all disciplinary actions, rather than only dismissals, the focus of OPM's investigation. In this chapter, our analysis and discussion is based largely on data collected by MSPB, including employment data from OPM's Central Personnel Data File (CPDF); responses to surveys of employees recently subject to disciplinary actions and their supervisors; and comments made by participants in focus groups. These data are supplemented with a discussion of existing research that may shed light on causes of such a disparity. Before undertaking that analysis, this chapter provides some background on the federal disciplinary process and the emergence of the disparity in discharge rates as an issue.

Disciplining Federal Employees

Like other employers, the federal government is at times confronted with employees who engage in misconduct or who do not perform satisfactorily in their jobs. Under current law, such employees may be subject to formal disciplinary actions, which include denial of within-grade pay increases, demotions, suspensions, and removal from their jobs. These actions occur fairly rarely, however. Out of the nearly 2 million civilian, nonpostal employees who worked for the government at the end of fiscal year 1995, only about 20,000 (or 1 percent) were subject to one of these formal actions (see Table 5.1).

Table 5.1 displays the numerical and percentage shares of total employment, removals, and other disciplinary actions taken against each race/ethnic group in fiscal year 1995. Only formal disciplinary actions are recorded in the government's CPDF, so these figures do not include informal actions such as oral or written reprimands.

TABLE 5.1   Total Employment and Disciplinary Actions by Race/Ethnicity, Fiscal Year 1995

RNO	Total employment	% of total	Removals	% of total	Other disciplinary actions	% of total
African American	326,129	17	3,238	38	4,056	34
Asian Pacific American	82,705	4	244	3	410	4
Latino	115,117	6	706	8	917	8
Native American	39,644	2	342	4	384	3
Euro-American	1,380,038	71	3,961	47	6,117	51
TOTAL	1,943,633	100	8,491	100	11,884	100

NOTES: Not included are those for whom race/ethnicity was unspecified. Total percentages may not equal 100 due to rounding. Workforce percentages are based on employment as of September 1995.
SOURCE: U.S. Office of Personnel Management, Central Personnel Data File.

The numbers presented in Table 5.1 highlight the disparity. Of the formal disciplinary actions (excluding removals) taken in FY 1995, 34 percent were taken against African Americans and 3 percent against Native Americans, although these two groups make up 17 and 2 percent of the federal civilian workforce, respectively. The same pattern is found, though to a lesser extent, with Latino employees. Their share of government jobs is 6 percent of the workforce, while they were subject to 8 percent of the non-removal disciplinary actions in 1995. Euro-American employees, who make up 71 percent of the federal workforce, were subject to only 51 percent of the total disciplinary actions taken,[1] disparities of about the same magnitude with respect to the proportion of actions taken to remove employees from their jobs (see Table 5.1).

A Disparity Comes to Light

Attention was first directed to this issue by studies completed by a task force of officials from the Internal Revenue Service (IRS) and the National Treasury Employees Union (NTEU) in 1991 and 1993 (National EEO Task Force Report 1991, 1993). Those reports noted a continuing pattern of disciplinary actions taken against African American employees at three times the rate of actions taken against Euro-American employees within the IRS. The disparity was found, to varying degrees, in all regions of the country, at all grade levels except GS 14, at all ages from 26 to 55, and regardless of years of service from the third year to the twenty-fifth. The task force was unable to identify a "root cause" for the disparity, suggesting instead that it was most likely a function of several interrelated factors that the task force was not in a position to adequately measure or document (National EEO Task Force Report 1993).

Meanwhile, in response to a request from Knight Ridder newspapers, OPM released statistics in late 1993 that showed the IRS was not unique. Government-wide, civil servants of color were fired at three times the rate of Euro-American workers in fiscal year 1992. Shortly thereafter, OPM undertook a data-gathering initiative to understand the nature of the disparity and to provide assistance to individual agencies also grappling with such a disparity. The OPM limited its focus to the rates at which federal employees were *discharged* from their jobs for poor performance or misconduct, rather than including other forms of discipline as well.

The OPM's final report, released in April 1995, included the following findings:

- The disparity in discharge rates is neither a new phenomenon nor a statistical aberration.
- African Americans and Native Americans are discharged at significantly higher rates than others. Latinos experience some disparity, while Asian Pacific Americans are fired at the same rate as Euro-Americans.
- The disparity with respect to Latinos disappears once other factors are controlled. In other words, Latino employees are no more likely to be fired when compared with Euro-Americans or Asian Pacific Americans who are comparable in terms of age, sex, occupation, and grade level. The disparity for African Americans remains even when like employees are compared.
- The disparity for Native Americans is difficult to analyze because they represent only 2 percent of the government's civilian workforce.
- The disparity with respect to African Americans cannot be explained on the basis of grade level, education, kind of work, agency, geographic location, age, performance rating, seniority, attendance records, or any other data collected by OPM. Accounting for these factors reduces the disparity, indicating that some of them do affect employees' likelihood of being discharged. However, none of these factors alone, or in combination, explains all of the disparity between discharge rates for African Americans and those for other employees.

The OPM analysts concluded that they did not know the cause of the disparity or how to resolve it. However, the report noted that feedback from agency reviews, combined with findings from focus groups of supervisors, employee relations specialists, and union members who had been involved in disciplinary actions during their federal careers suggested some possible explanations. The OPM sorted these explanations into the following four categories:

- Actual bias or lack of cultural awareness
- Factors other than race that bias the discipline process
- Poor selection, development, and accountability patterns for supervisors and managers
- Lack of understanding of "the System" on the part of minority employees (U.S. Office of Personnel Management 1995, ii–iii).

Similar patterns with regard to disparate discipline rates in employment have been found in a region of the U.S. Postal Service (Zwerling and Silver 1992), in the U.S. Navy (Halloran 1988), and in the state of California's public workforce (Harmon, Vaughn, and Cromwell 1987). It would be tempting to attribute such disparities to simple causes, ranging from discrimination on the one hand to a tendency to select poorly qualified people of color to meet affirmative action goals on the other. Despite their exhaustive analyses, neither the IRS, OPM, nor MSPB could marshal enough evidence to support such propositions. This chapter will not provide the answers either. Rather, it will show that in many subtle, sometimes indirect, and often immeasurable ways, race makes a difference in relationships between supervisors and subordinates. The most obvious manifestation of this difference is in the disparate impact of the disciplinary system. But it stands to reason that this is not the only arena in which race limits the opportunities and inclusion of people of color in the workplace; the others may be less visible.

The remainder of this chapter examines plausible explanations for the disparity as a means for understanding the ways race affects prospects for employees of color in the workplace.

Explaining the Disparity

Occupational and Grade Distribution

A common perception offered by many people who are aware of the disparity in discipline rates is that it reflects the fact that minorities are more often found in lower grades and in technical, clerical, and blue-collar occupations, in which rates of disciplinary action are highest. The OPM (1995) summarized responses from those who participated in its focus groups this way:

Most comments evidenced a feeling that supervisors/professional employees/ higher graded employees are far less likely to be disciplined, or [to] receive more lenient discipline, than lower graded employees who do the same things. A number of commenters believed lower graded employees are more likely to be minorities. (U.S. Office of Personnel Management 1995, E–3)

The greater prevalence of people of color at lower grades and in the occupational groups mentioned above may account for the high *number* of disciplinary actions taken against Native Americans, Latinos, and African Americans. However, it does not explain more than a small portion of the disparity. As shown in Tables 5.2 and 5.3, there is a consistent pattern of higher proportions of disciplinary actions taken against African Americans, Latinos, and Native Americans than their representation in every occupational category and grade level grouping.

Table 5.2 presents these breakdowns within each of the major occupational categories in the government. It is true that the largest proportion of disciplinary actions in FY 1995 (29 percent) were taken against blue-collar employees, who represent only 14 percent of the government's workforce. It is also true that African Americans hold a relatively high percentage of blue-collar jobs (20 percent). However, even within the category of blue-collar workers, African Americans were subject to nearly twice as many disciplinary actions (39 percent) as their representation within that workforce (20 percent). Euro-Americans, in contrast, hold more than three times as many blue-collar jobs as African Americans but were subject to only a slighter greater percentage of disciplinary actions (45 percent) than African Americans.

Disciplinary actions are fairly rare within the federal government's professional workforce. Nearly one-quarter of the workforce is classified as professional, but only about 9 percent of disciplinary actions were taken against employees in that category of jobs in FY 1995. However, even among professional employees, African Americans received a disproportionate share of the actions. Of the nearly 2,000 disciplinary actions taken against professional employees in FY 1995, 18 percent were taken against African American employees, while African Americans hold only about 8 percent of professional jobs. The disparity among racial/ethnic groups, then, does not disappear even when comparing employees who hold similar jobs.

Table 5.3 makes a comparison among employees in three grade level groups. Although a greater number of disciplinary actions was taken against employees in lower grades than in higher grades, a higher proportion of disciplinary actions were taken against African American, Native American, and Latino employees than their share of the employee population within every grade group. For example, 65 percent of the disciplinary actions taken against employees in white-collar jobs were taken against those in grades GS 1–8 even though this grade group represents only about 39 percent of the white-collar workforce. African Americans hold about

TABLE 5.2   Percentage of Workforce and of Disciplinary Actions Taken Against Employees by Occupational (PATCO) Category and Race/Ethnicity, FY 1995

Occupational category	African American % of Workers	African American % of Actions	Asian Pacific American % of Workers	Asian Pacific American % of Actions	Latino % of Workers	Latino % of Actions	Native American % of Workers	Native American % of Actions	Euro-American % of Workers	Euro-American % of Actions	Total Actions
Professional	7.8	18.3	6.9	6.2	4.0	4.9	1.2	2.8	80.0	67.6	1,767
Administrative	13.8	23.1	2.6	2.8	5.3	8.8	1.4	2.1	76.8	63.2	3,158
Technical	21.6	37.9	3.3	2.2	6.3	6.9	3.2	5.7	65.6	47.3	3,987
Clerical	29.1	47.4	3.5	2.5	7.0	7.6	2.5	2.9	57.9	39.6	4,351
Blue-collar	19.8	39.1	4.8	3.9	7.7	8.3	2.7	3.3	64.9	45.4	5,900
Other	18.7	29.4	3.0	2.6	11.8	13.5	2.3	4.9	64.1	49.5	1,221

NOTES: Workforce percentages are based on employment as of September 1995. Included in totals are those for whom no race/ethnicity was specified.
SOURCE: U.S. Office of Personnel Management, Central Personnel Data File.

one-quarter of jobs in grades GS 1–8, but were subject to 42 percent of disciplinary actions taken against employees in those grades. Even among employees in the highest grades (GS 13–15), who are subject to few disciplinary actions (910 in FY 1995), the rate of actions taken against African Americans was 54 percent higher than their share of that workforce. The rate of actions taken against Latinos was 88 percent higher than their workforce representation.

Disciplinary actions were taken against other racial/ethnic groups in numbers disproportionate to the percentage of jobs they hold in each grade group, although the disparity was not as marked. Asian Pacific Americans received a lower proportion of disciplinary actions in every grade group than their share of the workforce in that grouping. The proportion of disciplinary actions taken against Euro-Americans was considerably lower than their share of employment in all grade level groupings. Although Native Americans were subject to a greater percentage of disciplinary actions within each grade group than their proportion of that group's workforce, the overall percentages were small, making conclusions difficult to draw.

Thus, these tables demonstrate that some racial/ethnic groups, in particular African Americans, were more likely to be subject to disciplinary action in FY 1995 than Euro-Americans, regardless of occupational category or grade-level group. In fact, in an analysis of 1992 CPDF data performed for OPM, Dr. Hilary Silver controlled for twenty variables that could reasonably explain the disparity, including occupational category, grade level, work location, employment history (including demotions and suspensions),

TABLE 5.3   Percentage of Workforce and of Disciplinary Actions Taken Against Employees by GS and Related Grade and Race/Ethnicity, FY 1995

Grades	African American		Asian Pacific American		Latino		Native American		Euro-American		Total
	% of Workers	% of Actions	% of Workers	% of Actions	% of Workers	% of Actions	% of Workers	% of Actions	% of Workers	% of Actions	Actions
1 to 8	25.5	42.1	3.6	2.6	7.0	7.8	2.8	4.3	61.0	43.3	9,056
9 to 12	13.0	22.9	4.1	3.6	5.5	8.4	1.5	2.6	75.9	62.5	3,901
13 to 15	7.8	12.0	3.8	3.1	3.3	6.2	0.9	1.3	84.3	77.5	910

NOTES: Workforce percentages are based on employment as of September 1995. Included in totals are those for whom no race/ethnicity is specified.
SOURCE: U.S. Office of Personnel Management, Central Personnel Data File.

age, and sex. After taking these other variables into account, African Americans were still about two and one-half times more likely than Euro-Americans, Asian Pacific Americans, and Latinos to be discharged. Native Americans also had a significantly higher probability of being fired, but accounted for such a small portion of the sample of employees she analyzed that Dr. Silver could not assure reliable findings (U.S. Office of Personnel Management 1995, D–4–5).

If these factors accounting for many aspects of employees' backgrounds and work experience don't fully explain the disparate impact of the federal disciplinary system on people of color, then what does? One of the common refrains voiced by Euro-American participants in focus groups convened by MSPB in 1996 was that the high rate of discipline among employees of color was due, at least in part, to the fact that many had been placed in jobs for which they were not well-qualified because of affirmative action requirements. That possible explanation is addressed next.

What About Affirmative Action?

There are few policies as controversial as affirmative action. Scholars have attempted to explain the enduring discord by suggesting that it is indicative of the contradiction between values of individualism and egalitarianism (e.g., Lipset and Schneider, 1978), a disagreement over the meaning of concepts such as equality (Verba and Orren, 1985), or differences in the way the issue is framed (Fine 1992). David Shipler (1997, 499) suggests that, "More fundamentally, affirmative action raises objections because it acknowledges the mythical quality of the American dream." That is, that anyone with a brain who works hard can get ahead.

One specific source of debate is the impact of affirmative action on the workforce. Proponents of affirmative action programs argue that they are necessary to ensure women and minorities have an equal chance to compete for jobs at all levels (Lee 1995). Critics of affirmative action argue the opposite. They believe that in many instances employers pass over Euro-American applicants for less-qualified people of color (Gleckman et al. 1991). Hence, critics would argue that it is not surprising that many employees of color fail in their jobs and are disciplined or dismissed.

Unfortunately, there is no way to systematically test this hypothesis. Although the CPDF contains much information about federal employees, including the authority under which they were hired or removed from their job, there is no code to indicate whether the employee was hired under affirmative action requirements.

Coding such a designation would be problematic because there is no way to determine what constitutes an "affirmative action hire." Under the Veterans Preference Act of 1944 (58 Stat. 387), certain military veterans (and their widows) are entitled to three to five points added to their examination score and may not be passed over for a nonveteran with a lower score. This preference system, therefore, requires that individuals be formally designated as to whether they are veterans entitled to veterans' preference (and which type).

There is no comparable structured preference program for people of color or women. There is no place on federal employment applications for candidates to indicate their race or national origin. Therefore, any consideration of this factor would have to occur informally—*after* a list of best-qualified applicants has been referred to the selecting official.

As shown previously, in Table 5.3, the disparity exists even in higher-graded jobs, which are generally filled from within by employees who have been promoted through the ranks from entry levels. Recall from Chapter 4 that two of the most important factors affecting advancement are experience and education. The next two tables show that even when federal employees are matched with respect to amount of experience or educational attainment, African Americans, Latinos, and Native Americans are more often subject to disciplinary action than Euro-Americans or Asian Pacific Americans.

As shown in Tables 5.4 and 5.5, there is a relationship between employees' experience and education and their likelihood to be disciplined. Fifty percent of disciplinary actions taken in FY 1995 were taken against employees without a college degree. However, even among employees with post-bachelor's degrees, African Americans, Native Americans, and Latinos were disciplined at disproportionate rates.

Table 5.5 shows that nearly one-third of disciplinary actions were taken in 1995 against employees with less than five years of federal experience.

TABLE 5.4 Percentage of Workforce and of Disciplinary Actions Taken Against Employees by Educational Attainment and Race/Ethnicity, FY 1995

Educational attainment	African American % of Workers	African American % of Actions	Asian Pacific American % of Workers	Asian Pacific American % of Actions	Latino % of Workers	Latino % of Actions	Native American % of Workers	Native American % of Actions	Euro-American % of Workers	Euro-American % of Actions	Total Actions
No college education	22.3	40.0	3.5	3.2	6.6	8.3	2.6	3.9	64.9	44.6	10,084
Some college education	20.3	38.6	3.3	2.5	7.3	8.7	2.2	3.0	66.8	47.2	6,195
Bachelor's degree	11.4	24.8	5.2	4.0	4.9	6.3	1.1	1.7	77.4	63.3	2,477
Post-bachelor's education	7.2	15.5	6.2	5.8	3.6	4.9	0.8	1.8	82.1	71.8	1,355

NOTES: Workforce percentages are based on employment as of September 1995. Included in totals are those for whom no race/ethnicity was specified.
SOURCE: U.S. Office of Personnel Management, Central Personnel Data File.

But even among employees with more than twenty years of service, African Americans, Native Americans, and Latinos were subject to disciplinary actions at a rate exceeding their representation among employees in that category. These findings cast doubt on the theory that the disparity in discipline rates is directly caused by the selection of under-prepared people of color. Dr. Silver's analysis of discharges showed that those with a college education, in white-collar jobs, making higher pay, and working outside of a metropolitan area were less likely to be dismissed, but the disparity based on race persisted even once these factors were controlled for.

It is true that the tools available to supervisors for measuring job applicants' knowledge, skills, and abilities are not as precise, nor effectual for predicting future performance on the job, as one might hope for (U.S. Merit Systems Protection Board 1996). Moreover, supervisors, often in a hurry to fill staffing vacancies, sometimes sacrifice quality for expediency when they make hiring decisions rather than ensuring that they have a broad pool of candidates to choose from (U.S. Merit Systems Protection Board 1995, 1996). This tendency, when combined with a desire to achieve a diverse workforce, may result in the selection of some employees of color who, on average, are not well qualified for their jobs.

Euro-Americans are also sometimes selected for jobs for which they are not well qualified. However, because people of color are few in number in most organizations, their failings are much more visible than those of Euro-

TABLE 5.5   Percentage of Workforce and of Disciplinary Actions Taken Against Employees by Years of Federal Experience and Race/Ethnicity, FY 1995

Federal experience	African American % of Workers	African American % of Actions	Asian Pacific American % of Workers	Asian Pacific American % of Actions	Latino % of Workers	Latino % of Actions	Native American % of Workers	Native American % of Actions	Euro- American % of Workers	Euro- American % of Actions	Total Actions
0–5 years	16.2	35.5	6.3	3.3	6.9	8.8	2.7	5.1	67.9	47.2	4,544
6–10 years	18.4	37.8	4.9	3.2	6.4	8.0	2.0	3.2	68.4	47.8	3,512
11–15 years	16.9	35.4	4.1	3.3	6.4	7.8	1.9	3.0	70.7	50.3	2,330
16–20 years	15.8	31.0	3.3	2.0	5.5	7.1	2.0	2.6	73.5	57.2	1,721
21–30 years	17.0	29.3	2.6	1.4	4.8	5.7	1.7	2.5	73.9	61.1	1,606
31–50 years	13.4	23.8	3.1	2.8	4.1	4.2	1.4	0.0	78.1	69.2	143

NOTES: Workforce percentages are based on employment as of September 1995. Included in totals are those for whom no race/ethnicity was specified.
SOURCE: U.S. Office of Personnel Management, Central Personnel Data File.

Americans who are not well suited for their jobs (see discussion of stereotypes in Chapter 4). Moreover, attention to shortcomings on the part of employees of color is likely to be heightened in light of the controversy surrounding affirmative action programs (Heilman 1994; Heilman, Block, and Lucas 1992; Heilman, Simon, and Repper 1987; Turner and Pratkanis 1994; Major, Feinstein, and Crocker 1994; Loury 1992).

The statutory requirement for federal agencies to achieve representative workforces is informal. Guidance issued by the U.S. Equal Employment Opportunity Commission (EEOC) in 1987, and still in effect, allows (but does not require) agencies to set numerical goals where there is "a manifest imbalance or conspicuous absence of EEO Group(s) in the workforce" (U.S. Equal Employment Opportunity Commission 1987, 13). The directive refers agencies to *Johnson v. Transportation Agency, Santa Clara County* (107 S. Ct. 1442 [1987]) in determining when an affirmative action program is appropriate. That decision set very narrow parameters under which such a program would be permissible. The more recent *Adarand* decision (115 S. Ct. 2097 [1995]) has made agencies even more cautious with respect to taking race or ethnicity into account in hiring or promotion decisions (see Chapter 1).

As discussed in Chapters 2 and 3, support for affirmative action waxed and waned over the last two decades of the twentieth century. Meanwhile, the employment of people of color steadily and gradually increased, and promotion rates have remained similar among people of color and Euro-

Americans. Chapter 3 presented survey data showing that less than half of federal supervisors say they take underrepresentation into account in their hiring decisions. That same survey asked supervisors whether they supervise someone hired under an affirmative action program, and only about one-fifth said yes. This suggests that affirmative action policies have not had a great impact on the employment of people of color. This finding is consistent with prior research (Kellough and Kay 1986; Kellough 1989; Kellough and Rosenbloom 1992).

Moreover, some research has found that affirmative action programs were more successful in bringing women into the federal government (Kellough and Kay 1986; Kellough 1989; Kellough and Rosenbloom 1992; Bayes 1995). Yet women are disciplined at a lower rate than men regardless of race or national origin (U.S Office of Personnel Management 1995).

On the other hand, there may well be a prevalent *perception* that affirmative action has resulted in the employment of poorly qualified people of color. This perception may have the unintended effect of branding even some well-qualified employees of color as unsuited for their jobs. Employees who are not viewed as well qualified are less likely to be given access to mentors, networks, or opportunities to carry out significant or visible job assignments, thus making their success on the job more difficult.

Thus, while the proposition that the disparity in discipline rates is a *direct* result of the implementation of affirmative action requirements cannot be definitively ruled out, neither is there much evidence to support it. On the other hand, it is reasonable to assume that affirmative action may have had an *indirect* effect by stigmatizing individuals as unqualified, setting off a string of events that can ultimately undermine their performance on the job. Whether the solution to that problem is to eliminate affirmative action is another issue. As is discussed in greater depth later in this chapter, considerable research has documented the continuing impact of racial stereotypes and stigmatization on people of color in the workplace. This impact exists even where affirmative action does not. Whether affirmative action contributes to the stigmatization remains a source of contention among experts (see, for example, Heilman 1994; Heilman, Simon, and Repper 1987; Taylor 1994; Loury 1992; Graves and Powell 1994; Clayton and Crosby 1992). But just as affirmative action is often blamed for problems supervisors have with their employees, so is the discrimination complaint system.

The EEO Complaint Process

There is also a widespread perception that government regulations make it nearly impossible to fire employees who are not performing their jobs at an acceptable level. In a recent study, MSPB (1999) noted that government regulations governing disciplinary actions are not, in fact, particularly burdensome. However, many agencies have developed formal and informal processes and procedures that often discourage supervisors from dealing aggressively with performance issues. Supervisors face disincentives such as a lack of higher management support and a requirement for extensive documentation (U.S. Merit Systems Protection Board 1999). Compounding these deterrents, in the view of many of the Euro-American participants in the focus groups convened by MSPB, is a fear that employees of color will respond to disciplinary actions by filing discrimination complaints. A respondent to MSPB's 1995 survey of employees who had been disciplined expressed this viewpoint this way:

> *It is well-known that if you are not of a specific minority group (i.e., African American), you are disciplined more frequently. Blacks tend to get away with more because supervisors are afraid they will run to the EEOC or other agencies and cry discrimination. Thus, many supervisors will allow poor performance or misconduct to go unpunished rather than having to risk being accused of racial discrimination.* (Male survey respondent, suspended for five days; reason and race/ethnicity not provided)

This does appear to be one reason supervisors do *not* take disciplinary action against employees whom they believe warrant such action. Thirty-nine percent of supervisors responding to a 1996 survey indicated that the possibility of the employee filing an EEO complaint affected their decision to not take action to a moderate or great extent (Fuertes 1999). Nevertheless, if very many supervisors are deterred from taking action by the threat of an EEO complaint, one would expect disproportionately *few* people of color would be subject to disciplinary action, rather than disproportionately more.

At this point it would be useful to look at how employees do respond to disciplinary actions. Table 5.6 presents responses of employees to a survey administered by MSPB in 1995. That survey was mailed to a random sample of federal employees who had recently been subject to one of the disciplinary actions tracked by the CPDF.[2] Because of the small sample size, non–African American people of color are combined.

Table 5.6 shows that there is actually little difference between the way people of color and Euro-Americans respond to disciplinary actions. Less than half of each group responded through a formal process such as an agency grievance procedure or the filing of an EEO complaint. A greater percentage of people of color than Euro-Americans did *consider* filing an EEO complaint. A greater percentage of people of color than Euro-Americans who considered filing an EEO complaint actually did so. However, a significant percentage of Euro-Americans used the EEO complaint process to respond to the disciplinary action as well. Moreover, a

TABLE 5.6   Responses to Disciplinary Actions by Race/Ethnicity

	African American	Other People of Color	Euro- American
Challenged action with oral/written response	50.7	55.7	51.4
Challenged through a formal procedure	42.9	44.7	36.4
Considered filing EEO complaint	58.5***	58.4	41.2
Of those who did consider filing EEO complaint, percentage who did file	30.8***	35.8	24.8
Sought union representation	41.8*	42.2	54.0
Sought representation from another (nonunion) organization	77.3*	73.1	86.4
Sought representation from an attorney	62.3**	52.5	70.4
Began looking for another job	68.2	59.5	58.1
Thought disciplinary process worked poorly	69.1	69.1	69.3
N	97–203	104–237	129–321

*p<.05, **p<.01, *** p<.001
SOURCE: U.S. Merit Systems Protection Board, *Survey on Employee Discipline,* 1995.

greater percentage of Euro-Americans than people of color sought representation from their unions, other employee organizations, and/or attorneys. Therefore, a belief that people of color are more likely than Euro-Americans to fight disciplinary actions is not well founded.

That does not mean the *perception* that people of color will respond more aggressively than Euro-Americans does not exist, however. It is possible that supervisors who fear discrimination complaints are more likely to formalize adverse actions involving employees of color and to handle more informally similar matters involving Euro-American employees.[3] Fred Romero, a retired senior Labor Department official, explained it this way to Knight Ridder reporter Frank Greve:

Everybody gets defensive [in response to criticism] but if they're black, or Hispanic, the first thing they think is, "the bastard wants to get rid of me be-

cause I'm a minority." At the very least, that angers the manager. He certainly doesn't think he's a racist. So he starts documenting everything, treating the minority worker very formally. (Greve 1994a, A12)

It is also important to note that while many Euro-Americans believe that people of color often use the potential to file a discrimination complaint as a shield against disciplinary action, many of the employees of color participating in MSPB focus groups expressed a very different perspective. Some expressed the view that the EEO office is in the pocket of management and will not come to their aid. The MSPB Survey on Workforce Diversity, administered to a representative sample of the federal workforce in 1993 (see Chapter 4) included a statement to which respondents were asked to agree or disagree: "If I filed an action charging race/national origin discrimination, I am confident that it would be resolved in a fair and just manner by my organization." Only one-quarter of employees of color agreed with the statement, while more than one-third disagreed. In contrast, 50 percent of Euro-American employees agreed with the statement, and only 17 percent disagreed. Clearly, many employees of color have a very different view of the EEO complaint process than Euro-Americans.

In summary, an employee's prerogative to file an EEO complaint may serve as a deterrent to some supervisors who are faced with problem employees. However, if this were true very often, people of color would not be subject to a disproportionate share of formal disciplinary actions. Instead, it seems more likely that some supervisors consider the potential threat of an EEO complaint a reason to deal more formally with a problem they are having with an employee rather than to handle it informally. Or, those supervisors may see the potential threat of an EEO complaint as yet another reason to avoid giving negative feedback to a difficult employee. If this were the case, it would not be surprising if that employee's poor performance or misconduct deteriorated to a point where formal disciplinary action was required.

However, the contrasting perceptions of people of color and Euro-Americans with respect to the EEO complaint process speak to another more fundamental point. As will be discussed in greater detail in Chapter 6, people of color—in particular African Americans—and Euro-Americans have very different interpretations of the world around them. Such different interpretations lend credence to the notion that some supervisors interpret the conduct of employees who are dissimilar to them differently—and more harshly—than those who share their cultural background. Some supervisors may also believe they have more informal options available for addressing misconduct when they feel comfortable with their subordinates than when they don't. Hence, the quotation from Arthur Cizek that opened this chapter.

The next sections of this chapter examine research on cognition and human behavior that provide additional, plausible explanations for the disparity in discipline rates.

The Continuing Impact of Race

In *Facing Up to the American Dream,* Jennifer Hochschild expresses the opinion of many who have studied race in this country: "Racial stereotypes are not new, however, and are declining if we can believe surveys. . . . What *is* largely new is elusive racial bias—subtle actions with the foreseeable effect but not necessarily the overt intention of fostering racial subordination" (Hochschild 1995, 114).

Although most observers agree that the kind of overt racism that led to passage of the Civil Rights Act of 1964 is largely gone (Pettigrew 1979; Pettigrew and Martin 1987; Cose 1993; Collins 1983; Greenhaus, Parasuraman, and Wormley 1990), people of color continue to face disparities in outcomes similar to those reported with respect to federal disciplinary actions by OPM. A recent study found that African Americans in the early stages of lung cancer are less likely than Euro-Americans to have life-saving surgery (Grady 1999). African Americans are twice as likely and Latinos one and one-half times as likely to be denied conventional home loans (Kilborn 1999). African Americans are half as likely as Euro-Americans to earn $50,000 per year (Bowen and Bok 1998). During the 1990–1991 recession African Americans were more likely to lose their jobs than Euro-Americans, even accounting for industrial and occupational affiliations, educational levels, and worker age (U.S. General Accounting Office 1994). An analysis of panel data of American families in the 1970s showed that African Americans were almost twice as likely to be fired as Euro-Americans, and that unlike Euro-Americans, education did not reduce the probability of their dismissal (Sorenson and Fuerst 1978). African American students are more than twice as likely as Euro-American students to be punished and 3.5 times more likely to be expelled (Meier, Stewart, and England 1989; see also Eyler, Cook, and Ward 1983; Taylor and Foster 1986; Hull 1994). African American prisoners receive longer jail sentences than Euro-Americans who had committed the same crimes (Maluso 1995).

Differences in rates of punishment and layoffs are partly explained by the reality that African Americans tend to have less job tenure, education, and economic resources than Euro-Americans (U.S. General Accounting Office 1994, Sorenson and Fuerst 1978). However, with respect to dismissal rates, human capital and other worker characteristics account for little of the racial differential (Zwerling and Silver 1992).

Survey research confirms the persistence of negative attitudes toward people of color. In a survey by the National Opinion Research Center, 78 percent of Euro-Americans thought African Americans were more likely to prefer living on welfare than Euro-Americans, and 74 percent thought Latinos were more likely to prefer welfare. Sixty-two percent of Euro-

Americans thought African Americans were less likely to be hard working, and 53 percent thought they were less intelligent (Bryant 1991).

Moreover, experimental research that holds everything constant but the race of the individual involved has confirmed the low regard in which some Euro-Americans hold people of color. Such research has shown, for example, that Euro-Americans disproportionately assign a resume with poor qualifications to an African American rather than a Euro-American (Hochschild 1995), that African American applicants are often treated less favorably in applying for jobs than equally qualified Euro-Americans, (Bendick, Jackson, and Reinoso 1994), and that African American performance is often evaluated more harshly than that of non-African Americans (Pettigrew and Martin 1979).

The Urban Institute and U.S. General Accounting Office, among others, have conducted hiring audits where pairs of job applicants matched on all characteristics except their race/ethnicity are sent to apply for jobs. Euro-American applicants are much more likely to receive favorable treatment and job offers (Tomaskovic-Devey 1994; Bendick, Jackson, and Reinoso 1994; Pettigrew and Martin 1987). In one study where identical applicants (except for their race) were sent to apply for jobs, 47 percent of Euro-Americans were offered jobs compared to 11 percent of African Americans (Bendick, Jackson, and Reinoso 1994).

These studies show that despite the nation's best efforts to ensure that race plays no part in the hiring process, a degree of subjectivity remains that makes people of color vulnerable to disparate treatment. These studies are evidence of "access discrimination," referring to greater difficulties people of color have in acquiring jobs that bear no relationship to their potential performance on those jobs (Ilgen and Youtz 1986). Research has also demonstrated the persistence of "treatment discrimination," or the limitations people of color face once they do gain entry into organizations (Ilgen and Youtz 1986).

Many employers, especially in the public sector, have taken great pains to ensure that mechanisms for evaluating applicants and on-board employees are objective and race/ethnic-neutral, but it is impossible to eradicate all opportunities for subjective judgments to come into play. Pettigrew and Martin (1987, 45–46) explain:

> During the recruitment process, it can be required that minority applicants be interviewed, but the content of that interaction and the recruiter's judgment processes are more difficult to control. Formal training for blacks can be improved, but much of the entry process involves informal learning from peers and supervisors, often in the course of ostensibly social interactions. Formal performance appraisals can be made more objective, but the process of evaluation is ongoing. Opinions are often formed and communicated during infor-

mal interactions that precede and supplement formal performance appraisals. . . . Formal, objectively verifiable rules and procedures cannot prevent
prejudice and discrimination in these situations.

As these authors suggest, disparate treatment is very real, but tends to occur in subtle and often unintentional ways. It is not likely that very many
federal supervisors deliberately discriminate against employees of color by
taking unwarranted actions against them. The reasons for this are addressed in the next section of this chapter.

Does the Disparity Reflect Overt Discrimination?

Although the OPM report on minority discharges neither confirmed nor
ruled out discrimination as a source of the disparity, an OPM specialist,
quoted in several newspaper articles discussing the disparity, said, "There's
no question that we've got residual discrimination" ("Records Show
Federal Firing Bias" 1993). Similarly, a spokesman for Blacks in Government attributed the disparity to discrimination ("Two Minority
Perspectives" 1996).

Many employees of color who have been disciplined also believe that discrimination was involved. In response to a question on the survey sent to
employees who had been subject to disciplinary action, more than half of
employees of color (55 percent) reported that discrimination contributed to
the supervisor taking the action against them. About half of all disciplined
employees who responded to the survey reported that the supervisor who
took the action against them had been more lenient with another employee
who committed comparable offenses. Nearly half (43 percent) of employees of color who responded positively to this question said that the other
employee had been treated more leniently because of his or her race or national origin. The following comment, made by one survey respondent, is
illustrative:

> I vehemently believe that the disciplinary actions are gender and racially bi-
> ased. I believe the disciplinary procedures are not equitably enforced.
> Management many times allows certain behaviors from employees who are
> liked and takes disciplinary actions on the others they don't like who do the
> exact same thing. (Latina survey respondent, suspended for four days for falsi-
> fying time and attendance)

Such perceptions should not be dismissed. But it is important to note that
when disciplinary actions are reviewed by third parties (e.g., arbitrators,
MSPB, and/or the courts), those actions are nearly always upheld, and discrimination is rarely found. It seems unlikely, then, that very many supervisors intentionally take unwarranted actions against employees of color.

However, it is possible that some supervisors interpret the conduct of people of color more harshly than that of Euro-American employees. In that case, they may more readily take action against people of color for behavior or performance they might otherwise ignore or handle more informally. Despite the government's best efforts to demand performance evaluations that are objective and neutral, it is a process that requires subjective judgments to be made and hence is vulnerable to unintended bias.

Evaluating the Performance of People of Color

How performance is perceived on the job is, of course, critical for retention and career advancement. Those whose performance is rated as unsatisfactory are likely to be subject to disciplinary action, whereas those whose performance is viewed as stellar are likely to be given advancement-related opportunities. Yet a meta-analysis of research on factors affecting performance appraisals found that both African American and Euro-American raters gave significantly higher ratings to members of their own race than to members of the other race (Kraiger and Ford 1985; see also Greenhaus, Parasuraman, and Wormley 1990; Hamner et al. 1974; Fernandez 1981, 213–214; Sherman, Smith, and Sherman 1983; but see also Tsui and O'Reilly 1989 for contrary finding). Because there are many more Euro-American supervisors than Native American or African American supervisors, this tendency will have a disproportionate impact on members of these groups.

Research has also shown that a Euro-American's successful work product is more likely to be attributed to his or her hard work and ability, while the same work product by a person of color would be attributed to luck and/or the ease of the task. In other words, the Euro-American's good work is attributed to *internal* and *stable* causes, while the person of color's work is attributed to *external, unstable* causes. The first suggests performance that should be rewarded and expected to continue, thereby providing a rationale for promotion. The second suggests performance that may not be worthy of reward and is not expected to continue (Ilgen and Youtz 1986; Greenhaus, Parasuraman 1993).

There is also evidence that when a person rates another's performance, that person tends to look for confirmation about any pre-existing belief he or she may have about that person. For example, if a rater believes African Americans are lazy, that rater is more likely to notice any instances of laziness among African Americans as opposed to among those racial/ethnic groups about which the rater doesn't hold such preconceived notions (Ilgen and Youtz 1986). If that same rater does not associate Euro-Americans with laziness, a similar instance on the part of Euro-American employees is seen as an aberration.

Employees are not completely passive in this process, either. When punished, their perceptions of the appropriateness of the punishment and its consistency with what has happened to others has an important impact on the likelihood for their behavior to improve (Ball, Trevino, and Sims 1994). Moreover, according to equity theory, individuals who feel under-rewarded for their efforts in relation to others sometimes attempt to restore balance by decreasing their efforts, refusing to comply with decisions, engaging in dishonest behavior, or withdrawing from the workplace through voluntary absenteeism or tardiness (Ilgen and Youtz 1986; Rutte and Messtick 1995). Rosabeth Moss Kanter put it this way: "Opportunity structures shape behavior in such a way that they confirm their own prophesies. . . Those set on low-mobility tracks tend to become indifferent, to give up, and thus to 'prove' that their initial placement was correct" (Kanter 1977, 158). Thus a vicious cycle is set in motion, which can ultimately lead to employees engaging in behavior that justifies disciplinary action.

The 1994 MSPB Survey of Supervisors (see Chapter 3) included questions asking supervisors about the last employee they supervised whose performance was less than "fully successful." The survey also asked responding supervisors to identify their own race/ethnicity and that of the unsuccessful employee. Nearly all supervisors (93 percent) reported that they had counseled their employees. However, when asked how the employee responded to the counseling, some interesting differences emerged.

As shown in Table 5.7, Euro-American supervisors reporting on the poor performance of a subordinate of color were less likely to say that the employee's performance had improved following counseling than were Euro-American supervisors reporting on Euro-American employees or supervisors of color reporting on their subordinates. These same Euro-American supervisors were also more likely to say that their employees of color became more difficult and/or ultimately left the job than Euro-American supervisors reporting on Euro-American employees. Euro-American employees working for Euro-American supervisors and employees of color working for supervisors of color were less likely to leave their jobs by retiring, resigning, or taking another job than those employees whose supervisors were more similar to themselves. We do not know whether these employees actually did improve their performance or become more difficult; the survey only captured the supervisors' perspectives on that issue. Nevertheless, these results add credence to the notion that Euro-American supervisors perceive a difference in the way subordinates of color and Euro-American subordinates respond to counseling about performance problems.

In addition to a *direct* effect of marring an employee's employment record, poor ratings can also have *indirect* adverse effects. Such evaluations can erode job satisfaction, reduce employees' expectations for their own

TABLE 5.7 Supervisors' Views of How Their Poor-Performing Employees
Responded to Counseling

After counseling, the employee ...	Euro-American Supervisor		Supervisor of Color	
	Euro-American	Employee of Color	Euro-American	Employee of Color
Improved performance	48.5***	39.6	45.5	45.7
Became more difficult	24.6***	30.3	24.6	22.3
Left the job	9.6*	13.0	12.1	8.9
N	1955	900	264	337

* p<.05, *** p<.001
NOTE: "Left job" includes resigning, retiring, or getting a job elsewhere.
SOURCE: U.S. Merit Systems Protection Board, *Supervisor Survey*, 1994.

performance, and deter them from applying for positions or taking on assignments where they know they are not expected to succeed (Pettigrew and Martin 1987; Alvarez 1979; Greenhaus, Parasuraman, and Wormley 1990). Without the benefit of such experience, the employees' knowledge and skills may deteriorate in relation to their coworkers, further eroding their likely retention and advancement. Another such "lost opportunity" that may ultimately degrade employees' performance is a lack of access to mentors or sponsors (Ilgen and Youtz 1986).

People of color are also vulnerable to being "tokens" in their work units. Tokens, or those who are very few in number in an organization, are often subject to greater scrutiny and excluded from informal networks made up of majority group members. Such networks often provide access to information that can improve effectiveness on the job (Kanter 1977). Research has shown that, at least in some contexts, ratings of women and people of color improve as their proportion in the workplace grows larger (Kraiger and Ford 1985; Sackett, DuBois, and Noe 1991). To overcome the barriers they face as tokens, people of color must appear to fit into the dominant group even while they stand out. This leaves a narrow band of acceptable behavior for those not part of the majority group (Tomaskovic-Devey 1994).

The conclusion that an employee is not well suited for his or her job, then, may not simply reflect rater bias. It may also reflect actual differences in performance. Clearly, if a supervisor finds an employee who is unable or unwilling to perform his or her job, that supervisor should consider demoting or removing the employee. However, it is important to recognize that performance deficiencies can also result from disparate treatment in the workplace, rather than from differences in ability (Pettigrew and

Martin 1987). And it is people of color who are most susceptible to disparate treatment.

Statistical Discrimination and Stereotype Threats

When appraising employee performance, supervisors must rely on their subjective judgments, judgments that are vulnerable to the imposition of stereotypes. Recall from Chapter 4 that stereotyping is a natural process that allows people to categorize information to make sense of it. However, stereotypes can also result in negative evaluations of individuals or their behavior when they are automatically and often unconsciously invoked in the process of making such assessments.

Research has shown that negative stereotypes about people of color persist. For example, one recent survey found that Euro-Americans were ten times as likely as African Americans to be stereotyped as having a superior inborn ability to perform abstract thinking (Plous and Williams 1995). Stereotypes were discussed in detail in Chapter 4, but a couple of points are worth reiterating here.

One way in which stereotypes affect employees is when employers engage in "statistical discrimination," a tendency to base employment decisions, at least in part, on the perceived likelihood that an individual will be a good or poor match for the job based on the individual's membership in a group (Tomaskovic-Devey 1994; Braddock and McPartland 1987; Kennelly 1999). An example would be an assumption that African Americans receive poorer educations than Euro-Americans and so would require more training and have less long-term potential for advancement. Employees who are subject to such stereotypes may receive fewer developmental opportunities, which can affect those employees' employment prospects for years to come (Tomaskovic-Devey 1994). Another version of statistical discrimination occurs when women or people of color are not selected for jobs or assignments because those making the selections believe that their clients or superiors prefer to deal with Euro-Americans or men (Larwood, Szwajkowski, and Rose 1988).

It is not difficult to see the impact that statistical discrimination can have on performance in the workplace. Supervisors who believe their African American employees are less capable of contributing fully to organizational performance are likely to give them less training and mentoring and fewer significant work assignments than employees of other races. This can result in either of the two outcomes described in the context of performance ratings above. Those employees may end up with fewer skills and less ability to perform successfully on the job, and/or they may perceive unfair treatment and respond by disengaging from their work and withdrawing their best effort.

Helen Duran, a Euro-American union president at the Department of Health and Human Services, gave an example of how stereotypes affect the evaluation of African Americans:

> *Stereotypes about race are amazingly powerful. If I call my supervisor and say my sink overflowed and I'm going to be late because I've got a mess to clean up, my manager is not going to question me for an instant. But if a minority calls and says the same thing, I guarantee they raise more of a suspicion that that's not true. White people can have emergencies; black people have emergencies and they're seen as a pretense for goofing off.* (Greve 1994b, A13)

Another important point is the self-fulfilling nature of stereotypes. Considerable research has shown that those who are stigmatized by stereotypes sometimes change their behavior so it is consistent with those negative stereotypes (Ilgen and Youtz 1986; Pettigrew and Martin 1987). For example, someone who is assumed to be a poor worker may start to produce inferior work products, at least partly because his or her self-confidence is undermined by the stereotype.

Stereotypes can be self-fulfilling in another way, and that is by inducing what psychologists call a "stereotype threat." This refers to the fact that in situations where a negative stereotype about a group is relevant, members of that group are at risk of confirming it. For example, experimental research has shown that African American performance on tests suffers when the test is presented as a measure of intellectual ability. When it is not presented that way, they do as well as others taking the test, confirming that their lower performance is not a result of less ability. The same occurs when women are given a math test, because of the stereotype that men are better than women at math (Steele 1999; Steele and Aronson 1995; Spencer, Steele, and Quinn 1999; Brown and Josephs 1999). There are many possible reasons for the deterioration in performance. The threat may be distracting or anxiety producing, cause a withdrawal of effort, or impel the person to spend too much time rechecking his or her work (Steele and Aronson 1995; Aronson, Quinn, and Spencer 1998).

However, there is also evidence that stigmatized individuals sometimes protect their own self-esteem by attributing negative feedback to prejudice (Crocker and Major 1989; Crocker et al. 1991; Major and Schmader 1998). In other words, if people assume the person judging them is prejudiced, they can then discount that negative feedback as stemming from prejudice rather than an objective assessment of their performance. In some cases, stigmatized individuals also discount *positive* feedback they receive, if they doubt the intentions of the person evaluating them (e.g., they assume the rater is trying to avoid appearing prejudiced) (Crocker et al. 1991). The tendency to discount feedback, whether positive or negative, has long-term consequences for employees' performance as it gives them reasons not to improve their work.

Research has also shown that people sometimes automatically and unconsciously respond to stereotypes of other people with behavior in line with those stereotypes (Bargh, Chen, and Burrows 1996; Devine 1989). For example, in one experiment the presentation of an African American image caused subjects to react with more hostility to a message instructing them to redo their work than those who had not seen the African American image (Bargh, Chen, and Burrows 1996). In the workplace, this could create an unconscious difference in the way a supervisor treats African American and other subordinates.

In short, there is considerable evidence that stereotypes play a part in creating a workplace environment in which the conduct or performance of people of color suffers or is perceived to suffer. The theory of statistical discrimination suggests that some supervisors may unconsciously assume that their employees of color will not perform as well as other subordinates and so invest less in their training and development. Employees of color who are aware of negative stereotypes may experience a stereotype threat, further impairing their performance, and deterring them from seeking skill-building assignments or even volunteering their best efforts. They may discount feedback from their supervisors, whether it is negative or positive. Thus, it seems likely that stereotypes may contribute to the disparity in discipline rates.

Communication

Considerable research has also demonstrated that race has an impact on relationships between subordinates and their supervisors in the workplace (Kirschenman and Neckerman 1991; Feagin and Sikes 1994). Communication is affected by the degree of demographic similarity or difference between employees and their bosses (Tsui and O'Reilly 1989; Dugan et al. 1993; Asante and Davis 1985; Coleman, Jussim, and Isaac 1991; Hoffman 1985). Homogeneity eases communication between individuals and makes their interaction more likely (Ilgen and Youtz 1986; Tsui and O'Reilly 1989), whereas people who are very dissimilar from one another often have more trouble communicating. Communication styles are grounded in culture, and different cultures assign different meaning to peoples' actions. For example, behavior that may be considered a sign of respect in one culture may be considered disrespectful in another culture (Fine 1995).

Some of these difficulties in communication or relating to one another also stem from stereotypes and the tendency to evaluate the performance of a member of a different race/ethnic group more harshly than a member of one's own group (Mamman 1996; Fernandez 1999). One study found that although greater familiarity with African Americans tended to diminish the tendency for Euro-Americans to rely on stereotypes, dealing with African Americans in subordinate roles in the workplace seemed to reinforce stereotypical thinking among Euro-Americans (Hudson and Hines-Hudson 1999). But the impact of race on supervisor-subordinate relationships goes beyond stereotypes.

Some research has shown, for example, that managers implicitly assign their subordinates to either an "outgroup" or an "ingroup." Managers are more likely to assign subordinates who are more similar to them to the ingroup and those that are less similar to the outgroup. Because most managers are Euro-Americans, it follows that more people of color will be assigned to outgroups. This has implications for their careers, as managers tend to provide more assistance, interesting work assignments, and greater resources and show more trust for ingroup members than outgroup members (Ilgen and Youtz 1986).

Molefi Asante and Alice Davis describe the ways in which culture causes misunderstandings between African Americans and Euro-Americans. It is not the specific language in every instance, but the "entire communication environment," which includes the situation in which the interaction occurs and the modalities of culture. They write, "Whites in America often assume that blacks 'cannot tell them anything' and consequently react negatively to blacks making requests. The black worker who makes a request or gives a suggestion often anticipates a negative response from the Euro-American person. This self-fulfilling prophecy makes communication difficult and masks the potential valuable interaction in the work place" (Asante and Davis 1985, 91).

Communication goes both ways, of course. Employees who suspect their supervisors are not treating them in an even-handed way may respond by not keeping their supervisors informed. The same union president from the Department of Health and Human Services quoted above went on to say:

> *By the same token, if a minority—or any worker—starts showing up late every day because they have family problems, they have a responsibility to let their supervisors know what's going on. So often I run into employees who just won't talk to their supervisors, who, I find, often will listen and make an accommodation. But the employee just lets the situation fester until their butts are on the line.* (Greve 1994b, A13)

Of course, lack of communication may also reflect employees' distrust of their supervisors (Cox 1994), which may or may not be justified. In such a situation, it is difficult to assign blame to either the employee or the supervisor.

The 1995 MSPB Matched Survey on Discipline was designed, in part, to assess the extent to which miscommunication and misunderstanding between subordinates of color and Euro-American supervisors contributes to the disparity in discipline rates in the federal government. The surveys, administered to employees who had been disciplined and their supervisors, asked about informal actions that may have preceded the formal disciplinary action taken. For example, supervisors were asked if they had counseled the employee, communicated with the employee in writing, etc., and employees were asked if their supervisors had done these things. Out of all those who responded, 527 matches could be made between the employee and the supervisor who took the action against that employee.

Responses to the surveys showed that there can be quite a gulf between employees' and their supervisors' understanding of the events that occurred regardless of the race/ethnicity of either. For example, 75 percent of supervisors reported that they had counseled the employee before taking disciplinary action, but only 30 percent of those same employees reported that they had been counseled. Similarly, nearly one-third of supervisors said they referred the employee to an Employee Assistance Program before taking action, while fewer than 10 percent of employees said they had been referred to such a program.

What is of more interest for the discussion in this chapter, however, is whether employees of color with Euro-American supervisors are less likely to agree on the steps taken by the supervisors than Euro-American employees with Euro-American supervisors. Such findings can be expected in light of the literature identifying communication difficulties between supervisors and subordinates of different races/ethnicities.

An index of agreement was computed by adding the number of times employees and their supervisors agreed that a particular step had been taken (range of zero to nine). The average index score, called an Index of Agreement, for Euro-American supervisor–Euro-American employee dyads and Euro-American employer–employees of color dyads is presented in Table 5.8.

The difference in the index score is small but significant (see Table 5.8). It suggests that there is greater agreement between Euro-American employees with Euro-American supervisors as to the events leading up to the disciplinary action than between employees of color with Euro-American supervisors.

Table 5.8 also shows the percentages of Euro-American employees and employees of color working for Euro-American supervisors, who reported that their supervisors had taken each of the steps. In most cases, Euro-American employees are more likely to report that their supervisor took the steps than people of color. In most cases, however, the differences are not statistically significant.

TABLE 5.8   Euro-American and Employee of Color Responses to the Steps Their Euro-American Supervisors Took Before Taking Disciplinary Action

	Euro-American Employee	Employee of Color
Index of agreement	5.5**	5.1
Action taken		
Counseled employee	35.5**	23.1
Communicated in writing	29.0	24.0
Gave oral warning or reprimand	24.9*	17.5
Gave written warning or reprimand	20.7	18.7
Referred to Employee Assistance		
Program	10.7	8.2
Gave chance to improve	19.4*	12.3
Suggested employee resign/retire	10.7	11.1
Suggested a different action than		
one taken	8.3	8.8
N	169	156

* p< .10, ** p< .05
SOURCE: U.S. Merit Systems Protection Board, *Survey on Employee Discipline,* 1995.

The primary exception is with respect to counseling. Thirty-five percent of Euro-American employees reported that their Euro-American supervisors had counseled them, compared to only 23 percent of employees of color. This is an important finding, because it is this action that speaks most directly to the level of communication. After all, there is much less room for interpretation when a supervisor puts his or her concerns in writing than when the concern is expressed verbally. This is consistent with Marlene Fine's (1995) notion that African American culture tends to place more importance on what is said than on what is written.

There are two other steps where differences between the two groups of employees, albeit small ones, can be found. The first is with respect to whether the supervisor issued an oral warning or reprimand. Twenty-five percent of Euro-American employees said that their Euro-American supervisors gave them an oral warning, compared to 17 percent of employees of color with Euro-American supervisors. The second is whether the employee was given the opportunity to improve his or her conduct or performance. Nineteen percent of Euro-American employees reported they were given the opportunity to improve, compared to only 12 percent of employees of color. These, again, are the steps where there is likely to be the greatest ambiguity. Suggesting the employee resign or retire, or that a different action be taken, is also fairly ambiguous, but very few employees or supervisors reported that these discussions had taken place.

Employees who don't believe they were counseled are also less likely to believe they were given timely, accurate feedback about their performance or conduct. In such a situation, people are left to find their own rationale for what appears to be disparate treatment. Given the long history of discrimination in this country, it is not surprising that people of color often conclude that the supervisor was prejudiced against their race/ethnicity (Fernandez 1999). That conclusion contributes to a poisoned atmosphere, as the employee and the supervisor become defensive. Thus, misunderstanding and misinterpretations may well also contribute, directly or indirectly, to the disparity in discipline rates.

Conclusion

It is not surprising that researchers were unable to pinpoint a specific cause for the disparity in discipline rates among racial/ethnic groups in the federal government. Neither has this chapter been able to provide "the answer." Instead, it has used the disparity in discipline rates as the lens through which to observe the ways in which race/ethnicity continues to affect relations between supervisors and subordinates in the workplace.

This chapter has suggested that the disparate rates of discipline probably are not caused by widespread discrimination that results in the discipline of minority employees who did not engage in misconduct or perform unsatisfactorily on their jobs. When such actions are appealed, the majority are upheld with no findings of discrimination.

Neither is the disparity simply the result of the grade and occupational distribution of employees of color. African American, Latino, and Native American federal employees are disciplined at higher rates in every grade level and every occupation. Nor does it simply reflect the selection of employees of color who are not well qualified for their jobs. There is little evidence that supervisors have felt compelled to make such selections, and even people of color with many years of experience and high levels of educational attainment are disciplined disproportionately.

Rather, in a variety of subtle and often unintentional ways, differences in the treatment and perceptions of Euro-American and employees of color can lead to situations in which some supervisors are more likely to take actions against the latter employees than the former. Because disciplinary actions are taken so rarely in federal agencies, it doesn't take many such situations to arise for the disparity in discipline rates to emerge.

Supervisors are often reluctant to confront and take formal action against employees with whom they are having problems. This reluctance is demonstrated by survey responses in which supervisors expressed their views about a wide range of obstacles to taking action against poor performers. It is also apparent in the data, which show that only about 1 percent of federal employees are subject to formal disciplinary actions each year. Thus, it is quite possible that for every employee subject to disciplinary action, there are others who also engaged in similar misconduct or poor performance who were not disciplined.

Research shows that people of color continue to be subject to stereotypes that cast aspersions on their abilities and performance. This natural tendency to stereotype may well mean that supervisors, most of whom are Euro-American, sometimes interpret the conduct or performance of an employee of color more harshly than that of a Euro-American employee. Because not all employees who engage in poor performance or misconduct are disciplined, it is likely that a higher proportion of those not disciplined are Euro-Americans.

When this occurs, it contributes to the likelihood that people of color will view their organizations as discriminatory. They may also give up trying to conform to standards they view as unfair and discount the feedback they receive from their supervisors. Some of the supervisors who are reluctant to confront problem employees may also fear that such confrontation would lead to an EEO complaint. Regardless of the accuracy of this perception, it no doubt reinforces a tendency to avoid giving unpleasant, informal feedback unless performance or conduct deteriorates to the point where it must be addressed through formal disciplinary action.

The disparity in discipline rates, then, is not a simple problem with an easy solution. In part it must be addressed by agencies finding effective ways to select supervisors based on their ability to impartially evaluate and communicate effectively with diverse subordinates. Most first-line supervisors now are selected based on their technical skills rather than their potential to carry out supervisory responsibilities (U.S. Merit Systems Protection Board 1989). The disparity in discipline rates must also be addressed by devising and diligently using training programs to bridge the cultural and perceptual gap between people of color and Euro-Americans, and to better prepare people of color for the expectations they will encounter in the workplace.

Some agencies may find it beneficial to create impartial "ombuds" to facilitate communication between employees and supervisors and to ensure that employees understand workplace rules, procedures, and their avenues of redress. Some agencies may find their supervisors need training in effective coaching techniques and the best means for confronting employees who are falling short of performance or conduct requirements. Supervisors could also benefit by gaining an awareness of the subtle ways in which stereotypes can affect their interpretation of employees' behavior and of the differences in perceptions between Euro-Americans and employees of color that can have an adverse impact on performance and morale.

The employee focus groups that MSPB conducted as part of its study suggest that the disparity in discipline rates is a serious issue, even though the number of employees disciplined each year is small. That is because it is symptomatic of the tension, miscommunication, and misunderstanding that seem to underlie the government's diverse work environment. To the extent that such dynamics undermine the authority, status, and opportunities available to people of color, they act as a barrier to the achievement of a representative and inclusive federal bureaucracy. As will become clear in Chapter 6, it is not just the actions people take or don't take that limit the influence of women or people of color. Rather, employees' own *perceptions* of such limitations can have a powerful effect on the career decisions they make and the prospects that an agency will retain talented women and people of color.

Notes

1. Normally, a distinction is made between disciplinary actions that are taken based on an employee's poor performance, discussed in part 432 of the Code of Federal Regulations (C.F.R.), and those taken because of employee misconduct, discussed in part 752 of the C.F.R. However, supervisors often do not make this distinction. Moreover, it seems logical that if employees are not doing their job, it isn't always clear whether they *can't* do it (poor performance) or *won't* do it (misconduct). Therefore, for simplicity of presentation, the distinction between the two disciplinary actions is not made in this chapter.

2. A random sample of about 2,300 employees who had recently been subject to disciplinary action was drawn from the CPDF. Surveys were mailed to those employees' personnel offices for distribution to employees. Simultaneously, those personnel offices were asked to deliver a similar survey to the supervisors of the same employees. About 2,100 surveys were returned, for a response rate of about 50 percent. Employees who had been discharged or who had left government voluntarily were not included because their home addresses were not available.

3. The same situations described here may also apply to situations in which the supervisor is a person of color and the employee Euro-American. However, that situation is much less common than the one being described here, an employee of color with a Euro-American supervisor.

6

Subjective Discrimination

I think one of the things you decide to do is confront, or get angry, or leave.
... Different people have different ways of dealing with it.

*A woman speaking about her perception of disparate treatment in
her agency during a 1990 focus group assembled by
the U.S. Merit Systems Protection Board (U.S. MSPB) for
its study of women and the glass ceiling in the federal government*

As should be evident from the previous chapter, much of the research addressing barriers to advancement faced by women and people of color has focused on those that are external to those employees. Examples of external barriers include assumptions that women and people of color lack the ability or commitment required for advancement and exclusion from informal networks that often provide the information and contacts necessary for promotion (Guy 1993; Naff 1994; Naff and Thomas 1994; Page 1994; Thomas and Mohai 1995; U.S. Department of Labor 1991b; Dugan et al. 1993). However, Rosabeth Moss Kanter (1977) theorized that *internal* barriers can be just as limiting. That is, when employees perceive that there is little opportunity for advancement, their own motivation and desire to succeed is diminished, and they behave accordingly.

Anne Hopkins (1980) used two terms to describe these kinds of limitations. She defined *objective discrimination* as differences in treatment that can be detected by an outside observer based on previously defined criteria. *Subjective discrimination*, on the other hand, "is said to exist when an individual or group on the basis of their own subjective perceptions, define their situation as discriminatory" (Hopkins 1980, 131). To the extent that perceptions of disparate treatment contribute to the desire of women or people of color to leave government employment, or deter them from applying for promotions, such perceptions make problematic the achievement

133

of a representative bureaucracy in even the passive sense. This chapter explores the nature and impact of subjective discrimination in the federal government.

Perceiving Discrimination

There has been little research on how women and people of color perceive their opportunities in the federal government, but that which has been done suggests that subjective discrimination is a reality. In a survey of employees in the regional office of one federal agency, 57 percent of women said women face unique obstacles to promotion, and 71 percent of people of color believed they faced obstacles to promotion based on their race/ethnicity (Fine, Johnson, and Ryan 1990). Similarly, 59 percent of Latino federal executives reported experiencing the assumption that people of color can only fill certain types of jobs (Sisneros 1992). A survey of Asian American employees at the U.S. Department of Agriculture found that 63 percent believe that they "have to be better performers than whites to get ahead" (Wong 1994, 27). More recently, a government-wide survey of federal employees found that more than half of employees of color believe they had been treated unfairly with regard to promotions in the past two years (U.S. Merit Systems Protection Board 1996, 36).

This focus on women and people of color is not meant to suggest that men and Euro-Americans never perceive their work environment as discriminatory, or that their perceptions are not important. But because the discussion in this chapter is taking place in a larger study of obstacles to the advancement and inclusion of women and people of color in the federal government, its focus is on these groups of employees. Moreover, survey data used for this analysis suggest that men are much less likely than women to experience gender-related subjective discrimination. For example, in responding to the 1991 MSPB Career Development Survey, 34 percent of women agreed with the statement: "In general, managers in my organization believe women are incompetent until they prove themselves competent." Only 8 percent of men agreed with the statement: "In general, managers in my organization believe men are incompetent until they prove themselves competent."

It is important to note, however, that the perspective held by many women and people of color that gender and race continue to affect how they are treated in organizations is not widely shared by men or Euro-Americans. In the regional federal office survey mentioned above, only 27 percent of men (compared to 57 percent of women) said that women face unique obstacles to promotion (Fine, Johnson, and Ryan 1990). Clayton Alderfer and colleagues determined from their analysis of the opinions of

African American and Euro-American managers at a large company that "black and white managers may hold cognitively different theories to explain what happens in the organizational world in which they live" (Alderfer et al. 1980, 148).

That Euro-Americans and people of color often live in very different perceptual worlds has been continually demonstrated by polling data (Sigelman and Welch 1991; Morin 1995; Sherman, Smith, and Sherman 1983). Recent polling data demonstrate the persistence of this divide: 58 percent of Euro-Americans, but only 23 percent of African Americans, believe that the average African American is likely to hold as good a quality job as the average Euro-American person (Morin 1995). In a survey of Detroit residents, Susan Welch et al. (1998) found that more than seven times as many African Americans as Euro-Americans said that African Americans are discriminated against in jobs in their communities. These differences in perspective are noteworthy because the extent to which people believe discrimination exists affects their views as to whether and what kinds of remedies are needed (Sigelman and Welch 1991). For example, those who think racism continues to be a major problem in this country are more likely to support affirmative action programs than those who think little racism persists (Cohn 1995; see also U.S. Merit Systems Protection Board 1996).

Not much is known about the extent to which federal civil servants perceive discrimination, but even less is known about the circumstances under which subjective discrimination is likely to occur in a work environment. Of particular importance are work-related factors such as the proportion of women or people of color in the work group or access to a mentor, as these are factors that federal agencies may be able to change to reduce subjective discrimination. To the extent that perceptions are related to personal attributes such as education or age, agencies may have more difficulty addressing them (Hopkins 1980). Although little research has looked directly at the correlates of subjective discrimination (an exception is Hopkins 1980), considerable research has examined the relationship between various factors and attitudes toward related issues such as sex roles, perceptions of injustice, and consciousness about inequality (see, for example, Adams and Dressler 1988; Ransford and Miller 1983; Thornton, Alwin, and Camburn 1983; Gurin 1985; Gruber and Bjorn 1988; Davis and Robinson 1991; Wilcox 1991; Banaszak and Plutzer 1993).

The final, and perhaps most important, concern is the impact of subjective discrimination on employees' employment-related decisions. Research outside the federal bureaucracy has demonstrated that perceptions of disparate treatment can adversely affect job satisfaction and commitment (Graves and Powell 1994; Witt 1990). Such perceptions can also reduce the likelihood of employees seeking promotion (Cannings and Montmarquette

1991; Gallese 1991) and increase the likelihood that they will leave the organization rather than pursue what they perceive to be a dead end (Morrison, White, and van Velsor 1987; Wick and Company 1990; Hale and Kelly 1989; Dailey and Kirk 1992; James, Lovato, and Cropanzano 1994).

What Is Subjective Discrimination?

In this chapter, subjective discrimination is defined as the perception that a work-irrelevant criterion—in this case gender or race/ethnicity—affects how one is evaluated or treated on the job. For example, a person of color may not have direct evidence that people of color are less likely than Euro-Americans to be promoted in his or her organization because no promotions have occurred for some time. Nevertheless, that employee may interpret comments from, or actions taken by, her or his superiors as an indication that people of color are not highly regarded. An example is the following comment made by an Asian Pacific American respondent on the Workforce Diversity Survey:

> *It was difficult to respond to some of the [survey] questions because [the] treatment and behavior of those above me are subtle and imperceptible, but I "feel" some sort of bias exists.* (U.S. Merit Systems Protection Board 1996, 55)

The frustration experienced by a woman who perceived that her supervisor was considering her sex in evaluating her career prospects was clear from her comments during a focus group of mid-level employees conducted by MSPB. When she expressed an interest in finding a different job opportunity, one particular key manager kept saying, "Well she's a good staff person; I want her in a staff job." Many times she told him that she was interested in being a supervisor and a manager, but he maintained his perception of her as a "feminine type." Consequently, she accepted his view and declined to take a supervisory role, which would involve confronting people.

This comment illustrates the point that whether or not her experience would meet some objective test of discrimination, a woman who perceives disparate treatment may be disheartened and not apply herself fully to the job or seek advancement. Research has suggested that women are particularly vulnerable to this kind of thinking. Even when they like their jobs, they often have less positive attitudes than men about their organizations and sense less opportunity (Dunivan 1988; Terborg 1977). Similarly, in the political arena women officeholders who see themselves as electorally vulnerable are unlikely to run for a higher office. However, such vulnerability apparently does not affect men's decisions (Bledsoe and Herring 1990).

There is also some evidence that those who perceive their opportunities as restricted have less commitment to their organizations, fewer aspirations, and lower self-esteem (Graves and Powell 1994; Kanter 1977). In some cases, confusion and frustration can result from not simply knowing where one stands. A participant in the MSPB focus group relayed this reaction:

> *If I perceive that maybe I'm being treated different, I really have to take the time to think through it. . . . I say . . . "Are you having a persecution complex because of the comment . . . are you being excluded because it's just oversight, or because you are a woman?"*

A self-perpetuating cycle can be created where women and people of color, sensing a lack of opportunity, do not aspire to top positions and so continue to be underrepresented at those levels (Alvarez and Lutterman 1979; Kanter 1977). They may engage in self-limiting behaviors (Greenhaus, Parasuraman, and Wormley 1990; Rowe 1990). Another woman's comment during a MSPB focus group is illustrative:

> *It affects your self-esteem, which can affect your career growth. I sometimes feel like oh God, I must be the stupidest person alive. . . . And then you think, well, I'm in this job and I can't do this job, why am I here? And it really affects how you feel about what you do and what you're capable of. You know, I'm getting a new boss. I could have applied for that job. I didn't feel qualified for that job, I didn't apply.*

An unwillingness to apply for supervisory positions means that fewer women and people of color will hold them, reinforcing the perception of a lack of opportunity for advancement. Although this is true for anyone, women and people of color are most likely to experience discrimination and therefore also to interpret their situation as discriminatory (Rowe 1990; Kanter 1977). Hence, in tandem, subjective discrimination and glass ceilings can have a forceful impact on the advancement and inclusion of women and people of color.

It is important to note at this juncture that perceptions of discrimination really can fall into either of two categories. Women or people of color may believe people from their group, in general, are discriminated against based on sex and/or race/ethnicity. Or, they can believe they *personally* have been discriminated against based on their sex and/or race/ethnicity.

Research has shown that those who perceive group discrimination may not perceive personal discrimination (Crosby 1982, 1984; Crosby et al. 1986; Clayton and Crosby 1992). In a study of working women in a Boston suburb, Faye Crosby found that despite clear evidence that women were being discriminated against, and despite their obvious awareness of sex discrimination in general, the women she surveyed did not believe they were personally discriminated against (Crosby 1984). Similar findings have occurred in studies of public opinion. For example, in the survey of Detroit residents mentioned previously, while 80 percent of African Americans said African Americans are discriminated against with respect to jobs in their communities, only 47 percent of African Americans said they personally have been discriminated against (Welch et al. 1998; see also Sigelman and Welch 1991).

Susan Clayton and Faye Crosby put it this way: "The upsets and grievances we experience on behalf of ourselves as individuals are distinguishable from the upsets that we feel on behalf of our membership groups" (Clayton and Crosby 1992, 64). Crosby offers several reasons for this conundrum. One explanation is that people tend to avoid attributing their own disappointments to discrimination because it is difficult to make inferences from individual cases. This is especially true in situations where the criteria are imprecise, as in promotion decisions. Seldom do two people have exactly the same qualifications, so an unsuccessful bid for promotion may be attributed to a difference in a particular qualification. Moreover, Crosby suggests, people don't like to see themselves as victims or to pinpoint others as villains. This is an almost inevitable reaction in a situation involving an individual incident, but doesn't usually take place in the context of a group being discriminated against (Crosby 1984).

Crosby bases much of her work on a theory of "relative deprivation." In part, this theory suggests that dissatisfaction with one's situation not only depends on the situation itself, but also on the feeling that one is being deprived based on reference to some standard (Clayton and Crosby 1992). For example, a worker who is poorly paid may not feel unjustly treated as long as she believes that others in her workplace are also poorly paid. But if she learns that her coworkers with the same qualifications and job duties as her are being paid more, it is likely that she will feel deprived.

In making the distinction between women believing that *women in general* are not afforded the same opportunities as men and women believing that *they personally* have been deprived, Clayton and Crosby (1992) use the terms *group deprivation* and *personal deprivation* respectively. For the purpose of the analysis of subjective discrimination in this chapter, then, the term *group subjective discrimination* is used to denote perceptions that one's race/ethnic or gender group is discriminated against. The term *personal subjective discrimination* refers to the perception that one personally has been subject to discriminatory practices.

Subjective discrimination in either form is a problem for any organization inasmuch as it affects job satisfaction and motivation. But because of the federal government's involvement in ensuring equal employment opportunity, and its stated objective of being a model employer in this respect (U.S. Merit Systems Protection Board 1996; Lawn-Day and Ballard 1996), perceptions of discrimination in a federal agency can be even more objectionable than in private sector firms. Where there are no barriers in theory, the existence of barriers becomes all the more invidious (Krislov 1967).

This chapter first examines subjective discrimination as experienced by female federal employees. The analysis is based on the responses of about 8,400 male and female employees at the GS 9–15 and senior executive levels to the Career Development Survey, administered in 1991 (described in Chapter 4). It then turns to perceptions of discrimination among civil servants of color. Data for that analysis come from the responses of approximately 13,000 federal employees to the Workforce Diversity Survey administered in 1993 (see Chapter 4).

Women and Subjective Discrimination

The Dichotomy in Perceptions

Table 6.1 shows the responses of female and male respondents to several items included on the Career Development Survey. The responses reported here make clear that a significant proportion of women in the federal government do experience group subjective discrimination, in that they believe women are not afforded the same opportunities as men. Table 6.1 also shows that men, in general, do not share their perceptions.

Over half of women but fewer than one in ten men believe that women must outperform men to be promoted. There is less disagreement between men and women about the notion that people are promoted because of whom they know, although the difference in responses is significant nevertheless. Nearly half of women but only about one in twenty men agree that standards are higher for women than men. About the same ratio believe women's views are overlooked at meetings until those same issues are raised by men.

Although a minority of women report that top management positions often lose their power and prestige when assumed by women, they still outnumber men by a margin of four to one. About one-third of women in the federal government believe, to at least some extent, that managers in their organizations assume women's incompetence until they prove their competence, while only less than 10 percent of men believe that to be the case.

To summarize, a substantial number of women in middle and higher grade levels in the government believe that women are not given the same respect and opportunities that are available to men. Although the numbers are considerable, it is not a majority of women who hold these perceptions

TABLE 6.1   Federal Employees' Perceptions of How Women Are Treated in Their
Organizations (Percent)

In general, in my organization ...	Women	Men
A woman must perform better than a man to be promoted		
Strongly agree/agree	55.4	9.2
Neither agree nor disagree	21.9	20.5
Strongly disagree/disagree	22.7	70.3
N	2,632	5,707
People are promoted because of whom they know		
Strongly agree/agree	62.2	57.3
Neither agree nor disagree	21.3	22.5
Strongly disagree/disagree	16.5	20.2
N	2,628	5,723
Standards are higher for women than men		
Strongly agree/agree	45.3	4.8
Neither agree nor disagree	24.5	21.8
Strongly disagree/disagree	30.2	73.4
N	2,597	5,686
The viewpoint of a woman is often not heard at a meeting until it is repeated by a man		
Strongly agree/agree	41.1	6.0
Neither agree nor disagree	29.4	26.2
Strongly disagree/disagree	29.5	67.8
N	2,636	5,728
Once a woman assumes a top management position, that position often loses much of its power and prestige		
Strongly agree/agree	22.3	5.6
Neither agree nor disagree	36.2	28.8
Strongly disagree/disagree	41.5	65.6
N	2,634	5,715
In general, I think that managers in my organization believe that women are incompetent until they prove themselves competent		
To a great extent/some extent	36.8	7.8
To little extent/no extent	63.2	92.2
N	2,401	5,083

NOTE: Ns reflect total responses, weighted. All differences are significant at $p < .001$.
SOURCE: U.S. Merit Systems Protection Board, *Career Development Survey,* 1991.

in most cases. The next question this chapter addresses, then, is, what differentiates those women who experience subjective discrimination from those who don't?

Correlates of Subjective Discrimination
Experienced by Women

For this analysis, only the 3,443 women who responded to the Career Development Survey are included.[1] Women's responses to the items in Table 6.1 are combined into an additive scale to serve as a measure of group subjective discrimination (alpha = .84). The items are recoded, where necessary, so that the higher the score, the greater the subjective discrimination experienced.

A second scale was developed to measure women's personal subjective discrimination (alpha = .71). This scale consists of only two items. One asked respondents whether gender had helped, had no effect on, or had hindered their career advancement. About one-quarter of women responded that gender had hindered their advancement, about one-sixth said it helped, and the remainder (61 percent) reported no effect. The second item asked respondents whether gender would have a positive effect, no effect, or a negative effect on their chances for promotion. Slightly more than one-quarter of women responded that gender would have a negative effect, one-fifth said it would have a positive effect, and the remaining 52 percent said there would be no effect. These items are recoded so that a higher score indicates a greater level of personal subjective discrimination.

Interestingly, the two scales are only moderately correlated (r = .35), indicating that the two types of subjective discrimination are imperfectly related, as Crosby and associates theorized (Crosby 1982, 1984; Crosby et al. 1986; Clayton and Crosby 1992). Consistent with their research findings, a smaller proportion of women experience personal subjective discrimination than experience group subjective discrimination.

Factors included on the Career Development Survey that potentially predict subjective discrimination were selected based on research identifying the correlates of related constructs, such as perceptions of injustice and consciousness about inequality (see, for example, Adams and Dressler 1988; Ransford and Miller 1983; Thornton, Alwin, and Camburn 1983; Gurin 1985; Gruber and Bjorn 1988; Davis and Robinson 1991; Wilcox 1991; Banaszak and Plutzer 1993; Sigelman and Welch 1991; Ospina 1996). These factors can be thought of in three categories:

- organizational experiences, e.g., was recently turned down for a promotion or developmental opportunity, has a mentor;

- the nature of the organization, e.g., relative proportion of men and women in the organization, representation of women in senior levels;
- personal attributes, e.g., education, age, supervisory status, amount of federal experience, marital/parental status, and race/ethnicity.

These factors are included in multiple regression models in which the dependent variables are group subjective discrimination and personal subjective discrimination. The results are shown in Table 6.2.[2]

Both models are statistically significant, although they explain only small portions of the variance in women's perceptions of discrimination. This is not unexpected, as psychologists have posited that perceptions of discrimination also depend on early socialization, the degree of identification with the group, the extent to which the individual desires or feels entitled to the outcome in question (Clayton and Crosby 1992), and individual cognitive styles (Witt 1990). This survey instrument did not measure these concepts.

The two strongest predictors of group subjective discrimination and two of the top three predictors of personal subjective discrimination are women's experiences on the job. Those who were turned down for a recent promotion or training or developmental opportunity for which they applied are more likely to believe that women are discriminated against and that they personally have been discriminated against, than those who either didn't apply or were not turned down. Of course, the direction of causation is not clear. It could be that women who perceive discrimination are also more likely to confront the system by repeatedly applying for promotions or developmental opportunities. This relationship is explored in greater depth at the end of this chapter.

It was expected that having a male or female mentor might reduce subjective discrimination, because such mentors provide role models and can often provide additional opportunities for their protégés (Vertz 1985; Dreher and Ash 1990; Hale 1992; Catalyst 1992). However, Table 6.2 shows no relationship between having a female mentor and either group or personal subjective discrimination. Women who have a male mentor do appear less likely to experience personal subjective discrimination. This suggests that these male mentors may have indeed been effective in opening doors for their protégés.

In the case of group subjective discrimination, the composition of respondents' work units also turns out to be a strong predictor. Where women are working with more men than women, they are more likely to perceive discrimination against women. This is consistent with Rosabeth Moss Kanter's discussion of how women who were few in number in the corporations she studied were more likely to report that they had to work twice as hard as men to prove their competence. She theorized that their rarity drew attention to their appearance and other non–ability related

TABLE 6.2   Factors Predicting Group and Personal Subjective Discrimination Experienced by Women (Regression Coefficients, Standard Errors)

Variable	Group Subjective Discrimination		Personal Subjective Discrimination	
	B	Beta	B	Beta
Organizational experiences				
Denied promotion	.274*** (.036)	.152	.233*** (.030)	.157
Denied training	.373 *** (.043)	.171	.246*** (.037)	.136
Female mentor	−.048 (.039)	−.027	.046 (.034)	.031
Male mentor	−.012 (.040)	−.006	−.079** (.034)	−.053
Organizational environment				
Work with more men than women	.358*** (.037)	.197	.004 (.031)	.002
More than 20% of SES are women	.257*** (.054)	−.103	.143** (.047)	.068
Less than 10% of SES are women	−.018 (.038)	−.010	.273*** (.032)	.187
Personal Attributes				
Supervisory status	−.058 (.030)	−.039	−.050* (.026)	−.041
Federal experience	.022 (.014)	.042	.045** (.012)	.105
Educational attainment	.057*** (.012)	.107	.059*** (.010)	.134
Woman of color	.180*** (.040)	.087	.001 (.034)	.006
Age	.046** (.018)	.062	.073*** (.015)	.117
Has spouse or partner	−.128*** (.035)	−.070	−.021 (.030)	−.014
(Constant)	1.808*** (.124)		1.641*** (.106)	
R^2	.15		.12	
N	2346		2271	

*p<.05, ** p<.01, *** p<.001
NOTE: See Appendix 3 for item coding.
SOURCE: U.S. Merit Systems Protection Board, *Career Development Survey*, 1991.

traits, while their accomplishments tended to be overlooked (Kanter 1977, 216–217).

Working in a majority-male organization does not affect personal subjective discrimination, however. This is consistent with Crosby's (1984) thesis that a perception of personal discrimination requires the identification of victims and villains. Because the question about who respondents work with addressed those they encounter "during a normal day," it may have hit too close to home for respondents to be willing to acknowledge that their own prospects for advancement are limited in their current work environment.

The model also includes two variables representing the degree to which women are represented in senior executive (SES) positions in their agencies, and these prove to be important predictors of subjective discrimination as well.[3] Where women are well represented in top positions, women are less likely to experience group subjective discrimination. Women in agencies with low female representation in the SES are not more or less likely than women in the excluded category (10–20 percent representation) to believe women are discriminated against. It may be that relatively high numbers of women in high-level positions, in this case, do signal greater opportunities for women. Another possible explanation could be that agencies where women hold many SES positions also happen to be those that have service delivery–related missions (the departments of Health and Human Services, Education, the Small Business Administration, and the Office of Personnel Management). This type of mission is consistent with women's traditional roles, so there might be a greater receptiveness to women's advancement as a result of that factor.

The impact of women's representation in the SES on personal subjective discrimination is more complicated, however. Poor representation of women in the SES turns out to be the strongest predictor of personal subjective discrimination in the model, controlling for all else. Interestingly, a high representation of women in the SES also contributes to women's likelihood to believe they have been personally discriminated against. This counterintuitive finding is actually consistent with the theory of relative deprivation. That theory says that a precondition for perceptions of discrimination against one personally is a comparison with others (Clayton and Crosby 1992). Where women have high representation in the SES, women at lower levels might expect that they should be afforded greater opportunities for advancement and are personally affronted when they are not promoted.

A number of personal attributes are related to group and personal subjective discrimination. Older women are more likely than younger women to experience personal and group subjective discrimination, perhaps because they are products of the women's movement of the 1960s. Education is positively related to both types of perception of discrimination, a finding consistent with previous research (Hopkins 1980; Davis and Robinson 1991). It is likely that higher educational attainment leads to greater career ambitions, so better-educated women are more sensitive to obstacles that may impede their progress.

Not surprisingly given the perceptions of discrimination based on race/national origin that also exist in the government, women of color are more likely than Euro-American women to believe opportunities for women are limited. When one perceives discrimination, it is not always possible to identify whether it is based on one's race/national origin or gender and, indeed, it may be both (James, Lovato, and Cropanzano 1994). Single women are also more likely to experience group subjective discrimination than married women, perhaps because they are harder hit than those in a dual income situation by the lower pay they receive relative to men. They may be more sharply attuned to differences in the way women are treated (Davis and Robinson 1991).

Neither supervisory status nor tenure in the federal workforce turn out to be related to group subjective discrimination, controlling for all else. This is contrary to Hopkins's (1980) finding that women in higher status occupations were more likely to experience subjective discrimination. (Of course, it is not clear whether Hopkins's survey asked questions related to group or personal discrimination, as she did not include question wording in her article.)

In contrast, nonsupervisors are more likely to experience personal subjective discrimination, perhaps because they have not succeeded in moving into supervisory ranks. Women with more federal experience are more likely to perceive discrimination against themselves, possibly because their added tenure has given them more opportunities to try to advance. Women of color are not more likely to report personal discrimination based on sex. They might attribute obstacles to their own advancement to race/ethnic discrimination, even if they believe women are discriminated against in their organizations.

In summary, women's perceptions of discrimination against women in general and against themselves personally are strongly influenced by several factors related to their experience on the job and the organizational environment. The factors affecting the two types of subjective discrimination are not identical because group and personal subjective discrimination are different constructs. Nevertheless, it is important to identify the contributors to both because organizations may be able to take steps to reduce subjective discrimination.

For example, even though it is obviously impossible for an organization to ensure that women are never denied training opportunities or promotions for which they apply, it would be worthwhile to make an effort to provide an explanation for why the opportunity was denied. In other words, rather than the experiences themselves, it may be employees' perceptions of how the decision was made that have a lasting impact on their evaluation of the organization's commitment to equal employment opportunity. Research has demonstrated how perceptions of the fairness of management decisions regarding pay, promotions, and other job rewards have an impact on employees' job satisfaction and commitment. Robert Dailey and Delaney Kirk, for example, found strong correlations between job satisfaction and perceptions of distributive and procedural justice. They recommended that managers could help shape positive employee perceptions of the fairness of organizational systems by showing respect for employees and by allowing employee input (Dailey and Kirk 1992).

Federal agencies may have a more difficult time changing the composition of their SES corps or individual work units. However, they should be aware that these factors affect women's perceptions as well. The fact that women in organizations with a high representation of women in the SES are more likely than women in middle range agencies to experience personal subjective discrimination should not be interpreted as a reason to maintain female representation below 10 percent! Rather, women should be informed of the steps required to be more competitive for advancement. Although a number of personal attributes also contribute to subjective discrimination, there is less that an organization can do to mitigate their effect.

Crosby suggests that women also have a role in eliminating barriers to their own advancement. She urges women to draw attention to disparate treatment and question those in decision-making positions about the reasons for the perceived imbalance (Crosby 1984). However, Clayton and Crosby (1992) further argue that because women are less likely to perceive discrimination against themselves than they are to perceive limited opportunities for women in general, it is incumbent on the organization to take proactive steps to mitigate the circumstances under which discrimination may be occurring. Recall Crosby's research that found women unwilling to perceive personal discrimination despite clear evidence that this was the case, and despite their acknowledgment of bias against women in general. For that reason, Clayton and Crosby (1992) argue, it is not sufficient for organizations to rely on self-reports of incidents of discrimination to ensure fair treatment.

People of Color and Subjective Discrimination

Another Dichotomy in Perceptions

Table 6.3 presents the responses to items from the Workforce Diversity Survey reflecting group subjective discrimination by race/ethnicity. It is clear that a significant proportion of people of color believe their organiza-

TABLE 6.3   Federal Employees' Perceptions of How People of Color Are Treated in Their Organizations (Percent)

	African American	Asian Pacific American	Latino	Native American	Euro- American
In my organization, nonminorities receive preferential treatment compared to minorities					
Strongly agree/agree	58.0	34.6	40.0	26.0	8.2
Neither agree nor disagree	14.5	23.5	20.9	16.2	16.0
Strongly disagree/disagree	16.2	29.7	29.2	39.6	65.6
N	2,066	451	708	265	9,589
Minority women face extra obstacles to advancement					
Strongly agree/agree	61.4	34.4	48.7	37.2	23.4
Neither agree nor disagree	10.1	18.0	13.9	14.3	14.3
Strongly disagree/disagree	20.7	32.4	26.3	38.0	51.1
N	2,065	450	696	266	9,577
The viewpoint of a minority is often not heard at a meeting until it is repeated by a nonminority					
Strongly agree/agree	50.9	25.7	38.2	25.3	8.3
Neither agree nor disagree	19.9	21.2	16.9	14.3	12.5
Strongly disagree/disagree	15.1	32.1	31.4	40.4	62.8
N	2,056	452	697	265	9591
Once a minority assumes a top management position, that position often loses much of its power and prestige					
Strongly agree/agree	44.1	18.2	24.7	25.9	7.5
Neither agree nor disagree	18.5	18.7	18.3	16.5	14.2
Strongly disagree/disagree	17.9	39.3	40.6	38.7	59.9
N	2,078	450	699	266	9589
My organization is reluctant to promote minorities to supervisory or management positions					
Strongly agree/agree	46.2	26.5	27.5	20.8	7.7
Neither agree nor disagree	21.3	22.7	22.0	18.9	12.3
Strongly disagree/disagree	20.9	34.2	37.8	49.1	65.3
N	2,096	453	706	265	9,617

NOTE: Those responding "don't know" are not included, so percentages do not total to 100. Ns reflect total responses, weighted.
All differences significant at the p<.001 level.
SOURCE: U.S. Merit Systems Protection Board, *Workforce Diversity Survey*, 1993.

tion does not treat them fairly. The table also shows that a likelihood to experience group subjective discrimination varies by group. For example, whereas 58 percent of African Americans believe that in their organizations "nonminorities receive preferential treatment compared to people of color," only 26 percent of Native Americans believe that to be true. This is consistent with previous research in private sector organizations, which found Asian Americans and Native Americans to be less critical of how people of color are treated in their organizations than were African Americans or Latinos (Fernandez 1981).

Native Americans are not uniformly the most positive about their organizations. Only 18 percent of Asian Pacific Americans, compared with 26 percent of Native Americans, agreed that in their organizations "once a minority assumes a top management position, that position often loses much of its power and prestige."

In each case, however, African Americans are the most disparaging of their organizations. Fernandez suggests that African Americans are the most critical of the treatment of people of color at least in part because they have faced dual liabilities of the stigma of slavery and color. Moreover, as the largest minority group, they present the greatest threat to Euro-Americans and therefore have likely experienced the most discriminatory treatment (Fernandez 1981).

Table 6.3 also shows that, as expected, Euro-Americans do not, by and large, share these skeptical views of how people of color are treated within federal organizations. With the exception of the statement concerning disadvantages faced by women of color, fewer than one in ten Euro-Americans agreed with any of the statements regarding the adverse treatment of people of color in the government. Thus, as seems to be true in the country as a whole (see, for example, Morin 1995; Sigelman and Welch 1991), people of color and Euro-Americans within the government live in very different perceptual worlds regarding the reality of equal employment opportunity. This is important to recognize because such a conflict in interpretations of workplace dynamics can erode collegiality. Moreover, those who don't believe there is a problem are not likely to support remedies aimed at correcting that problem.

Table 6.4 shows the responses of the four racial/ethnic groups to questions reflecting personal subjective discrimination. Again, a substantial number of federal civil servants of color believe their race/ethnicity has worked to their own personal disadvantage. In most cases, African Americans are the most critical; 40 percent responded that advancement would require playing down their ethnic customs, and the same proportion reported that racial stereotypes have adversely affected their treatment in their organizations. More than one-third of African Americans believe they had been discriminated against one or more times with respect to promo-

TABLE 6.4 Federal Employees' Perceptions of Their Own Treatment Within Their Organizations

	African American	Asian Pacific Islander	Latino	Native American
If I want to advance my career, I will have to play down my ethnic customs				
To a great or moderate extent	40.5	23.4	28.7	20.9
To a minimal or no extent	46.8	59.6	58.2	66.8
N	2,023	411	658	196
I would strive harder for promotions if I saw other members of my race/ethnic group get promoted				
To a great or moderate extent	51.7	44.4	49.8	47.2
To a minimal or no extent	40.2	41.3	40.1	40.5
N	2,008	414	664	195
My motivation on the job has suffered because of the way people from my race/ethnic group have been treated				
To a great or moderate extent	40.9	21.3	28.3	24.5
To a minimal or no extent	52.3	63.8	60.8	62.0
N	2,002	414	653	200
How much have racial/ethnic stereotypes adversely affected your treatment?				
Greatly or moderately	46.7	30.0	37.3	33.8
Minimally or not at all	44.8	56.4	50.9	54.4
N	2,035	420	668	204
Were you not selected for a promotion or developmental opportunity because of racial/ethnic discrimination in the last three years?				
Yes, more than once	22.6	13.1	17.4	8.8
Yes, once	15.1	10.5	13.5	10.7
No	38.4	52.3	45.3	57.4
N	2,091	459	711	272

NOTE: Those responding "don't know" are not included, so percentages do not total to 100. Ns reflect total responses, weighted.
All differences significant at the p<.001 level.
SOURCE: U.S. Merit Systems Protection Board, *Workforce Diversity Survey*, 1993.

tions or developmental opportunities for which they had applied in the preceding three years.

Native Americans and Asian Pacific Americans appear to be least concerned about the treatment they personally experience at work, although nearly one-fifth of Native Americans and nearly one-fourth of Asian Pacific Americans believed they have been discriminated against at least once in the preceding three years. About one-third of Native Americans, Latinos, and Asian Pacific Islanders report that they have been adversely affected by stereotypes to a moderate or great extent.

The next question to address, then, is whether there are factors related to the work environment or experiences on the job that contribute to the likelihood that each racial/ethnic group will experience group or personal subjective discrimination. If so, federal agencies may be able to take steps to reduce the likelihood that employees will perceive discrimination.

Correlates of Subjective Discrimination as Experienced by People of Color

This analysis is based on the responses of the 6,251[4] people of color who responded to the MSPB Workforce Diversity Survey. Two scales were created to measure personal and group subjective discrimination. The first is based on the mean responses to the five items shown in Table 6.3 and measures group subjective discrimination (alpha = .81). The second is designed to measure personal subjective discrimination and is based on the mean responses to the five items shown in Table 6.4 (alpha = .82). (The two scales are moderately correlated, r = .58.) In both cases, items are recoded, where necessary, so that a higher score means a higher level of subjective discrimination.

Independent variables represent work-related experiences and personal attributes that are likely to have an impact on subjective discrimination. Because this analysis is based on a different survey instrument, the independent variables here do not match those used in the analysis of subjective discrimination as it affects women. The included variables are:

- Organizational experiences: turned down for a promotion, number of cash awards received, amount of diversity training received, and having a mentor.
- Personal attributes: tenure in federal workforce, educational attainment, supervisory status, age, gender, and race/ethnicity.

The results of these analyses are presented in Table 6.5.[5]

TABLE 6.5 Factors Predicting Group and Personal Subjective Discrimination as Experienced by People of Color (Regression Coefficients, Standard Errors)

Variable	Group Subjective Discrimination		Personal Subjective Discrimination	
	B	Beta	B	Beta
Organizational experiences				
Denied promotion	.410*** (.036)	.228	.416*** (.038)	.228
Cash awards	−.020 (.013)	−.031	−.007 (.014)	−.010
Has mentor	−.109** (.036)	−.059	−.156*** (.039)	−.083
Diversity training	−.084*** (.014)	−.120	−.058*** (.015)	−.081
Personal attributes				
Federal experience	.008** (.002)	.073	.005* (.003)	.050
Educational attainment	.033** (.011)	.059	.046*** (.012)	.080
Supervisory status	−.121** (.036)	−.069	−.116** (.039)	−.065
Age	.019 (.018)	.024	.003 (.020)	.004
Gender (female)	.226*** (.037)	.126	−.070 (.040)	−.038
African American	.570*** (.036)	.314	.420*** (.039)	.228
(Constant)	2.500*** (.119)		1.524*** (.129)	
R^2	.25		.15	
N	2050		2059	

*p<.05, ** p<.01, *** p<.001
NOTE: See Appendix 3 for item coding.
SOURCE: U.S. Merit Systems Protection Board, *Workforce Diversity Survey*, 1993.

Three of the four variables representing organizational experiences predict the likelihood of people of color experiencing both group and personal subjective discrimination. As with women (see Table 6.2), having been turned down for a promotion is one of the two strongest factors, controlling for all else. Surprisingly, the number of cash awards received does not seem to make a difference in employees' outlook. This is unexpected in light of previous research showing a relationship between how employees perceive the distribution of awards and their attitudes about their jobs (Dailey and Kirk 1992). It may be that the employees believe the distribution system for cash awards is just, even if they believe the organization is denying them opportunities in other respects.

In the analysis of women's perceptions, we found that a female mentor had no effect on perceptions of discrimination, while a male mentor reduced personal subjective discrimination. The Workforce Diversity Survey did not distinguish the sex or race/ethnicity of the mentor. However, in this case, having a mentor mitigates both types of perceptions of discrimination among civil servants of color. This would suggest that some people of color have found mentors who serve as examples of opportunities open to them as well as mentors who can open doors for them. Also effective in reducing personal and group subjective discrimination is attendance at diversity training. This should be welcome news to organizations that invest resources in providing training that will, among other positive effects, reassure employees that their organization is committed to fair treatment for all.

Among personal attributes, years of federal experience, educational attainment, and supervisory status all predict both types of subjective discrimination. As noted with respect to women, more education may lead employees to have greater ambitions and therefore to be more likely to see those ambitions thwarted. Nonsupervisors are more likely to perceive discrimination than supervisors. This is not surprising given that supervisors have more control over their work environments than nonsupervisors while also enjoying a higher status. Age does not appear to affect perceptions of discrimination of employees of color either against their group or personally, controlling for all else.

The strongest predictor of both group and subjective discrimination is being African American. In this model, the inclusion of a dummy variable representing African Americans compares them with all other people of color. The size of this coefficient means that they are much more likely than other people of color to perceive discrimination. This is not surprising given the results reported in Tables 6.3 and 6.4. Nevertheless, it would be important for organizations to take note of these differences among racial/ethnic groups.

In concert with previous research (Sherman, Smith, and Sherman 1983), female civil servants of color are more likely than men of color to believe that people of color are discriminated against. However, they are not more likely than men of color to report that they have personally been discriminated against on the basis of race/ethnicity. This is consistent with a previous finding that women of color were more likely than Euro-American women to perceive discrimination against women, but not more likely to believe they had personally experienced sex discrimination (see Table 6.2). These findings suggest either that female civil servants of color have not personally experienced any discriminatory treatment or, more likely, that they attribute such experiences to something other than discrimination (e.g., more qualified competitors for promotions). Lee Sigelman and Susan Welch (1991) also found that African American women were less likely to perceive discrimination against themselves personally than were African American men.

There is, of course, much unexplained variance in both models, suggesting that there are many other factors that lead people of color to experience subjective discrimination. Nevertheless, these models do suggest steps that organizations can take to reduce both group and personal subjective discrimination. This is not to say that the same strategies will work for each racial/ethnic group, as different racial/ethnic groups think about discrimination-related issues in different ways (see Naff 1995).

It is clear, however, that those who have been denied promotions for which they have applied are more likely to perceive both group and personal discrimination. This is further evidence that it is important for supervisors to ensure that those who unsuccessfully apply for promotions are given adequate explanations. Data from the Workforce Diversity Survey indicate that only 8 percent of employees surveyed received useful feedback when they were denied a promotion. Organizations can also reduce perceptions of discrimination through providing diversity-related training and setting up mentoring programs.

This analysis has provided some insight into the circumstances under which subjective discrimination is likely to occur, and therefore what federal agencies can do to abate such perceptions. It has also shown that although many of the variables included in these models do appear to contribute to subjective discrimination, there are likely many others that do so also. Further research should explore and measure additional work-related variables and their relationship with subjective discrimination. What remains to be seen is whether such perceptions have an impact on employees' career choices, and therefore whether such perceptions contribute to the dearth of women and people of color in senior-level positions in the federal bureaucracy.

The Consequences of Subjective Discrimination

As noted at the beginning of this chapter, subjective discrimination is of particular concern when it has an impact on employees' job satisfaction, commitment, and career-related decisions. Previous research has, in fact, shown the adverse consequences that can occur when employees believe they are not being treated fairly and uniformly by their organizations (Graves and Powell 1994; Witt 1990; Cannings and Monmarquette 1991; Gallese 1991; Morrison, White, and vanVelsor 1987; Wick and Company 1990; Hale and Kelly 1989; Dailey and Kirk 1992; James, Lovato, and Cropanzano 1994). The final piece of this chapter is an examination of the effect of personal and group subjective discrimination on career decisions of federally employed women. Unfortunately, the MSPB Workforce Diversity Survey did not directly ask respondents about their career plans, so an examination of the relationship between subjective discrimination and those plans is not possible.

The MSPB Career Development Survey asked respondents about their plans for the next three to five years (see Table 6.6). Possible responses included whether respondents would seek promotion within their agencies or within the federal government but at different agencies. In addition, respondents were offered several options that would require leaving their agencies (e.g., retiring, resigning, seeking reassignment in another agency, taking a leave of absence). The two promotion options and a composite measure of desire to leave the agency are the dependent variables in this analysis.

We undertake this analysis by estimating models in which the primary independent variables are the two scales measuring group and personal subjective discrimination. Because the dependent variables are dichotomous (i.e., take the action or not), logistic regression is used. Controls are included reflecting factors that might also influence a woman's career-related decisions. These include current age, grade level, and experience, as older women with more experience and higher grades are less likely to apply for promotions and are probably more likely to consider leaving their agencies than are younger, lower-graded employees with less tenure (Kellough and Osuna 1995). Parental status is also included, because mothers may be less likely to apply for promotions or more likely to consider taking a leave of absence than childless women. A variable is also included representing work location (field or headquarters), because there are more opportunities for advancement in the headquarters locations of most agencies. Previous research has also found a relationship between organizational size and turnover or likelihood to apply for promotion (Kellough and Osuna 1995; Jackson et al. 1991), so a factor representing the total number of white-collar positions in respondents' agencies at the time of the survey is also included in the model. The results are shown in Table 6.7.

TABLE 6.6   Items from Career Development Survey Used to Evaluate Women's Career Plans

	Percent Checking Box	N
Which of the following best describes your plans affecting your career for the next three to five years? (Mark all that apply)		
No change planned	20.1	693
Seek promotion within this agency	52.5	1,809
*Seek promotion within the federal government but in another agency/department	24.2	840
*Leave the federal service to work outside the federal government	11.0	380
*Retire from the federal service	11.2	385
*Seek reassignment outside this agency at the same grade level	8.7	299
Seek reassignment within this agency at the same grade level	9.9	341
*Take a leave of absence	2.3	79
*Resign from my current job	2.0	68
Other	2.2	76

*These items are used to develop composite indicator of plans to leave agency.
SOURCE: U.S. Merit Systems Protection Board, *Career Development Survey*, 1991.

As it turns out, neither group nor personal subjective discrimination has an impact on a woman's thoughts about applying for promotion within her own agency, controlling for all else. This is contrary to prior research indicating that women who perceive disparate treatment are less likely to seek advancement (Cannings and Montmarquette 1991; Gallese 1991). However, a recent article summarizing the results of interviews with some of the few African American women holding senior executive jobs helps to put these findings in perspective. According to that article, these women credit their own success in the face of "careers littered with incidents of bias" (Laurent 1996, 13) to hard work, self-confidence, and perseverance. Rather than filing complaints, they "gritted their teeth, bit their tongues and, when no other avenue offered relief, confronted their managers" (Laurent 1996, 21). It could be that women who enter federal

TABLE 6.7   Effect of Subjective Discrimination on Career Plans (Logistic Regression Coefficients, Standard Errors)

	Seek Promotion Within Agency	Seek Promotion Outside Agency	Leave Agency
Group subjective discrimination	.090	.595***	.394***
	(.052)	(.067)	(.055)
Personal subjective discrimination	.005	.268***	.205**
	(.061)	(.072)	(.063)
Size of agency	−.002***	.002*	.002**
	(.001)	(.001)	(.001)
Works at headquarters	−.118	.222	.358**
	(.126)	(.144)	(.126)
Works at a field office	−.357**	−.468***	−.177
	(.116)	(.139)	(.118)
Age	−.223***	−.273***	.168***
	(.048)	(.062)	(.048)
Current grade level	−.070**	−.061	−.051
	(.027)	(.034)	(.028)
Federal experience	−.104**	−.061	−.040
	(.032)	(.039)	(.033)
Has children	.329***	.219*	−.325***
	(.089)	(.107)	(.091)
Constant	2.447***	−2.241***	−2.350***
	(.417)	(.499)	(.426)
Chi Sq	131.410***	206.085***	175.023***
Percent of cases in modal category	52.5%	75.6%	56.2%
Percent predicted correctly	62.4%	77.9%	64.5%
Proportional reduction in error	14.2%	2.1%	11.2%

N = 2901, * p<.05, ** p<.01, ***p<.001
NOTE: See Appendix 3 for item coding.
SOURCE: U.S. Merit Systems Protection Board, *Career Development Survey*, 1991.

service are more determined to advance than women in other sectors, or that women's consciousness of discrimination in the 1990s has reached the point where such perceptions only make them more determined to succeed.

Note also the size of the coefficient representing the impact of motherhood in this model. It could be that as a mother a woman believes it is important to seek promotion to earn a better income but doesn't have the time to look outside her agency. She may also fear that she will have to prove her job commitment all over again in a new organization, because women with children tend to be viewed as less committed to their careers than women without children (see Chapter 4).

Personal and group subjective discrimination do appear to contribute to the likelihood that a woman will consider seeking a promotion in another agency rather than her own, however. In fact, in this second model, group subjective discrimination is the greatest predictor of her likelihood to apply elsewhere. It may well be that although she wants to advance, she would rather do so in another agency that she believes to be less prone to what she considers to be discriminatory treatment against women. The woman's aspirations to advance are not damaged, but the agency may well lose her to another employer. This is also consistent with Anne Laurent's finding from her interviews with African American female senior executives. She reported that when they found their careers had stalled or they received lower ratings than they believed they deserved, these women took different jobs, switched agencies, or even moved across the country to find new opportunities (Laurent 1996).

The third model predicts a woman's likelihood to leave her agency altogether, and again both types of subjective discrimination are significant predictors. The results presented in Table 6.7 suggest that although a woman may be deterred from leaving her agency by having children, her perception of discrimination against women has a much stronger effect on her decision to leave.

In Table 6.8, the independent impact that group and subjective personal discrimination have on women's career choices is determined by holding covariates constant. (Plans to apply for promotion within one's own agency are not included because the impact of subjective discrimination turned out to be negligible.) The effect of subjective discrimination is assessed by using the characteristics of the "average woman" responding to the survey (i.e., the modal response) and varying only the level of subjective discrimination as measured by the scale.[6] The "average woman" is a thirty- to thirty-nine-year-old mother, with ten to fifteen years of federal experience, currently holding a GS 11 job at headquarters in an agency with approximately 73,000 white-collar employees.

Findings presented in Table 6.8 indicate that group and personal subjective discrimination have a substantial impact on the "typical" mid-level, female federal employee's decision to apply for promotion outside her own agency or to leave that agency altogether. A woman who experiences little or no group subjective discrimination has only a 7 percent probability of applying for promotion outside her own agency. For a woman who perceives a great deal of inequitable treatment, that likelihood is 69 percent. Similarly, a woman who strongly believes her own opportunities and those of women in general are limited in her organization has a 62 percent prob-

TABLE 6.8   Probability of Making a Career Move (Percent)

| | Degree of Subjective Discrimination | | |
	Little/None	Neutral	High
		Probability	
Apply for promotion outside agency	7	29	69
Leave agency	13	33	62

N = 3,443
SOURCE: U.S. Merit Systems Protection Board, *Career Development Survey*, 1991.

ability of leaving her agency. If she were to see no such disadvantages based on gender, the likelihood of her leaving would be only 13 percent.

Conclusion

This analysis has suggested that although the assessment of barriers faced by women and people of color to their inclusion and advancement in the government is important, it is incomplete. *Perceptions* of inequitable treatment are also important. This is particularly critical in the federal government, where a strong commitment to equal employment opportunity and a merit system has no doubt raised the expectations of its employees (see Chapter 1).

This chapter has shown that a substantial number of women and people of color in the government do perceive their opportunities to be limited. More than half of women believe they must outperform their male colleagues to be promoted, and nearly half of African Americans and more than one-quarter of Asian Pacific Americans and Latinos believe that their organizations are reluctant to promote people of color into supervisory positions. Data presented in this chapter also show that the extent to which people of color believe their opportunities are limited varies considerably by race/ethnicity. Moreover, men and Euro-Americans, by and large, do not share those views. It seems that colleagues working side by side in an agency often have very different views of the environment in which they are working with respect to equal employment opportunities.

The chapter has also identified work-related factors that affect the chances that a woman or person of color will perceive discrimination. Although only a small portion of the variance in perceptions was explained by these factors, these analyses do suggest that there are remedies organizations can impose to reduce the prevalence of subjective discrimination. These include providing feedback to those who unsuccessfully apply for promotions and making mentors and diversity training courses available.

In assessing employees' views and designing programs to mitigate perceptions of unequal treatment, it is crucial that agencies recognize that there are really two types of subjective discrimination. Women and people of color may believe that their group is treated inequitably while expressing no concerns about their own treatment (or vice versa). The factors that contribute to these different types are not necessarily the same. However, because men and Euro-Americans don't share these perceptions, convincing them that remedies are necessary may be an additional challenge faced by an agency striving to ensure employee confidence in its commitment to equal employment opportunity.

Finally, this analysis has provided evidence that such perceptions do have an impact on the career choices made at least by women in federal agencies. Even though they are not discouraged from applying for promotions within their own agencies, women are likely to jump ship and try to find another position elsewhere. Thus, it is clear that agencies that wish to improve the underrepresentation of women in management in their own organizations must not only eradicate any "objective" discrimination that continues to exist but also address employees' perceptions of discrimination. Such perceptions, indeed, appear to constitute a barrier to achieving a bureaucracy fully representative of women and people of color at all grade levels, and in all agencies.

Notes

1. After weighting to correct for oversampling, this number is 2,645 women.

2. A model was estimated that included the gender of respondents' supervisors and whether or not they had children, as these could logically affect perceptions of discrimination. In the interest of parsimony, they were eliminated from the final model because they did not contribute at all to the variance explained.

3. Bivariate analysis showed that there is not a linear relationship between women's representation in the SES and subjective discrimination. However, there were indications that women in agencies where female representation in the SES is below 10 percent are more likely to experience personal subjective discrimination, and that women in agencies where women represent more than 20 percent of senior executives were less likely to experience group subjective discrimination. Therefore, two dummy variables were included representing these two extremes. The proportions represent women's representation in the SES at the time of the survey.

4. After weighting to correct for oversampling, this number is 3,585, of which 2,123 are African American, 463 are Asian Pacific American, 722 are Latino, and 276 are Native American.

5. There were no items in this survey that would reflect the organizational environment. An examination of the bivariate relationships between the two scales measuring subjective discrimination and the representation of people of color in the SES showed no relationship. Whether the job was white collar or blue collar was also eliminated from the final model, as it did not contribute anything to explaining the variance in perceptions.

6. The degree of subjective discrimination represents the sum of the highest, middle, and lowest possible scores on the two scales.

7

Sexual Harassment

If she confronts the harasser, she is being overly sensitive. If she files a grievance, she is a troublemaker. If she fails to respond to the harassment, she is leading on the harasser and "sending double messages." If she even serves as a witness to a sexual harassment complaint she is marginalized as being no longer one of "the team."

(Guy 1994, 86)

In October 1991, Americans sat glued to their television sets watching Anita Hill testify before the Senate Judiciary Committee. Supreme Court nominee Clarence Thomas, she asserted, had sexually harassed her when she was in his employ years earlier at the Equal Employment Opportunity Commission. Many citizens were caught by surprise upon learning that a woman would endure sexual harassment and not speak out against it until years later. This, and subsequent coverage of the "Tailhook" incident, in which Navy women complained of being sexually abused at a conference by male colleagues, brought heightened attention to the issue.

As with subjective discrimination, prior research has shown that sexual harassment can have dire consequences for those who experience it. It can lead to physical and psychological maladies, declines in productivity, and reduced job satisfaction and ambition (U.S. Merit Systems Protection Board 1995; Fitzgerald 1990; Morrow, McElroy, and Philips 1994; Murrell, Olson, and Frieze 1995; Kelly and Stambaugh 1992; LeMoncheck 1997; Vinciguerra 1994). Sexual harassment clearly represents a barrier to the achievement of bureaucracy by impeding the ability of its victims to contribute their maximum potential to their jobs.

The purpose of this chapter is to assess the incidence of sexual harassment among women in the federal government, how they respond to it, and its impact on them. It further examines the extent to which federally em-

161

ployed men and women share similar perceptions of sexual harassment, as considerable research outside the federal sector has shown that they do not (Glazer 1996; Tata 1993; Jones, Remland, and Brunner 1987; Riger 1991; Baugh 1997; Thacker and Gohmann 1993). An important question is whether the heightened attention brought about by such events as the Thomas hearings and the Tailhook incident has narrowed that divide.

My analysis is based on responses to two government-wide surveys administered by the U.S. Merit Systems Protection Board (MSPB) in 1987 and 1994. Each of those surveys was administered to broad cross-sections of federal employees and included many of the same questions, thus making some comparisons over time possible. Before undertaking that enterprise, some background on the development of sexual harassment as a legal and managerial issue is provided.

Sexual Harassment as a Legal Issue

That sexual harassment is a violation of the law is a relatively recent phenomenon and one that is undergoing continual development. There still is no statute that specifically prohibits sexual harassment. Rather, since a 1976 district court decision, *Williams v. Saxbe* (413 F. Supp. 654), courts have held that, under some circumstances, sexual harassment constitutes a form of sex discrimination under Title VII of the Civil Rights Act (Vinciguerra 1994).

Following that and similar decisions, the Equal Employment Opportunity Commission (EEOC) issued guidelines (29 C.F.R. § 1604.11) in 1980 defining two types of sexual harassment as violations of Title VII. One is "quid quo pro" harassment, which occurs if an individual is required to submit to sexual advances as a condition of continuing employment or to receive a promotion, pay raise, or other work-related benefit. The other type of sexual harassment occurs when a "hostile environment" is created by sexual behavior that makes it difficult for employees to work effectively (U.S. Merit Systems Protection Board 1995; see also Lee and Greenlaw 1995 for further explanation). The Supreme Court upheld these definitions of sexual harassment as violations of Title VII of the Civil Rights Act in *Meritor Savings Bank, FSB v. Vinson* (477 U.S. 57 [1986]).

Included in the EEOC's 1980 guidelines was a five-element test for the establishment of quid pro quo sexual harassment that has been endorsed by most circuit courts (Lee and Greenlaw 1996). Plaintiffs must show that (1) they belong to a protected class and (2) were subject to unwelcome sexual advances or demands; the (3) behavior was based on sex; (4) they were expected to submit to sexual demands to avoid negative employment actions or to receive job benefits; and (5) the employer is liable under Title VII (see

Lee and Greenlaw 1996 for further details). In practice, it can be difficult for plaintiffs to meet all five elements. For example, if the defendant denies the allegations, the plaintiff may have difficulty showing that the unwelcome sexual advances occurred or that the refusal to submit to the defendant's demands would have resulted or did result in retaliation (Lee and Greenlaw 1996).

Neither the EEOC guidelines nor the *Meritor Savings Bank* decision provided much clarity as to what specific behavior was to be considered sexual harassment nor what the burden of proof should be (Lee and Greenlaw 1995). In this regard, an important case in the development of sexual harassment law was *Harris v. Forklift Systems, Inc.* (114 S. Ct. 367 [1993]). In that case, the Supreme Court ruled that the harassment need not be so severe that it caused "concrete psychological harm" for it to be considered sexual harassment. The Court indicated that judgment as to whether a work environment was indeed hostile would be based on such factors as the frequency of the conduct, whether it was physically or psychologically threatening, and whether it unreasonably interfered with an employee's work (Lee and Greenlaw 1995). The Court said that it was taking a "middle path" between defining any offensive conduct as actionable and requiring that psychological injury be demonstrated. In *Oncale v. Sundowner Offshore Services, Inc.* (118 S. Ct. 998 [1998]), the Court provided further clarification that the conduct must be "so objectively offensive as to alter the 'conditions' of the victim's employment."

Another important milestone in the development of sexual harassment law was the 1991 Civil Rights Act, which gave plaintiffs, for the first time, the right to collect punitive damages in addition to compensatory damages for the abuse they endured. Although the law limits the damages that can be collected to $300,000, some plaintiffs have been awarded higher amounts by invoking state employment discrimination laws or bringing additional actions for personal injuries. In one of the most notorious cases, Wal-Mart was ordered to pay $50 million for the offensive and degrading remarks its female employees endured (Glazer 1996).

In addressing whether behavior is sufficiently severe to be actionable, some courts have relied on whether a hypothetical "reasonable person" would have found it offensive. In other cases the courts have held that such a standard would be male-biased and a more appropriate standard would be whether a "reasonable woman" would find the behavior offensive (see *Ellison v. Brady,* 924 F.2d 878 [1991]). Unfortunately, the Supreme Court has not addressed this issue. The courts have also had to address such issues as whether the conduct was really "unwelcome" as required by the law, whether off-work activities would establish a hostile working environment, and the sufficiency of the employer's sexual harassment policies (see Guy 1997). In other words, there is a lot of defining still left to do.

Recently, the Supreme Court decided two more cases further delineating employers' responsibilities for preventing sexual harassment. In *Burlington Industries, Inc. v. Ellerth* (118 S. Ct. 2257 [1998]) and *Faragher v. City of Boca Raton* (118 S. Ct. 2275 [1998]), the Court ruled that an employer is subject to vicarious liability when its supervisors commit unlawful sexual harassment.[1] One result of these decisions is that rather than distinguishing between quid pro quo harassment and that which creates a hostile environment, *Ellerth* distinguished between harassment that culminates in a "tangible employment action" and one that does not. If the harassment results in a tangible employment action (e.g., the supervisor fired, failed to promote, or gave an undesirable work assignment to the complainant), an employer cannot raise an affirmative defense. Rather, the employer must produce evidence showing that the action was taken for nondiscriminatory reasons. If the harassment does *not* result in a tangible employment action, the employer can raise an affirmative defense to liability or damages, which must consist of two elements. The first is that the employer must show that it exercised reasonable care to prevent and correct harassing behavior. The second element is that the employee failed to take advantage of any corrective or preventative opportunities the employer provided (U.S. Equal Employment Opportunity Commission 1999b).

In guidance issued on June 18, 1999, the EEOC describes steps management can take to meet the requirement of exercising reasonable care to prevent and correct harassing behavior. Such steps include establishing, publicizing, and enforcing anti-harassment policies; designing effective complaint and investigation processes; and making clear that it will take immediate corrective action (including discipline) when it determines that harassment has occurred. The Court also held that employees should take steps to avoid the harassment by alerting management before it becomes severe (U.S. Equal Employment Opportunity Commission 1999b).

The latest decisions make it clear that the Supreme Court has recognized that harassment in the workplace, whether it results in a negative employment action or not, is a violation of the Civil Rights Act. Although these decisions clarify employer responsibilities for preventing and correcting harassment, many other issues remain uncertain. Still to be determined is when social interaction becomes "unwelcome" sexual harassment, and just how severe or widespread offensive conduct must be to constitute a hostile work environment (Burns 1995). However, because of the pervasiveness of sexual harassment and its adverse impact on those who experience it, it is clear that an employer should not merely be concerned with whether steps have been taken to ensure that an affirmative defense can be raised in the event of a sexual harassment suit. Rather, employers should address whether mechanisms are in place for evaluating the extent to which employees perceive conduct of a sexual nature to be offensive and the effect of those perceptions on their esteem and work performance. In other words, sexual harassment is not simply a legal issue, it is a management issue.

Sexual Harassment as a Management Issue

Clearly, understanding and complying with the evolving statutes and case law governing sexual harassment in the workplace is necessary, but it is not sufficient to ensure that sexual harassment does not serve as a barrier to the inclusion and advancement of women in the workplace. As the quote opening the chapter suggests, sexual harassment can undermine women's experiences in and contributions to the workplace in many pernicious ways, regardless of how they respond to it.

Moreover, the issue is unlikely to go away any time soon. The number of harassment charges filed with the EEOC and state fair employment practice agencies rose from 6,883 in 1991 to 15,618 in 1998 (U.S. Equal Employment Opportunity Commission 1999b). This does not necessarily mean that more harassment is occurring. At least some of the increase is probably attributable to the heightened attention to the issue following the Thomas hearings, Tailhook incident, and other high-profile events. Also contributing to the increase in claims is the 1991 Civil Rights Act, which permitted plaintiffs to seek damages for the first time (Glazer 1996). Nevertheless, sexual harassment is something few employers can choose to ignore.

This section of this chapter summarizes some of the matters that make sexual harassment difficult but important to address, as documented by a growing literature on the subject. These include definitional issues, how victims choose to respond to harassment, and its impact on them emotionally, physically, and professionally. We then turn to examination of these topics in the context of the federal government. The literature summarized here will make clear that sexual harassment is particularly difficult to investigate, for several reasons.

First, the lack of a commonly accepted definition makes sexual harassment difficult to measure. Compounding this measurement problem is evidence that suggests the number of individuals who experience sexual harassment is not the same as the numbers who believe they have been harassed. As with personal subjective discrimination (see Chapter 6), not all victims are willing to admit that they have been harassed, even to themselves.

Second, there remains disagreement as to whether behavior labeled as sexual harassment is a private issue resulting from misunderstandings among individuals or a public issue that is rooted in organizational power structures biased against women (Baugh 1997; Reese and Lindenberg 1999; Stringer et al. 1990; Riger 1991; Hotelling 1991). That disagreement then leads to questions about how individual women and the organizations they work for should respond to allegations of harassment. Finally, although it is commonly believed that sexual harassment harms its victims, in practice it is difficult to isolate that impact from other sources of potential harm in the workplace.

Mane Hajdin (1997, 97–98) is right on target when she says that the controversy about such issues makes "the debate about sexual harassment less straightforward and more difficult than are the debates about most other contemporary moral issues." Unlike other volatile issues such as abortion or affirmative action, different viewpoints about sexual harassment don't line up in direct opposition to one another in a way that can structure debate and inquiry. This chapter is not going to resolve that dilemma. Rather, after discussing previous research that has attempted to shed light on this complex issue, it focuses on sexual harassment as it affects women in the federal government. It will attempt to further our understanding of sexual harassment by examining, in the context of the federal government:

- Women and men's definitions of sexual harassment and how, if at all, they changed following the renewed attention to the issue in the early 1990s;
- The incidence of harassment and whether it has declined given the scramble to draft or update policy statements condemning sexual harassment, institute mandatory training, and ensure redress procedures following the Thomas and Tailhook incidents;
- Women's responses to sexual harassment and what factors may affect their choice of response ; and
- The impact of sexual harassment on women and whether organizational or individual factors make harmful consequences more likely.

Before proceeding with this examination, it is important to look at the issues that make it difficult to even arrive at a consensus as to how sexual harassment should be studied.

Defining Sexual Harassment

In its 1980 regulations, the EEOC defined sexual harassment thus:

> Unwelcome sexual advances, requests for sexual favors, and other verbal or physical conduct of a sexual nature constitute sexual harassment when (1) submission to such conduct is made either explicitly or implicitly a term or condition of an individual's employment, (2) submission to or rejection of such conduct by an individual is used as the basis for employment decisions affect-

ing such individual, or (3) such conduct has the purpose or effect of unreasonably interfering with an individual's work performance, or creating an intimidating, hostile or offensive working environment. (29 C.F.R. § 1604.11)

Despite this attempt at clarification, researchers still have not agreed as to which specific behaviors constitute sexual harassment (Gillespie and Leffler 1987). One basis of criticism is that these guidelines place the burden of determining whether behavior was unwelcome and constitutes harassment on the victim (Dougherty et al. 1996). In some cases that determination is obvious, as when a supervisor demands sexual favors in return for a promotion or pay increase. However, deciding whether an "implicit" rather than explicit demand has been made or whether particular conduct creates an intimidating or offensive work environment requires subjective judgment that differs among individuals. What one may perceive as flirtatious and welcome, another may perceive as unwelcome harassment (Solomon and Williams 1997).

Some researchers have undertaken experimental studies to determine when behavior will be interpreted as harassment rather than a more innocuous form of social-sexual communication. For example, Thomas Dougherty and colleagues (1996) found that his subjects' assessments as to whether the conduct was harassment were affected by the context in which it occurred, that is, whether the man and woman had socialized before the incident occurred, and where the incident occurred (i.e., in the office or at happy hour), as well as the position of the initiator. Although understanding the importance of context in defining sexual harassment is important, it does not settle the debate between those who believe women should be protected from harassment in every context and those who believe that under some circumstances similar behavior should be considered benign.

In another experimental study, Denise Solomon and Mary Lynn Williams (1997) gave participants a newsletter describing hypothetical workplace scenarios and manipulated the explicitness of the message (high or low), the initiator's position (supervisor or subordinate), the initiator's attractiveness, the target's attractiveness, and the initiator's sex. They found that study participants based their assessment as to what was harassment almost entirely on the explicitness of the message rather than the other factors. A study by Tricia Jones, Martin Remland, and Claire Brunner (1987) similarly found that outside observers' judgments as to whether sexual harassment occurred was most affected by the recipient's response to the behavior and the sex of the observer. It should be clear from even these three studies that there is nearly an infinite number of dimensions to sexual harassment that could be tested in what would probably be an unsuccessful quest to find a single definition of sexual harassment.

These last two studies illustrate another difficulty as well. The Solomon and Williams (1997) and Jones, Remland, and Brunner (1987) studies represent two exceptions to an otherwise persistent finding: that behavior on the part of someone with power over the recipient (e.g., a supervisor) is more likely to be viewed as harassment than the same behavior engaged in by someone who does not wield such power (Fitzgerald 1990; U.S. Merit Systems Protection Board 1995).

Assuming such differences in findings could be resolved, one would assume that these kinds of studies could then be used to develop an operational definition of sexual harassment that could be used to measure incidence (Gruber 1992). The problem is, however, that these studies assess the judgments of outside observers, rather than those of the recipients themselves. It can reasonably be argued that it is the recipients who suffer the consequences of harassment and who decide whether and how to respond.

However, some research has shown that individuals may experience conduct that meets the legal definition of harassment, that may even meet their *own* definition of harassment, and yet fail to perceive it as such (Reese and Lindenberg 1999; Arvey and Cavanaugh 1995; Morrow, McElroy, and Phillips 1994). When this occurs, incidence of sexual harassment is likely to be underreported (Reese and Lindenberg 1997).

Recall from Chapter 6 that women who believe women are discriminated against often do not believe they personally have been discriminated against. Researchers have postulated that this paradox occurs in part because it is uncomfortable to identify oneself as a victim and those that one works for as villains (Crosby 1982, 1984; Crosby et al. 1986; Clayton and Crosby 1992). It is likely that the same phenomenon occurs, in many cases, with respect to sexual harassment. Moreover, perceiving oneself as a "victim" of sexual harassment implies a loss of control over life circumstances and can make one feel vulnerable (Koss 1990; Reese and Lindenberg 1999).

Another recurrent theme in the literature, however, is that men are less likely to view certain behaviors as harassment than women, although the gap is narrowing (Glazer 1996; Tata 1993; Jones, Remland, and Brunner 1987; Riger 1991; Baugh 1997; Thacker and Gohmann 1993). From this arises the controversy being played out in the courts as to whether a claim is valid if a "reasonable *person*" would view a situation as harassment or whether the standard should be the judgment of a "reasonable *woman*." In the first case, women who genuinely perceive harassment may not be given their due. In the second case, men may be punished for behavior they did not realize was unlawful.

Most studies have found that there is likely to be more agreement between men and women as to whether behavior constitutes sexual harassment when that behavior is serious (e.g., pressure for sexual favors rather than sexual teasing) (Riger 1991; Reese and Lindenberg 1997; Tata 1993; U.S. Merit Systems Protection Board 1995; Baugh 1997). There are exceptions to this finding as well, however. In their study of two public sector organizations, Laura Reese and Karen Lindenberg (1999) found that men and women agreed that half of sixteen behaviors listed on a survey constituted sexual harassment. The behaviors upon which they agreed spanned the spectrum from complimentary looks to unwelcome pressure for sex and physical assault.

Alison Konrad and Barbara Gutek (1986) suggest that such differences in definitions are in part based on gender stereotyping, the fact that women are more likely to have negative experiences with sex at work, and by different personal orientations toward sexual overtures in the workplace. S. Gayle Baugh (1997) suggests that contributing to the difference in perceptions between men and women is a woman's sensitivity to the fact that attention to her sex role can undermine her work role. Moreover, those with less power in organizations tend to be more sensitive to the behavior and potential coercion of more powerful people rather than the other way around.

The lack of a commonly accepted definition, then, makes it difficult to ascertain how widespread sexual harassment is in any organization or at any point in time (Arvey and Cavanaugh 1995; Hotelling 1991). Having said that, the consistently high number of women who indicate on surveys that they have been harassed suggests that it indeed is pervasive enough in the workplace to be of concern.

Incidence of Sexual Harassment

When *Redbook* magazine surveyed its readers in 1976, of the more than 9,000 people who responded, 88 percent reported that they had been sexually harassed (Kaplan 1991). More recently, in response to a survey included in the February 1992 issue of *Working Women* magazine, more than 60 percent of 9,000 female respondents reported that they had been personally harassed (Sandroff 1992). One can certainly criticize these findings as unscientific and nongeneralizable because they are based on nonrandom, convenience samples of readers (Gillespie and Leffler 1987). Nevertheless, those women probably would not have responded had they been satisfied with their treatment at work.

The MSPB administered surveys to probability samples representative of the federal workforce in 1980, 1987, and 1994, a more defensible approach, and in each case more than 40 percent of women reported they had been sexually harassed in the previous two years (U.S. Merit Systems Protection Board 1995). Surveys administered to women in five state governments revealed that between 33 and 60 percent of women experienced harassment (Kelly and Stambaugh 1992). In a survey of women who had earned Masters of Public Administration degrees, 44 percent reported that they had experienced sexual harassment (Lawn-Day and Ballard 1996). Hence, sampling issues aside, it is probably fair to state that a significant proportion of women in these environments believe they have been sexually harassed.

Regardless of how it is defined or measured, then, it seems likely that sexual harassment is a problem with which management should be concerned. Research has shown that it can have serious consequences for both individuals and their employers.

The Impact of Sexual Harassment

Research has documented the considerable repercussions of sexual harassment for women and the organizations they work for. Such consequences include decreased morale and job satisfaction, tardiness and absenteeism, reduced productivity, deterioration in interpersonal relationships, depression, symptoms of post-traumatic stress disorder, and other physical and health problems (U.S. Merit Systems Protection Board 1995; Schneider, Swan, and Fitzgerald 1997; Murrell, Olson, and Frieze 1995; Kaplan 1991; Koss 1990; Sandroff 1992; Vinciguerra 1994; Kelly and Stambaugh 1992). Harassment can derail a woman's career either because of pressure to quit, fear of being fired, or a desire to escape the organization by taking a job with reduced opportunities (Murrell, Olson, and Frieze 1995). Such effects can even occur at low levels of sexual harassment (Schneider, Swan, and Fitzgerald 1997). These harmful outcomes can also take place when the victim does not believe she was harassed (Schneider, Swan, and Fitzgerald 1997; Morrow, McElroy, and Phillips 1994).

The adverse effects on individuals who experience harassment also have negative consequences for their organizations. The MSPB (1995) estimated, based on its 1994 survey, that sexual harassment cost the federal government about $327 million in the two-year period addressed in the survey. Expenses borne by the government and other employers include unwanted turnover, the use of sick leave, and declines in productivity (U.S. Merit Systems Protection Board 1995; Kaplan 1991; Murrell, Olson, and Frieze 1995). The employer also may have to endure direct costs for litigation, out-of-court settlements, higher unemployment compensation, and workers' compensation claims (Kaplan 1991).

Given such consequences, it seems that women would be likely to report the harassment so that measures could be taken to stop it. This is not usually the case, however.

Responding to Sexual Harassment

Once they encounter offensive behavior, women have to decide whether to respond with a formal complaint, handle the incident informally, or not respond at all. Prior research indicates that the majority of women choose not to respond outwardly; they merely avoid the harasser, find excuses for the behavior, deny that it happened, or blame themselves (Kaplan 1991; Riger 1991; Fitzgerald, Swan, and Fischer 1995). All of these strategies can have unwanted consequences, however. Avoidance is not possible if the nature of the work requires continued interaction with the harasser (Schneider, Swan, and Fitzgerald 1997). Moreover, not responding at all often results in more harassment (Kaplan 1991), but a complaint can result in retaliation (Murrell, Olson, and Frieze 1995). Not surprisingly, then, victims tend to turn to formal strategies as a last resort when everything else fails (Fitzgerald, Swan, and Fischer 1995). A more active response also requires acknowledging that one has been a victim and, as discussed previously, there is a strong tendency to avoid that (Reese and Lindenberg 1999).

The response chosen by the victim generally depends on the severity of the harassment, with more severe harassment resulting in a more assertive response. Studies have produced mixed findings with respect to whether victims are more likely to report harassment by a supervisor or by a coworker (Fitzgerald, Swan, and Fischer 1995). Affecting that decision, of course, is whether the policy calls for reporting the harassment to the supervisor who may also be the perpetrator (Eberhardt, Moser, and McFadden 1999).

Also affecting victims' responses are organizational culture and norms (Fitzgerald, Swan, and Fischer 1995). One study examined women's responses to sexist remarks and found that although most would have liked to respond, they felt constrained from doing so by social pressure not to confront others. Those who did respond were more likely to be personally committed to fighting sexism (Swim and Hyers 1999). Another potential deterrent is an assumption by recipients of sexual harassment that they will not be believed or nothing will be done (Lindenberg and Reese 1995).

S. Gayle Baugh (1997) contends that a woman who attempts to make a claim faces a male-biased power structure that does not share her definition of sexual harassment. Even if those hearing her complaint do agree that harassment has occurred, they often do not share her perspective on the appropriate response. As noted in the previous section of this chapter, defining conduct as sexual harassment often involves assessing a variety of contextual factors (e.g., the explicitness of the message, whether the behavior occurred on the job or after hours), and therefore there is considerable latitude for blaming the victim. As long as the male bias in organizational responses to sexual harassment persists, Baugh maintains, there will be a chilling effect on victims' willingness to take action.

Stephanie Riger (1991) focuses her critique on the grievance process that victims must use to seek redress. She argues that more women don't make use of grievance procedures because gender bias in sexual harassment policies discourages them from doing so. Such policies appear to be gender-neutral, but they assume that men and women view harassment the same way (which they don't) and that the complainant and accused have equal power (which is often not the case, either). Women who are harassed by their supervisors are surely not dealing with someone with equal authority, and in many cases women may not have the same resources at their disposal as male coworkers, either.

Women who are apprehensive that their complaint won't be taken seriously have cause for concern. Studies have shown that those judging the complaint are likely to look for other explanations for the charge, including that the woman has a feminist orientation or is in career competition with the accused (Summers 1991). Many officials charged with responding to sexual harassment complaints simply do not believe that sexual harassment is widespread. In response to a survey of human resource officials in county and city governments in a large Midwestern state, 56 percent agreed with the statement that, "Individuals today are too sensitive about their work environment," and 47 percent agreed that, "Most claims of sexual harassment are really personal disagreements between two individuals without work-related ramifications" (Eberhardt, Moser, and McFadden 1999). These attitudes are not likely to result in an atmosphere receptive to women's complaints.

The growing body of literature, briefly discussed here, demonstrates an increasing concern about sexual harassment and its impact on its victims. However, as this review has suggested, that research has yet to coalesce into a stream of universally accepted principles that can guide further inquiry, let alone suggest the best means for ensuring harassment-free work environments. There is no indisputable definition of sexual harassment, which makes tracking it and enforcing policies against it difficult. Moreover, men and women often have very different perceptions of harassment, leading women to fear that if they do report it, they will not be taken seriously.

Women face many other constraints in responding to sexual harassment, including a natural reluctance to view themselves as victims and a fear that they will be marginalized or even retaliated against. Whether or not they do respond, it is likely that they will suffer psychological and/or physical maladies that will lower their job satisfaction and performance and possibly derail their careers in the long run. Hence sexual harassment can be as powerful a barrier to the inclusion and advancement of women as a glass ceiling or other forms of overt or oblique discrimination. As with other aspects of discrimination, the federal government, as the enforcer of laws with respect to sexual harassment, has an even greater responsibility to ensure its agencies are harassment-free.

Sexual Harassment in the Federal Government

Concern about sexual harassment in the federal government dates back to at least 1979, when Chairman James M. Hanley of the U.S. House of

Representatives Subcommittee on Investigations of the Committee on Post Office and Civil Service undertook an investigation of sexual harassment by examining 100 complaints. This was followed by a request that the MSPB carry out an extensive study of sexual harassment in the federal government (U.S. Merit Systems Protection Board 1981).

Shortly thereafter, the newly created Office of Personnel Management (OPM) issued a memorandum to all federal departments and agencies stating that sexual harassment was a "form of employee misconduct which undermines the integrity of the employment relationship" and "a prohibited personnel practice when it results in discrimination for or against an employee on the basis of conduct not related to performance" (U.S. Office of Personnel Management 1979, 2). The OPM further recommended that department and agency heads issue "very strong" management statements defining the policy of the federal government with regard to sexual harassment (U.S. Office of Personnel Management 1979).

The following March, the EEOC issued Management Directive 704 instructing agencies to submit plans for the prevention of sexual harassment as supplements to their Affirmative Action Plans. The plans were to identify steps taken by agencies to inform employees that sexual harassment is a form of sex discrimination and enumerate proposed methods to ensure accountability for a workplace free of discrimination (U.S. Equal Employment Opportunity Commission 1980).

In May 1980, MSPB administered a survey to a random sample of over 23,000 men and women in the government. Of the nearly 20,000 who responded, 42 percent of women and 15 percent of men reported that they had received uninvited and unwanted sexual attention in the previous two-year period (U.S. Merit Systems Protection Board 1981). The survey also listed eight behaviors and asked respondents if they would consider each to be sexual harassment if performed by a supervisor or if performed by a coworker. As would be expected, there was more agreement by both men and women that more serious behaviors constituted sexual harassment. Eighty-four percent of men and 91 percent of women indicated that pressure for sexual favors by a supervisor "probably" or "definitely" was sexual harassment. In contrast, only 42 percent of men and 54 percent of women agreed that sexual teasing, jokes, and remarks by a coworker constituted sexual harassment.

The results of that survey, published in March 1981, continue to be referred to as a landmark study and to be cited in many scholarly publications on sexual harassment. The MSPB decided to update its study in 1987, and this time administered a survey to about 13,000 federal employees, selected at random. As will be shown shortly, by that time a greater percentage of male and female federal employees defined the listed behaviors as harassment than had done so in the 1980 survey. The proportion of the 8,500 respondents who indicated they had been subject to unwanted sexual attention in the previous two years remained the same as in 1980 (U.S. Merit Systems Protection Board 1988).

In 1994 MSPB again surveyed a random sample of 13,200 employees across government agencies. Again, respondents were asked if they considered specific behaviors to be harassment, and the proportion identifying most behaviors as such increased from 1987. The proportion of employees who reported being harassed also increased slightly from 1987. Of the more than 8,000 employees who responded, 44 percent of women and 19 percent of men indicated they had received such unwanted attention in the previous two years (U.S. Merit Systems Protection Board 1995).

In this chapter, data from the 1987 and 1994 MSPB surveys are used to examine changes in definitions and incidence of sexual harassment over time. The 1994 survey data are used to examine women's responses to harassment and its consequences.

Federal Employees' Definitions of Sexual Harassment

Previous researchers have attempted to develop categories of sexual harassment to facilitate analysis and provide a means for ranking behaviors by severity (Till 1980; Gruber 1992; Reese and Lindenberg 1999). Such categorizations help to reduce a wide number of behaviors to a manageable size and account for the varying severity among those behaviors. Most of these categorizations have been conceptual rather than empirical, however. Reese and Lindenberg (1999) used factor analysis to develop a categorization based on empirical relationships among the behaviors and found that women tended to group together behaviors based on their severity. For example, one factor (which they called Level 1) included comments on personal appearance and touching, while another factor (Level 3) included unwelcome pressure for dates and pressure for sex. It is clear that there are differences in the ways men and women define sexual harassment, but few studies have examined the extent to which the underlying constructs of men's and women's views of sexual harassment are similar or different. We address that deficiency here with a factor analysis of responses to the 1994 MSPB survey.

Each of the MSPB surveys asked respondents to indicate whether eight specific behaviors would constitute sexual harassment if done by a supervisor or done by a coworker. The items were structured as they are in Table 7.1; that is, the behavior is presented and respondents are asked, if a supervisor did it, would it be harassment, and then if a coworker did it, would it be considered harassment? Respondents were asked to indicate the extent to which each represented sexual harassment with a five-point scale: definitely yes, probably yes, don't know, probably not, definitely not. Separate

TABLE 7.1   Results of Factor Analysis: Men's and Women's Views of Sexual Harassment (Factor Loading)

Women		Men	
Factor 1		**Factor 1**	
Sexual teasing, remarks, questions		Sexual teasing, remarks, questions	
By supervisor	.77	By supervisor	.81
By coworker	.76	By coworker	.82
Sexually suggestive looks or gestures		Sexually suggestive looks or gestures	
By supervisor	.73	By supervisor	.69
By coworker	.75	By coworker	.72
Letters, phone calls, materials of sexual nature		Pressure for dates	
From supervisor	.56	By supervisor	.56
From coworker	.57	By coworker	.62
Factor 2		**Factor 2**	
Pressure for dates		Deliberate touching, leaning, cornering	
By supervisor	.76	By supervisor	.77
By coworker	.83	By coworker	.74
Factor 3			
Pressure for sexual favors		Pressure for sexual favors	
By supervisor	.75	By supervisor	.72
By coworker	.74	By coworker	.69
Deliberate touching, leaning, cornering		Letters, phone calls, materials of sexual nature	
By supervisor	.69	From supervisor	.67
By coworker	.66	From coworker	.63
N	3,426		4,364

NOTE: In each case, the behavior was described as "uninvited." See Appendix 4 for complete question wording.
SOURCE: U.S. Merit Systems Protection Board, *Sexual Harassment Survey*, 1994.

exploratory factor analyses were employed to identify the underlying constructs represented by these sixteen behaviors, for men and for women. The results are presented in Table 7.1.

It is interesting to note that for both men and women the same behaviors by a supervisor or by a coworker load on the same factors. This suggests that when presented with the question in this fashion, it is the behavior that drives people to label it as harassment or not, rather than who is doing it. The results suggest that women tend to view teasing and remarks, suggestive looks, and phone calls and letters similarly. That factor, which accounts for 49 percent of the variance in women's definitions of sexual harassment, can be seen as the most commonly encountered and least-threatening behaviors. The second factor, representing 8 percent of the variance, is more serious. It consists of only two items: pressure for dates by a supervisor and pressure for dates by a coworker. It seems logical that women would view this behavior more seriously than those listed under factor one because it is difficult to simply ignore a direct invitation. The third factor, representing 9 percent of the variance, is more serious still. It includes pressure for sexual favors and deliberate touching by supervisors and coworkers.

For men, the sixteen behaviors loaded on just two factors. The first represents 56 percent of the variance in defining sexual harassment and includes uninvited teasing, suggestive looks, and pressure for dates. The second, representing just 7 percent of the variance, includes uninvited deliberate touching, pressure for sexual favors, and uninvited letters or phone calls. One possible interpretation of men's and women's respective categorizations is that women view the behaviors in terms of which are more threatening, whereas men view them in terms of which are more damning. To women, letters and phone calls are no more threatening than teasing or suggestive looks. But to men, letters, phone calls, or other materials of a sexual nature can provide a record of the incident for which they may be called to account if it is reported. Men see pressure for dates in the same light as teasing or suggestive looks. Women see pressure for dates as more threatening than teasing, suggestive looks, or letters and phone calls, but not as threatening as pressure for sexual favors or deliberate touching.

This analysis sorted behaviors into empirical and logical categories representing increasing levels of seriousness. The three levels identified by women serve as a shorthand means for referring to mild (level one), moderate (level two), and severe (level three) sexual harassment for the remainder of this chapter.[2]

The next task is to determine the extent to which male and female federal employees similarly define sexual harassment, and whether the level of agreement has improved given the recent emphasis on sexual harassment training. Table 7.2 presents the percentages of men and women who indicated on the 1987 and 1994 surveys that these behaviors *definitely* were sexual harassment. Consistent with previous research, in all cases more women than men perceived each behavior to be sexual harassment. In some cases the difference in proportions of men and women who had no doubt that these behaviors constituted sexual harassment was more than twenty percentage points. Table 7.2 also shows how responses have changed since 1987. In each case,

TABLE 7.2   Men's and Women's Definitions of Behaviors as *Definitely* Sexual Harassment (Percent)

	1994		1987	
	Men	Women	Men	Women
Level 1				
Sexual teasing, remarks, questions				
By supervisor	38.4	54.7	25.9	39.3
By coworker	29.7	46.5	18.7	31.2
Sexually suggestive looks or gestures				
By supervisor	41.1	64.1	32.3	48.9
By coworker	33.3	58.1	24.6	41.8
Letters, phone calls, materials of sexual nature				
From supervisor	58.6	76.1	45.1	62.0
From coworker	46.9	67.8	32.9	51.7
Level 2				
Pressure for dates				
By supervisor	60.7	74.8	54.6	65.1
By coworker	45.1	62.6	37.4	49.0
Level 3				
Pressure for sexual favors				
By supervisor	84.6	94.7	82.1	92.9
By coworker	74.9	91.8	69.1	86.5
Deliberate touching, leaning, cornering				
By supervisor	70.3	87.0	63.1	80.2
By coworker	61.5	82.9	51.9	72.9
Average number of behaviors that definitely are sexual harassment	6.6	8.7	5.4	7.1
Percent indicating none of the behaviors was definitely sexual harassment	12.0	3.5	14.5	5.1
Percent indicating that *all* of the behaviors were definitely sexual harassment	20.3	36.0	10.3	19.2
N	3464– 3530	4164– 4233	3903– 3934	4335– 4369

NOTE: All differences between men and women and between years are significant at p>.001 level, except pressure for sexual favors from supervisor, where differences between years are significant at p<.05. Percentages reflect unweighted data because weighting methodologies differed between the two surveys.
NOTE: See Appendix 4 for item wording.
SOURCE: U.S. Merit Systems Protection Board, *Sexual Harassment Surveys*, 1987 and 1994.

the percentage of men and women who believe each behavior to constitute sexual harassment increased significantly over the six-year period.

When MSPB (1995, 7) reported differences between men's and women's definitions of harassment on each of the surveys, it grouped together those who responded "probably yes" and "definitely yes." The percentage of women who responded in that way increased between 1987 and 1994 by anywhere from zero points (for pressure for sexual favors by a supervisor) to thirteen points (for sexual teasing and jokes by a coworker). Similarly, the increase over that nine-year period in the percentage of men who responded that these behaviors were probably or definitely sexual ranged from 2 percent (for pressure for sexual favors by a supervisor) to 15 percent (for sexual teasing and jokes by a coworker). It is interesting to note, then, that the increase in the proportion of men and women who believe that these behaviors are *definitely* sexual harassment is even greater. Although increased awareness of the problems caused by sexual harassment in the workplace has led to an increase in the proportion of men and women who believe specific behaviors constitute sexual harassment, the divide between them has not narrowed.

Counting the total number of behaviors men and women define as definitely harassment is another indicator of the differences between the two genders. For men, the average number of behaviors in 1994 was 6.6; an average of 1.2 behaviors more than in 1987. For women, the average number of behaviors defined as definitely sexual harassment in 1994 was 8.7, up from 7.1 in 1987.

Thus, findings from the 1994 MSPB sexual harassment survey confirm what one would expect based on previous research. Men and women think about sexual harassment in different ways, and women label more behaviors as harassment than do men. In the arena of sexual harassment, then, there is again a significant divide between how men and women view the dynamics of their work environments. This makes it more likely that women will experience sexual harassment and its consequences and more difficult to develop a means for preventing it. Some might find it hopeful that the proportion of men and women that consider each behavior to definitely constitute harassment has increased dramatically since 1987, as this may imply greater awareness of unacceptable behavior. However it is also important to note that the divide between women and men has actually increased. The difference in the proportion of men and women labeling all the listed behaviors as definitely sexual harassment in 1994 was 12.7 percentage points, up from 8.9 points in 1987.

Incidence of Sexual Harassment in the Government

Overall, 44 and 42 percent of women respondents to the 1994 and 1987 surveys, respectively, indicated that they had experienced at least one form of unwanted sexual attention in the previous two years. Table 7.3 provides the percentage of each form of harassment experienced by women once, or more than once, as reported on the two surveys. The most frequent behaviors encountered continue to be unwanted sexually suggestive looks or gestures and sexual teasing and remarks. More than one-third of women experienced sexual teasing or remarks in both time periods; more than one-quarter encountered such behavior more than once. More than one-quarter of women were confronted with sexually suggestive looks or gestures at least once, and about one-quarter experienced deliberate touching, leaning, and cornering at least once in the time periods addressed by the surveys.

As noted previously, the reasons for the stability in the proportion of women who report sexual harassment aren't clear. One interpretation is that federal employees are now more aware of behaviors that constitute sexual harassment and so are reporting unwanted sexual attention that they would have assumed did not meet the definition of sexual harassment some years ago. Certainly both men and women are defining more behaviors as sexual harassment than they did in 1987. Moreover, nearly 80 percent of survey respondents reported attending sexual harassment awareness training, nearly 90 percent of those in the previous two years. It is likely that awareness has increased.

Another interpretation of the durability of the proportions of women reporting harassment is that the increased focus on defining and educating employees about it has failed to reduce its occurrence. One test of this proposition is to examine the behaviors that nearly all women defined as "probably" or "definitely" sexual harassment even in 1987. These are the behaviors that constitute level three harassment: pressure for sexual favors and deliberate touching and cornering. If women were just as likely to report experiencing these behaviors in 1994 as they were in 1987, it suggests that the education effort has not achieved its goal of reducing the incidence of these forms of harassment. If there has not been a decline in the incidence of these behaviors, it is not because more women believe that these behaviors constitute sexual harassment. Rather, the occurrence of these behaviors has persisted despite the heightened attention to sexual harassment.

As shown in Table 7.3, the proportion of women reporting that they had been pressured for sexual favors did not change significantly between 1987 and 1994. The proportion of women indicating that they had experienced deliberate touching, leaning, or cornering *one time* increased slightly. But the proportion of women indicating they had experienced these behaviors *more than once* dropped. This suggests that over the eight-year period women may have become more assertive after encountering these behaviors once, reducing the likelihood that the conduct would be repeated. Another possible explanation is that men have become more willing to back off after one confrontation. That same pattern is evident for sexually suggestive looks or gestures and pressure for dates.

TABLE 7.3 Incidence of Sexual Harassment of Women (Percent)

Behavior	1994		1987	
	Once	More Than Once	Once	More Than Once
Level 1				
Sexual teasing, remarks, questions***	11.1	27.2	7.8	26.7
Sexually suggestive looks or gestures***	9.0	20.2	6.8	20.2
Letters, phone calls, materials of sexual nature	4.9	5.0	5.2	4.5
Level 2				
Pressure for dates*	6.2	5.9	5.6	7.3
Level 3				
Pressure for sexual favors	3.8	3.6	4.0	3.7
Deliberate touching, leaning, cornering**	10.4	12.4	9.5	14.8
Actual or attempted rape***	2.7	2.1	.7	.1
Stalking	3.5	3.3	Not asked	
N	4,021–4,186		4,257–4,299	

* p<.05, ** p< .01, *** p<.001
NOTE: Percentages reflect unweighted responses.
See Appendix 4 for item wording.
SOURCE: U.S. Merit Systems Protection Board, *Sexual Harassment Surveys*, 1987 and 1994.

Another indicator of whether the climate for women has improved since 1987 is the proportion indicating they had experienced actual or attempted rape. This behavior was not included on the list of behaviors that respondents were asked to define as sexual harassment or not. However, clearly few men or women would disagree that this behavior is very serious and cannot be tolerated. Although the percentage of women experiencing this behavior remains very small, it has nevertheless increased significantly, from 0.8 percent in 1987 to 4.8 percent in 1994.

In summary, the most common forms of harassment are those that constitute level one: teasing, remarks, or gestures. A smaller, but still significant, number of women report experiences with a behavior they consider to be more serious: deliberate touching, leaning, or cornering. The percentage of women experiencing each behavior remained fairly stable between

1987 and 1994, with some notable increases. The most positive finding is that women are less likely to encounter some behaviors more than once than they were in 1987.

Responding to Sexual Harassment in the Government

Women who experience sexual harassment must decide how to respond to it. This can be a difficult choice because reporting the behavior and not reporting it can have equally adverse consequences. The 1994 MSPB survey asked respondents who had experienced sexual harassment to consider the *one* experience that either was the most recent or had the greatest effect on them. Respondents were asked questions about that specific event, including how they responded.

Louise Fitzgerald, Suzanne Swan, and Karla Fischer (1995) suggest that the responses of victims of sexual harassment can be categorized as either internally focused or externally focused. Internal responses are those that try to manage the cognitions and emotions by ignoring the behaviors, doing nothing, or just enduring the situation. Externally focused responses involve more active problem solving, including asking the perpetrator to stop or notifying a supervisor.

In Table 7.4, a similar categorization is employed. It presents the percentage of sexually harassed women who took each of eight actions in response to the specific incident they had been asked to consider.[3] The specific incidents are grouped according to level of severity.[4] As would be expected, those who experienced the more serious level three form of harassment were more likely to take three of the external actions—asking the person to stop, threatening to tell or telling others, and reporting the behavior to a supervisor or other official—than those who experienced the more milder forms. Those who experienced more serious harassment were also more likely to try to avoid the person than those who experienced milder forms. Those who experienced the milder forms of harassment were slightly more likely to simply ignore the behavior than the other two levels, but the difference is not significant.

Of course, other factors are likely to contribute to the way a victim chooses to respond besides the severity of the harassment. These include how often the harassment occurs and organizational norms (Fitzgerald, Swan, and Fischer 1995; Reese and Lindenberg 1999). According to Fitzgerald, Swan, and Fischer (1995), less is known about the relationship between the status of the harasser and response. For example, some studies have found that victims are more likely to report a supervisor than a coworker, while others suggest they are less likely to do so.

Neither is much known about individual characteristics that might affect the likelihood for a woman to choose any particular response (Fitzgerald,

TABLE 7.4 Women's Responses to Unwanted Sexual Attention (Percent)

	Level 1 (Least Serious)	Level 2	Level 3 (Most Serious)
Internal Responses			
Ignored the behavior	58.2	47.5	52.1
Avoided the person	30.5**	45.9	46.7
Made a joke of the behavior	17.0	26.2	16.6
Went along with the behavior	8.4	6.6	7.6
External Responses			
Asked the person to stop	35.5**	62.3	60.2
Threatened to or did tell others	8.4**	13.1	21.4
Reported behavior to a supervisor or other official	13.1**	4.9	19.6
Changed jobs	2.7*	0	5.0
Took a formal action	5.1*	1.7	8.6
N	488	61	674

* p<.05,   ** p<.001
NOTE: Respondents were asked to mark "all that apply."
See Appendix 4 for item wording.
SOURCE: U.S. Merit Systems Protection Board, *Sexual Harassment Survey*, 1994.

Swan, and Fischer 1995). Karen Lindenberg and Laura Reese (1995) hypothesized that awareness of the organization's sexual harassment policy would influence the decision as to whether to report the harassment, although they found no such relationship. Janet Swim and Lauri Hyers (1999) found women were more likely to respond to sexist remarks if they were the only women in the organization rather than when they were in the majority. Carol Ford and Francisco Donis (1996) found that women under forty years old have less tolerance of harassment, which presumably would mean that they would be more likely to respond with an active (external) response than merely a passive (internal) one.

Table 7.5 presents the results of a multivariate analysis designed to identify factors that contribute to the likelihood that a woman will respond to harassment with an external response rather than just an internal one. Because the dependent variable is dichotomous (external response or not), logistic regression is used. As expected, those who experienced the more serious forms of harassment—level two and level three—were more likely than

TABLE 7.5   Factors Contributing to Likelihood Women Responded Externally to Harassment (Logistic Regression Coefficients)

Variable	B	S.E.	Sig	Odds Ratio
Experienced level 2 harassment	1.309	.338	.000	3.701
Experienced level 3 harassment	1.152	.136	.000	3.166
Harasser was supervisor	−.170	.152	.262	.843
Frequency of harassment	.192	.081	.017	1.212
Duration of harassment				
Harassment lasted less than 1 week	.438	.210	.037	1.550
Harassment lasted 1–4 weeks	1.015	.263	.000	2.759
Harassment lasted 1–3 months	.506	.222	.023	1.658
Harassment lasted 4 to 6 months	.096	.233	.681	1.101
Number of behaviors considered to be harassment	.018	.020	.370	1.018
Aware of formal complaint channels	.320	.151	.034	1.377
Proportion of women (versus men) worked with on a normal day	−.201	.070	.004	.818
Young (under 45 years)	.332	.146	.023	1.393
Educational attainment	−.108	.049	.026	.898
Constant	−.925	.538	.086	

Chi sq. = 144.9, p<.001, N = 1474
NOTE: For item coding, see Appendix 4.
SOURCE: U.S. Merit Systems Protection Board, *Sexual Harassment Survey*, 1994.

those who experienced the milder form (level one) to respond externally, even controlling for all else. In fact, women experiencing level three harassment are more than three times as likely to respond externally as women who experience level one harassment. Whether the harasser was in the respondents' supervisory chain rather than a coworker or other employee does not appear to influence the form of response, controlling for all else.

Not surprisingly, the number of times the harassment occurred is positively related to the likelihood that victims would respond externally. The survey also asked respondents how long the unwanted sexual attention went on. Because this variable has a bimodal distribution with respect to the dependent variable, dummy variables were created to represent each of the time options given respondents. The longest time frame (more than six months) was omitted as the reference category. Those who experienced the behavior for three months or less were more likely to take external action than those who experienced it for more than four months. It seems, then, that when the behavior persists for that many months, women conclude that even external action will not be enough to stop it.

To examine whether the breadth with which one defines sexual harassment has an effect on the response, the variable representing the number of behaviors that respondents classified as "definitely" harassment was included. That variable, however, turned out not to be related to the type of response, controlling for all else. As would be expected, those who were aware of the procedures in their organization for filing a formal complaint were more likely to actively respond than those who weren't.

Consistent with Swim and Hyers (1999), the composition of the organization makes a difference. The greater the number of men the victim interacts with during a normal work day, the more likely it is that she will respond externally to the harassment. Perhaps under these circumstances, women believe that they must respond actively for the behavior to cease. Also as hypothesized, younger women (under forty-five) are more likely to respond externally than women over forty-five. Less-educated women are more likely to respond than more-educated ones, although the effect is small. It is not clear why this would be the case.

In summary, many women respond to sexual harassment only internally; that is, they ignore the behavior or attempt to avoid the harasser. Table 7.4 suggests that if that doesn't resolve the issue for them, many then go on to respond externally, particularly if the harassment takes one of the more severe (level two or level three) forms. In many cases victims choose not to respond because they assume nothing will be done or because they fear retaliation (Fitzgerald, Swan, and Fischer 1995). The MSPB survey only asked respondents why they did not choose to take *formal* action in response to the harassment. Common responses included that they didn't think anything would be done (21.3 percent) or thought it would make the work environment unpleasant (30.5 percent).

Fitzgerald, Swan, and Fischer (1995) warn that it should not be asserted *a priori* whether an internal or external response is appropriate or effective. Rather, the outcomes associated with different responses should be evaluated empirically. That is, in part, the next task undertaken in this chapter.

The Consequences of Sexual Harassment

Many researchers have been concerned with the extent to which sexual harassment has an adverse impact on women. Richard Arvey and Marcie Cavanaugh (1995) point out, quite correctly, the problems inherent in asking respondents simultaneously to report the existence of sexual harassment and its impact on them. When asked about both in the same survey, respondents are likely to judge that any performance decrements were a direct result of the harassment, without taking into account other factors that can affect performance. Arvey and Cavanaugh (1995) suggest that impact (poor performance evaluations, productivity losses) really should be measured independently of self-reported instances of harassment.

Of course, it can be very expensive to gather such independent measures along with survey data, and it was for this reason that MSPB relied on self-reports of both experience with harassment and its impact. Another weakness in MSPB's reliance on survey data is that only current employees are surveyed, and so those who were fired or left government employment because of the harassment would not be among the respondents. The survey data may, then, either underreport or overreport the actual impact of sexual harassment in the aggregate.

Still, the survey data do provide some evidence of women's perceptions of the consequences they face as a result of the harassment, and their perceptions are as important as any "objective" assessment as to what took place. It seems unlikely that the perceived consequences were significantly overreported in this case because only a relatively small proportion of women reported adverse effects. Only about 10 percent of respondents indicated that they had faced retaliation (e.g., denial of promotion or pay increase, reassignment, deterioration in working conditions). About 10 percent reported that they had used sick leave as a result of the harassment, and about 8 percent reported using annual leave. Slightly more (22 percent) reported a reduction in productivity. Altogether, one-quarter of women who had been harassed indicated that they had been harmed in some way as a result of the experience.

One important question is whether there is a relationship between women's response to the harassment (external or internal) and her likelihood to report adverse consequences as a result of the harassment. It is also important to determine if the position of the harasser (supervisor or coworker) has an impact on whether women are ultimately harmed by the behavior. In Table 7.6 these and other relevant variables are included in a logistic regression model designed to identify factors that contribute to the likelihood that women will report injury as a result of the harassment.

In this model, level one and level three harassment are included, with level two left out as the reference category. Both level one and level three harassment have a substantial impact on the likelihood that a woman will report an adverse impact as a result of the harassment. Those who experience level three harassment are nearly eight times as likely to believe they have been harmed by the experience as those who experienced level two harassment. Those who experienced level one harassment are nearly four times as likely as those experiencing level two harassment to believe they were harmed. This suggests that how women perceive the severity of sexual

TABLE 7.6 Factors Affecting Women's Likelihood of Experiencing Harmful Effects as Result of Harassment (Logistic Regression Coefficients)

Variable	B	S.E.	Sig	Odds Ratio
Level 1 harassment	1.415	.363	.000	4.116
Level 3 harassment	2.036	.357	.000	7.661
Harasser was supervisor	1.323	.151	.000	3.755
Responded externally	.554	.154	.000	1.740
Proportion of women (versus men) worked with on a normal day	–.186	.076	.014	.831
Married	–.340	.143	.017	.712
Educational attainment	.148	.053	.006	1.159
Young (under 45 years)	.413	.168	.014	1.511
Constant	–3.747	.486	.000	

Chi Sq. = 249.82, p<.001, n = 1768
Percent of cases in modal category = 76.4%
Percent predicted correctly = 78.4%
Proportional reduction in error = 8.1%
NOTE: See Appendix 4 for item wording.
SOURCE: U.S. Merit Systems Protection Board, *Sexual Harassment Survey*, 1994.

harassment may not correspond to the perceived consequences of the behavior. It supports Reese and Lindenberg's (1999) point that categorizing behavior on the basis of how women *experience* it is not the same as basing such a typology on their *definitions* of sexual harassment. Further research should explore this relationship.

Women who were harassed by someone in their supervisory chain of command were nearly four times as likely to report that they had suffered some adverse consequences than those who were harassed by a coworker. Recall that whether the harasser was a supervisor or a coworker did not affect women's definitions of harassment (see Table 7.1) nor their response to it (see Table 7.5). That the position of the harasser has such an important effect on her likelihood to be harmed is another indication of the complex relationship between how one views harassment and how one is affected by it.

There is a positive relationship between externally responding to the harassment and facing consequences as a result of the harassment. Three times as many women who responded externally as did not do so reported retaliation. Although both response choice and impact are related to the severity of the harassment, Table 7.6 shows that the effect for response type persists even when the level of severity is controlled. Further research will be required to explore the possible cause-and-effect relationship between response and impact.

Women who work with more men than women are more likely to report suffering adverse effects, as are unmarried women and young women. In contrast with the inverse effect of educational attainment on whether women respond externally or not, there is a positive relationship between education and the perception of adverse consequences.

In summary, only a minority of the women who were harassed reported harmful consequences, at least in terms of the response options presented by the MSPB survey. Previous research has suggested that harassment can also adversely affect job satisfaction and teamwork (Murrell, Olson, and Frieze 1995) and other important work-related attitudes (Kelly and Stambaugh 1992) and cause depression, self-blame, and disillusionment (Koss 1990). These issues were not addressed by the MSPB survey. However, the analysis of this survey does suggest some factors that might contribute to a perception of harmful consequences that organizations should pay attention to. These include how women choose to respond to the harassment, whether the harasser is a supervisor rather than a coworker, and the proportion of male and female employees that the victim interacts with on a day-to-day basis.

Conclusion

During the last two decades of the twentieth century the law evolved to where sexual harassment is now recognized as a form of unlawful sex discrimination. Moreover, the law recognizes that harassment need not take the form of an explicit demand for sexual favors as a condition of employment, but can also result from a hostile work environment. Congress has added teeth to anti-harassment policies by allowing victims to collect compensatory and punitive damages. In its two most recent decisions, the Supreme Court reaffirmed employers' responsibilities in preventing harassment and taking corrective measures where it occurs.

Although still evolving as a legal matter, sexual harassment is an important management issue for any employer. It is a particularly thorny concern because sexual harassment lacks a single, universally accepted definition. Moreover, male and female coworkers do not necessarily identify the same behaviors as harassment. In the federal government, there is a growing acknowledgment by men and women that certain behaviors like sexual teasing, remarks, or gestures constitute sexual harassment. However, women continue to be far more likely than men to include such behaviors in their definitions of sexual harassment. Moreover, the factor analysis employed in this chapter suggests that women and men think about sexual harassment in very different ways.

Even in the aftermath of highly publicized incidents of sexual harassment, the proportion of federal employees reporting that they experienced sexual harassment did not decline. This may be partly a function of increased awareness of what constitutes sexual harassment. However, reports of even some of the behaviors that the majority of federal employees have always considered to be sexual harassment, such as pressure for sexual favors, did not drop.

Perhaps the most difficult decision that a harassed woman must make is how to respond. Should she respond internally, just ignoring the behavior or avoiding the harasser? Or should she respond externally by telling the harasser to stop, notifying a supervisor, or filing a formal complaint? The analysis presented in this chapter confirmed that this decision is affected by the severity of the harassment, how frequently it occurred, how long the behavior has gone on, and whether the victim is aware of the agency grievance procedures. Less than two-thirds of women who experienced the most serious harassment went as far as asking the person to stop. Even fewer reported the behavior to someone else, and fewer than one in ten took formal action. This suggests that merely having a grievance procedure in place is not sufficient to significantly reduce the incidence of sexual harassment. Many women evidently wish to avoid the confrontation.

Women's decisions as to how to respond are likely to be affected also by their perceptions of the consequences of doing so or not doing so. Very few women reported retaliation against them, but those who responded externally were much more likely than those who didn't to report reprisal.

In short, sexual harassment can be seen as a barrier to the full participation and advancement of women in the federal civil service. It is an example of the differences in the way men and women view the dynamics of the workplace. More important, intentionally or not, sexual harassment undermines women's status in their organization by highlighting their gender and demeaning their status and authority. Legally prescribed solutions such as anti-harassment policies and grievance procedures are important, but insufficient, to address harassment (Riger 1991). As Reese and Lindenberg (1997, 39) note: "Thus, legal definitions provide a framework of employer liability but are not the critical variable with respect to policy impact. Rather, characteristics, attitudes, perceptions, and experiences of individuals determine the nature of interpersonal relations in the workplace and how a policy is actually implemented."

Federal managers seeking to measure the nature and extent of sexual harassment in their organizations need to broaden their perspective to include attitudes, perceptions, and experiences that don't appear to be directly related to sexual harassment. That is, they need to determine if, for example, perceptions of discrimination are contributing to a feeling of powerlessness among women, as suggested in Chapter 6. They need to examine whether stereotypes about women's abilities and commitment to their jobs is undermining their authority, as suggested in Chapter 4. These managers must bear in mind that when a woman reports, or even acquiesces in sexual harassment rather than confronting the perpetrator, a stereotype of women using their sexuality to advance rather than their talent and experience may be confirmed (Gutek 1989).

Anti–sexual harassment policies are important. Also essential is training designed to bridge the divide between men and women's understanding of the nature of sexual harassment and to teach supervisors and those at other reporting points to handle allegations of harassment with care (Reese and Lindenberg 1999; Thacker and Gohman 1993; Moynahan 1993; Gutek 1989). Given the relationship between unequal power relationships and sexual harassment, organizational restructuring to bring those relationships into greater alignment may be the ultimate solution. It is clear that the government will not become fully representative and inclusive until there has been much greater success in reducing the instance of sexual harassment within the civil service.

Notes

1. These decisions apply to harassment by supervisors based on race, color, religion, national origin, age, or disability in addition to sex (of a sexual nature or not) (U.S. Equal Employment Opportunity Commission 1999b).

2. Note that Reese and Lindenberg (1999) used these same terms (levels one through three) to identify the categories of behavior that emerged from their factor analysis of women's responses. However, the behaviors corresponding to each factor in their analysis are not always the same as those identified in Table 7.1, probably because the survey instrument and population surveyed were different.

3. Another option included on the survey, "I transferred, disciplined, or gave a poor performance rating to the person(s)" was excluded because only three people checked this response.

4. The survey noted that a particular sexual harassment experience could include more than one type of unwanted sexual attention, and asked them to mark all that applied. Respondents were grouped into level one, two, or three based on the most serious of the behaviors they reported. Similarly, respondents were asked to mark all the ways in which they responded to the harassment.

8

Strategies for
Fostering Inclusion

NASA will set the Equal Opportunity Standard for Excellence through a highly
skilled workforce which is representative, at all levels, of America's diversity
and built upon trust, respect, teamwork, communication, empowerment, and
commitment in an environment which is free of discrimination.

NASA's Equal Opportunity and Diversity Management Vision, May 1994

In explaining why she suggested the Merit Systems Protection Board spon-
sor a symposium on diversity in the fall of 1993, then-Member of the
Board Jessica Parks related that she was inspired by the Federal Aviation
Administration's (FAA) diversity program in the Great Lakes Region. "I
was so impressed that I thought FAA's story should be widely shared with
other agencies," she remarked (U.S. Merit Systems Protection Board
1993b, 26). A year later the FAA was forced to reach a settlement with the
union representing air traffic controllers, who claimed they were trauma-
tized by the cultural diversity training they were required to attend (Larson
1994a). According to *The Washington Times,* men were required to pass
through lines of female coworkers who patted their crotches and made sexually suggestive remarks. One air traffic controller from the Great Lakes
Region filed a sexual harassment complaint seeking $300,000 in damages,
the maximum permitted by law. "It was a government-sponsored
Tailhook," his lawyer said. "The only differences were that the harassers
were female, and the action was encouraged, sponsored and paid for by
Uncle Sam" (Larson 1994b).

    This incident points to the difficulty of developing strategies to achieve a
truly representative bureaucracy, i.e., methods for eliminating barriers to

the inclusion of women and people of color in federal agencies. Training is often a fundamental part of such efforts, but the FAA experience suggests that it can backfire.

This book has analyzed some of the subtle obstacles that stand in the way of full inclusion of people of color and women. It has noted some specific ways in which inclusivity might be enhanced, as suggested by the findings that emerged from the data analyses. These include making sure that employees have accurate information about hiring and promotion rates and re-examining informal and formal criteria for advancement that may have an adverse impact on some groups.

The purpose of this chapter is to examine other strategies that have been considered to be successful means for fostering inclusion. It begins with a review of the extensive literature on this topic that developed during the 1990s. The chapter then reports on the approaches federal agencies are undertaking to better "manage diversity." One of the premises of this book is that it is important for agencies to monitor their progress in creating an inclusive environment for people of color and women. That assessment should include an analysis of the extent to which specific strategies designed to increase their inclusion are achieving their intended purpose. This chapter shows how such an assessment can be undertaken with existing data and concludes with recommendations for developing a more complete framework for assessment.

Managing Diversity: The Growth of an Industry

The publication of *Workforce 2000* in the late 1980s set off shock waves with its warnings that the workforce was becoming more diverse (Johnston and Packer 1987). Human resource managers scrambled to heed the call to reform work structures to better accommodate women and people of color. Not surprisingly, a vast literature accrued urging employers to develop strategies for managing diversity, warning them of dire consequences if they did not, assuring them of the benefits if they did, and recounting success stories of organizations that already had heeded such advice. This literature takes three forms:

1. Empirical descriptions of organizations that are considered to be models in workforce diversity. Examples are the Equal Employment Opportunity Commission's publication *Best Practices of Private Sector Employers* (1997b) and a publication by the Chicago Area Partnerships (Chicago Area Partnerships, 1996) entitled *Pathways and Progress: Corporate Best Practices to Shatter the Glass Ceiling.*

2. Summaries of "lessons learned" about managing diversity based on case studies or surveys of human resource professionals. Examples include two publications by Ann Morrison and the Center for Creative Leadership, entitled *Breaking the Glass Ceiling* (1987) and *The New Leaders* (1992). Another example is a publication issued by the Society of Human Resource Management/Commerce Clearing House (SHRM/CCH), describing the results of its 1993 survey of human resource management professionals.
3. Descriptions of consulting approaches to effectively manage diversity. Examples include books by well-known consultant R. Roosevelt Thomas (1991, 1996, 1999) along with many others (e.g., Wilson 1997; Norton and Fox 1997; Fernandez 1999).

Most of these (especially those that elucidate "success stories") focus on private sector companies. The second part of this chapter reports on what federal agencies are doing to create an inclusive environment for women and men of color. First, a brief summary of the development of this literature and what it prescribes for increasing inclusion is in order.

From Equal Employment Opportunity (EEO) to Diversity

There can be little doubt that in the 1990s, "diversity management" (or what Frederick Lynch [1997] cynically calls "the diversity machine") became a multi-million-dollar industry. Former Harvard Business Professor R. Roosevelt Thomas is often credited for creating the term *managing diversity*. The development of a new phrase was in part designed to distinguish between the approaches he recommended and "affirmative action." Thomas's 1990 article in the *Harvard Business Review* began with the prediction that "sooner or later, affirmative action will die a natural death. Its achievements have been stupendous, but if we look at the premises that underlie it, we find assumptions and priorities that look increasingly shopworn" (Thomas 1990, 107). Instead, he argued, "The goal is to manage diversity in such a way as to get from a diverse work force the same productivity we once got from a homogenous work force, and do it without artificial programs, standards—or barriers" (Thomas 1990, 112).

Many of those contributing to the literature on diversity in the 1990s followed Thomas's lead in charting a path distinct from EEO and affirmative action. A common theme of the literature today is that EEO and especially affirmative action have outlived their usefulness because they were only aimed at recruitment and do nothing to ensure advancement (Thomas 1990). Another reason for discarding (or at least de-emphasizing) these programs is that they are associated with the anathema called "quotas," or the explicit expectation that specific numbers of people of color and women will be hired or promoted. Affirmative action was also perceived as violating the deeply ingrained American precept that advancement should be based solely on merit. Worse, people who were hired under affirmative action programs were stigmatized as not deserving of their positions (Thomas 1991, 1996; Norton and Fox 1997; Morrison 1992; Cox 1994). Many organizations have gone to great lengths to make this distinction between equal employment opportunity/affirmative action (EEO/AA) and managing diversity explicit. Table 8.1, which is taken from the National Institutes of Health's (NIH) Diversity Initiative Home Page, is illustrative.

Thomas drew a distinction between his methods and traditional approaches to EEO and affirmative action in another way as well. He did so by defining *diversity* as focusing not just on race, ethnicity, gender, etc., but rather on *all* of the ways in which individuals may differ from one another, including age, background, education, and personality traits (Thomas 1990). Note that the NIH table emphasizes that managing diversity focuses on "all elements of diversity."

Some organizations and consultants continue to emphasize race and sex as the most important issues that organizations must address. Ann Morrison (1992, 9) warns, for example: "The most frightening aspect of moving too hurriedly from affirmative action for targeted groups to promoting the diversity in everyone is that this becomes an excuse for avoiding the continuing problems in achieving equity for people of color and white women." Shari Caudron and Cassandra Hayes (1997) agree that positioning diversity as a global issue has diluted its original focus on creating opportunities for women and people of color, suggesting that this approach may be management's effort to pander to white male fears. Charles Moskos and John Butler (1996) take that argument one step further. In their book suggesting how lessons learned from the successful integration of the military can be applied to promoting inclusion elsewhere, these authors advise that such efforts should *only* focus on African Americans, whose experience is unique and whose predicament is trivialized by the notion of multiculturalism.

But as Caudron and Hays (1997) acknowledge, most authors have adopted Thomas's notion of diversity as including a wide variety of differences (Norton and Fox 1997; Fernandez 1999; Wilson 1997). One reason for doing so is to avoid the image of "us versus them" that many believe has undermined the acceptance of traditional EEO and affirmative action programs. An example of casting the diversity net very widely is NASA's Equal Opportunity and Diversity Management Plan, in which cultural diversity is defined as "simply that NASA employees are diverse because they bring a variety of different backgrounds, customs, beliefs, religions, languages, knowledge, superstitions, values, social characteristics, etc. with them to the workplace. . . . [In addition to racial and ethnic cultural groups] there are also

TABLE 8.1   National Institutes of Health Definitions of EEO/Affirmative Action and Managing Diversity

EEO/AFFIRMATIVE ACTION	MANAGING DIVERSITY
Mandatory	Voluntary
Legal, social, moral justification	Productivity, efficiency, and quality
Focuses on race, gender, ethnicity	Focuses on all elements of diversity
Change the mix of people	Changes the systems/operations
Perception of preference	Perception of equality
Short-term and limited	Long-term and ongoing
Grounded in assimilation	Grounded in individuality

SOURCE: National Institutes of Health Diversity Home Page, http://www1.od.nih.gov/ohrm/eoe/wdi.

class cultures, age cultures, gender cultures, and regional cultures to name a few" (National Aeronautics and Space Administration 1994, 3). By defining diversity so broadly, organizations such as NASA hope that all employees will support the program, rather than feel excluded from or offended by it.

More recently, some authors have suggested that even managing diversity is no longer relevant and promote an even broader effort. R. Roosevelt Thomas, in his 1996 book, *Redefining Diversity,* suggests that "diversity" has become a "semantic umbrella" that includes a wide assortment of programs. He offers a new definition of diversity as "any mixture of items characterized by differences and similarities" (Thomas 1996, 5). John Fernandez (1999) also finds fault with the term *diversity.* He proposes the notion of "constituent capitalization," defined as a business strategy aimed at respecting the broad array of people's skills, perspectives, and styles and integrating them into a postbureaucratic organizational structure. J. Renae Norton and Ronald Fox (1997) insist that *managing diversity* is too narrow, with its focus on developing interpersonal skills, and risks fragmenting or polarizing the workplace. Instead, they promote "organizational plurality" that works to remove barriers to the maximum utilization of employee talents and integrates organizational change with diversity.

In summary, it is important to recognize that in the interest of regaining the declining support for improving the lot of women and people of color in organizations, the focus of many organizational policies has shifted in two fundamental ways. First, the emphasis of such policies has shifted from legally mandated EEO and affirmative action programs to voluntary efforts to manage diversity. Second, these policies have redefined diversity to include everyone. Even the concept of managing diversity is under fire, as experts search for more effective ways to create a more inclusive work environment.

The Rationale for Managing Diversity

In case the commonsense notion that organizations should accept that all employees are different from one another in some ways is not enough, this literature also goes to great lengths to state the "business case" for managing diversity. Note that the NIH chart (see Table 8.1) distinguishes the reasons for managing diversity from those in which EEO/AA were grounded. EEO/AA were justified on legal, social, and moral grounds. Managing diversity is justified based on presumably more palatable grounds; that is, that it increases productivity, efficiency, and quality.

Much of the literature uses similar utilitarian rationales to justify supporting diversity management programs. Authors remind us of the *Workforce 2000* admonition that the workforce is becoming increasingly diverse (at least in terms of gender, ethnicity, and age), and employers have no choice but to accept nontraditional workers. Moreover, employers who refuse to manage diversity are missing out on the untapped productivity of workers whose potential can be thwarted by a traditional work environment (Morrison 1992; Norton and Fox 1997; Cox 1994; Thomas 1996; Fernandez 1999; Chambers and Riccucci 1997; Wilson 1997; Mathews 1998; Wylie 1996; Gardenswartz and Rowe 1993).

Another common theme for profit-making concerns is that the global marketplace in which businesses have to compete is becoming more diverse, and only a diverse workforce can appropriately respond to it. Trevor Wilson (1997, 14–15) puts it this way: "As an organization begins to reflect the diversity of its marketplace, it is far more likely to be able to relate to its customers' needs. This will allow it to improve the value of goods and services offered to its customers, which will ultimately lead to more sales." (See also Morrison 1992; Norton and Fox 1997; Cox 1994; Fernandez 1999; Wylie 1996.) Moreover, Wilson (1997) admonishes, satisfied employees mean satisfied customers.

Thus, this literature provides employers with another reason to support diversity programs. Diversity management translates into a real return on investment for organizations that adopt it as a strategy. What, then, is required for an organization to be successful in its endeavor to manage diversity?

What Works?

What value would the extensive literature on managing diversity have if it did not provide insights into what organizations should do to effectively manage diversity? Among the more common prescriptions found in this literature are the following:

- *Commitment from top management.* Tacit support is not enough; the CEO or equivalent must personally intervene and be willing to support the effort with organizational resources and communicate that support throughout the organization (Morrison 1992; Norton and Fox 1997; Thomas and Gabarro 1999; Cox 1994; Chambers and Riccucci 1997; Clayton and Crosby 1992; Fernandez 1999; Wilson 1997; Dobbs 1996; Chicago Area Partnerships 1996; Thomas 1996).
- *Management accountability.* Management officials' performance ratings and compensation should depend in part on their success in achieving diversity-related goals (Morrison 1992; Cox 1994; Fernandez 1999; Wilson 1997; Chicago Area Partnerships 1996; Dobbs 1996).
- *Re-examination of the organization's structure, culture, and management systems.* As discussed in depth in previous chapters of this book, there are many ways an organization's formal or informal policies and procedures can (often unintentionally) work to the disadvantage of nontraditional groups. Selection, promotion, performance appraisal criteria, and career development programs must be examined for potential bias, and where necessary, be revamped (Norton and Fox 1997; Thomas 1996; Mathews 1998; Wilson 1997; Morrison 1992; Cox 1994; Fernandez 1999; Dugan et al. 1993; Chicago Area Partnerships 1996; Fine 1995).
- *Attention to the numbers.* The representation of groups in various levels and occupations in the organization should be closely monitored (Morrison 1992; Norton and Fox 1997; Cox 1994; Chicago Area Partnerships 1996; Thomas 1996). Imbalances in representation may signal that biased selection and promotion criteria or other employment actions are working to the disadvantage of nontraditional employees. Wilson (1997) and Ann Morrison (1992) also emphasize the importance of monitoring employees' perceptions of the organizational environment.
- *Targeted recruitment.* Employers should make special efforts to encourage nontraditional employees to apply for openings in entry level and/or management positions (Morrison 1992; Fernandez 1999; Thomas and Gabarro 1999; Chambers and Riccucci 1997; Wilson 1997; Dugan et al. 1993; Chicago Area Partnerships 1996; Fine 1995).
- *Training.* Employers should provide training so that employees understand the importance of diversity goals and develop the skills required to work effectively in a diverse workforce (Cox 1994; Thomas 1996; Fernandez 1999; Chambers and Riccucci 1997;

Wilson 1997; Hudson and Hines-Hudson 1996; Chicago Area Partnerships 1996; Mathews 1998; Gardenswartz and Rowe 1993).

* *Mentoring programs.* A mentor can serve an important role in communicating organizational expectations to employees who are interested in advancement. Employers should facilitate the development of mentoring arrangements so that nontraditional employees can benefit from the experience and wisdom of more seasoned employees (Morrison 1992; Fernandez 1999; Cox 1994; Payne 1998; Thomas and Gabarro 1999; Wilson 1997; Chicago Area Partnerships 1996; Dugan et al. 1993; Fine 1995).

* *Internal identity or advocacy groups.* Formally or informally constituted groups representing specific categories of nontraditional employees such as women, African Americans, or gays and lesbians can serve a useful purpose in mitigating the potential isolation of members of these groups and by providing leadership in resolving differences (Morrison 1992; Cox 1994; Thomas and Gabarro 1999; Dobbs 1996; Digh 1997). Norton and Fox (1997), however, advise against creating such groups, arguing that they draw too much attention to differences among groups. A variant of this approach is to establish "advisory" groups that include representatives from many distinct groups in the workforce (Wilson 1997; Chicago Area Partnerships 1996; Fine 1995).

* *Shared values among employees, customers, and stakeholders.* The values underlying many organizations' cultures and structures reflect the orientation of Euro-American men. Organizations need to recognize this and strive to create a more inclusive climate, linking diversity to their business strategy (Fernandez 1999; Thomas and Gabarro 1999; Wilson 1997; Chicago Area Partnerships 1996; Norton and Fox 1997).

Other recommendations made by experts or coming out of case studies that are less popular, but worth mentioning, are:

* Providing education to people of color to increase their competitiveness for high-level jobs (Payne 1998)
* Creating an environment that has zero tolerance for racism and sexism (Fernandez 1999, Fine 1995)
* Continually assessing the needs and concerns of employees rather than making assumptions about what they may want from the organization (Fine 1995)
* Having employees complete a self-assessment of their proficiency in skills necessary to work in a "multicultural" environment. Such

skills include respect for other cultures, awareness of stereotypes, and effective and compassionate communication (Fernandez 1999)

- Ensuring effective job design to encourage nontraditional employees to remain with the organization and to counter any ill effects of corporate racism or sexism. An effective job design includes ensuring a successful match between employee skills and tasks and a variety in assigned work tasks, granting autonomy, and providing ongoing feedback from multiple sources (Fernandez 1999)
- Hiring and placing women and people of color in "batches" to avoid tokenism (Dugan et al. 1993)
- Using "flex management" including offering flexible work hours and locations, and rewards.

Fernandez (1999), Wylie (1996), and Chicago Area Partnerships (1996) remind readers that employees have some responsibility as well for gaining the education and experience needed to be competitive for selection and advancement. Still, this list suggests that there are many steps that employers can take to foster an inclusive environment. Many of these steps are promoted by literature that describes "best practices" for achieving an inclusive work environment. Much of this literature lacks a critical component, however: an empirical means for validating that a particular practice has been effective in improving the climate for diversity.

Documenting Best Practices

A growing number of reports highlight best practices as a means for encouraging organizations to successfully manage diversity and achieve the benefits therein. In many cases, this involves surveying employers about their diversity-related initiatives. If the practices submitted by those employers appear to be ones that would indeed lower barriers to the full inclusion of nontraditional workers, they are reported as such. Examples of such reports are *Best Practices of Private Sector Employers,* released by the EEOC in 1997, and the "Corporate Practice Tables" included in the Federal Glass Ceiling Commission's fact-finding report (1995b). *Fortune* magazine, in 1998 and 1999, also assembled a list of the best companies for people of color.

But how does one determine if these practices really are effective in increasing the inclusion of nontraditional groups? Some authors stress the importance of monitoring numbers to gauge improvement. Such numbers include representation at various levels within the organization (Morrison 1992; Norton and Fox 1997; Cox 1994; Chicago Area Partnerships 1996; Thomas 1996). Some also suggest that it is vital to monitor employees' perceptions (Wilson 1997; Morrison 1992). The trouble with most of the best practices reports is that they fail to offer any concrete evidence that the approaches to fostering inclusion that they highlight are successful. Reporting improvements in the representation of women and people of color or employee attitudes are incomplete indicators, but they are better than nothing.

One indicator that may be appealing is the number of EEO complaints filed over time. It would be tempting to assume that effective diversity efforts would lead to a decline in complaints. An article in *Government Executive* magazine in 1994 employed this line of reasoning. The author noted rather cynically that despite an increase in diversity training, the number of EEO complaints based on race or sex discrimination filed by federal employees had increased from 10,500 in 1989 to 13,200 in 1992 (Kaufman 1994, 16).[1] However, the increase could reflect a growing number of employees who are aware of their rights and how to go about filing a formal protest rather than a stable or deteriorating diversity climate.

In the 1999 report on the top companies for the employment of people of color, *Fortune* magazine analysts decided to strengthen their ratings by including an assessment of the impact of the companies' diversity efforts. They asked employers to report the number of employees affected by their diversity programs, the number of employees of color who were hired from historically black colleges, and whether compensation practices are used to hold managers accountable for their success in meeting diversity goals. The results were factored into scores assigned to the companies and used to develop a rank order of those most favorable for employees of color (Robinson and Hickman 1999). The *Fortune* report also indicates, for each of the top-rated companies, the number of people of color on its board of directors and among the top twenty-five paid officials. It includes the representation (expressed as a percentage) of people of color within the overall workforce, among officials and managers, and among new hires.

These numbers help to shore up the claim that the companies highly ranked by *Fortune* are engaged in practices that are effective in promoting inclusiveness. However, the *Fortune* report did not reveal how scores were assigned to specific elements, nor how the final tally was computed, leaving questions about their reliability and validity. Despite this drawback, however, the *Fortune* approach does contribute to diversity efforts by encouraging such practices among employers who would like to be recognized nationally as exemplary employers.

In short, a popular strategy for encouraging the adoption of measures to create a climate for diversity is to publish success stories about model practices that other employers can adopt. What the rest of employers concerned about diversity are doing is the next question to be addressed.

What Are Organizations Doing?

It should be clear by now that there is an extensive literature that offers ample advice on how to best manage diversity and do so in a way that goes beyond traditional equal employment opportunity and affirmative action practices. What is less clear is how many organizations have jumped on this bandwagon. The Society for Human Resource Management and Commerce Clearing House (1993) co-sponsored a survey of human resource specialists to try to find out. The authors concluded from the responses (which were nearly all from private sector firms) that the most popular initiatives to promote diversity are focused on legal concerns. The most prevalent activities reported by respondents were having a sexual harassment policy (93 percent) and ensuring physical access for the disabled (76 percent). A majority of respondents also reported offering flexible work schedules and parental leave (57 percent). The authors noted that only 33 percent said they had an explicit promotion policy to break through glass ceilings. In the authors' view, this lack of attention to career advancement means that "companies are not making a long-term commitment to diversity" (Society for Human Resource Management/Commerce Clearing House 1993, 5).

A central premise of this book is that public sector employers have even more reasons to promote inclusive work environments than do private sector organizations. This is because of the important role a representative bureaucracy plays in a democratic polity (see Chapter 1). And yet surveys of public sector officials, at least in the early 1990s, revealed that most of these organizations were not any more proactive than the private sector companies that responded to the SHRM/CCH survey.

For example, a survey of public sector human relations officials revealed that fewer than half (41 percent) worked in organizations that had written policies or programs that included the concept of employee diversity. When asked to indicate which activities were associated with such policies or programs, the most often cited activities were recruitment (77 percent) and selection (64 percent). These numbers actually exceed the number of respondents reporting that they had a written diversity policy or program. This led the study's authors to conclude that the respondents must consider diversity as inherent within recruitment and selection, rather than being part of a special effort (Carrell and Mann 1995).

Similarly, MSPB concluded from its 1991 survey of federal agencies that most (twenty-five of thirty-three responding agencies) were emphasizing affirmative employment rather than any other diversity-related initiatives (U.S. Merit Systems Protection Board 1993a). This survey was conducted many years ago, however, even before President Clinton took office with a commitment to create a government that "looks like America." Given the relentless attention that is being given to diversity among all sectors, there is every reason to believe that agencies have increased their efforts to promote inclusiveness over the course of the decade. That is the subject to which this chapter now turns.

Federal Agency Approaches

This section discusses the results of an "organizational assessment" survey administered to 160 federal departments, agencies, and subagencies by the National Partnership for Reinventing Government's (formerly National Performance Review or NPR) Diversity Task Force in the spring of 1999.[2] The questionnaire was designed to gather information about any diversity initiatives that these agencies may have undertaken, including their scope and resource commitment. The instrument defined *diversity initiative* very broadly: "any activities that your organization has undertaken to foster an inclusive workforce." Agencies were asked to respond to questions and to supply documentation where indicated. Responses were received from 137 agencies, for a response rate of 86 percent. Of those, 124 indicated that they had already adopted, or were planning to adopt, a diversity initiative in fiscal year 1999. Only 13 reported that they had not undertaken an initiative and did not plan to in FY 1999.

What Are Federal Agencies Up To?

Responses to the NPR survey suggest that agencies have come a long way since MSPB inquired about workforce diversity programs in 1991. At that time, MSPB estimated that 75 percent of agencies' diversity programs really did not consist of much more than the equal employment opportunity/affirmative employment programs (EEO/AEP) that had been in place for many years (U.S. Merit Systems Protection Board 1993a). This time, only 20 percent of the 124 agencies that responded to the NPR survey that had diversity initiatives in place reported that they primarily encompassed the agency's EEO/AEP program. Two-thirds (68 percent) of agencies indicated that their diversity initiatives address workplace diversity issues not previously addressed by the organization's EEO/AEP (the remaining 12 percent checked "other" or did not respond).

Table 8.2 shows the percent of federal agency respondents that reported undertaking various activities as part of their diversity initiatives. The activities are grouped into four dimensions: training, top management commitment and communication, accountability, and resource commitment. The table demonstrates that many agencies have indeed broadened their focus

TABLE 8.2   Proportion of Agencies Including Select Components as Part of Their Diversity Initiatives (Percent)

	Percent of Agencies
Training	
Diversity training is a part of the diversity initiative	82.3
Training is designed to accomplish specific objectives	83.0
Training objectives are communicated to employees	78.6
Training effectiveness is evaluated	71.8
Top management commitment and communication	
Diversity is incorporated into agency vision or mission statement	46.0
Agency head has issued a diversity statement	56.5
Diversity initiative is linked to the organization's strategic plan	57.3
Diversity initiative includes communication media (e.g., newsletter, intranet)	41.9
Accountability	
Organization uses measures (e.g., productivity, performance) to measure initiative's effectiveness	53.2
Employees are held accountable for achieving diversity objectives	75.8
Diversity initiative is linked to organization's annual performance plan	43.5
Diversity initiative includes awards and incentives	44.4
There is a diversity accomplishment or status report	52.4
Resource commitment	
There is a diversity initiative implementation plan	54.8
The initiative includes a formal mentoring program	33.1
The initiative includes an informal mentoring program	30.6
The initiative includes an internship program	46.8
There is more than one employee who performs significant duties related to the initiative	76.6
There is a specific budget for the diversity initiative	34.7
Total agencies with diversity initiatives	124

SOURCE: National Partnership for Reinventing Government (NPR), *Diversity Task Force Survey*, 1999.

from EEO/AEP. Many report that they are implementing the prescriptions discussed in the literature, as summarized earlier in this chapter. These include incorporating diversity into the organization's vision and/or strategic plan, holding employees accountable for diversity-related accomplishments, and committing resources to the initiatives. The commitment of resources often includes the establishment of internship and/or mentorship programs. Each of these dimensions is discussed in turn.

Diversity Training. The most popular of these components is the provision of diversity training. Nearly all agencies that have a diversity initiative in place include training as one component. Most of these agencies also report that the training has specific objectives. However, when asked what these specific objectives were, answers varied considerably. Some agencies were fairly explicit, saying that the purpose is the "prevention of sexual harassment," or an "increased knowledge of legal and regulatory requirements." Other agencies described the goals of their diversity training in terms that were more vague. For example, one agency reported that it is designed to "educate and raise awareness about diversity." Another simply said the training's purpose is to create "awareness." Of agencies that conduct diversity training, just under half indicated that it is required for supervisors and team leaders and for managers and executives. Only about one-third of agencies require training for their nonsupervisory employees.

Clearly, it is important for agencies to evaluate the effectiveness of such training to ensure that it is accomplishing its objectives. If not done well, training can have little effect on attitudes or behavior or, worse, alienate employees, as was evidently the case for some FAA employees (Society for Human Resource Management/Commerce Clearing House 1993; Dugan et al. 1993). Such a backlash may even muddy the government's image and legitimacy because skeptical employees sometimes alert the press. *The New York Times* reported that a $1 million dollar diversity training program for Washington State Ferry System workers left many feeling more polarized than they were before the training (Egan 1993). A distrustful employee of the Bureau of Labor Statistics took a tape recorder to a training session and then wrote about it for *The Washington Post* (Harris 1995). *The Washington Times* reported that, "The Navy is urging uniformed personnel to attend a diversity training program today during which homosexual activists will promote their lifestyle, discuss cross-dressers and liken gay sex to heterosexual sex" (Scarborough 1994).

Nearly three-quarters of agencies reported that they do evaluate the effectiveness of their diversity training. The most popular form of evaluation is to assess participants' reactions immediately following the training. This form of evaluation is of limited use in that it really measures participants' responses to the trainer more than whether the training has had a lasting impact on their behavior or attitudes (Society for Human Resource Management/Commerce Clearing House 1993). That is not to say that participants' reactions are not important—they are less likely to be motivated by training they didn't like.

However, a more complete training evaluation *also* measures the extent to which participants gained new knowledge, changed their behavior, and did so in such a way that demonstrates measurable results for the organization (e.g., greater productivity, decreased turnover) (Kirkpatrick 1998). Of the agencies that indicated that they evaluate the training, 39 percent report that they assess participant learning. Only 13 percent appraise participants' application of what they learned to the job, and 11 percent assess whether the learning is achieving desired results.

In sum, training is the most widely adopted component of federal agency diversity programs. Still, fewer than half require classroom diversity training for their employees at any level (e.g., supervisory, nonsupervisory) training. Although most agencies understand the importance of evaluating that training, their means for doing so is generally limited to gauging participants' reactions immediately following the training.

Top Management Commitment and Communication.   The effectiveness of diversity initiatives is enhanced if top management affirms its support for such efforts, and that support is communicated throughout the organization (Cox 1994; Thomas 1996; Fernandez 1999; Chambers and Riccucci 1997; Wilson 1997; Hudson and Hines-Hudson 1996; Chicago Area Partnerships 1996; Mathews 1998). Still, not all agencies with diversity initiatives take steps to ensure that all employees are aware of the initiative or its importance. Slightly more than half of the agencies indicated that diversity goals have been communicated to employees via a statement issued by the agency (see Table 8.2). The same percentage reported that diversity goals are linked to the agency's strategic plan, which, presumably, is disseminated to all employees. Just under half make use of communication media such as a newsletter or the agency's intranet. It appears, then, that many agencies may be relying primarily on training for communicating diversity objectives, rather than supplementing training with other forms of communication. And, as noted previously, most agencies don't even require most employees to take the training.

Accountability.   Many authors suggest that the communication of diversity goals must be backed up with mechanisms to hold employees accountable for making efforts to achieve those goals (Morrison 1992; Cox 1994; Fernandez 1999; Wilson 1997; Chicago Area Partnerships 1996; Dobbs 1996). Three-quarters of agencies reported that employees are held responsible for "taking appropriate actions to achieve the objectives of the diversity initiative." Two-thirds of agencies reported that a diversity element is included in the performance plans of senior executives, supervisors, managers, and team leaders. Fewer agencies (11 percent) include a diversity element in the performance plans of nonsupervisory employees.

Another important follow-up to implementation of diversity strategies is to assess their effectiveness and monitor progress toward achieving intended results (Morrison 1992; Norton and Fox 1997; Cox 1994; Chicago Area Partnerships 1996; Thomas 1996). Such measurements could include an assessment of employees' attitudes and perceptions and whether any disparities in rates of promotion, discipline, or turnover among groups (not attributable to non-racial/ethnic- or gender-related factors) have been reduced. Another measure could be an increase in team productivity, as a healthy climate for diversity is clearly required for effective performance of teams (Fernandez 1999). About half of the respondents answered affirmatively when asked if they "use measures (e.g., productivity, performance) to assess the effectiveness of [their] diversity initiatives in achieving stated objectives." The same number report that accomplishment or status reports are part of their diversity initiatives.

Agencies are already required to compare representation by grade level grouping and occupational grouping in their workforce with representation in the civilian labor force and report changes in workforce profiles annually to the EEOC. The most common response to an open-ended question asking about the measures used to assess the effectiveness of their diversity initiatives was that kind of demographic analysis. This suggests that many agencies have not expanded their means of assessing their diversity initiatives beyond the ones the EEOC has required for many years. Some agencies also monitor the rate at which racial/ethnic groups are being recruited, hired, given training, given awards, and the like.

As we shall see later in this chapter, most agencies' diversity efforts are focused on more than just the traditional categories of race, ethnicity, sex, and disability. They *also* include an emphasis on such attributes as geographic origin, educational attainment, and communication styles. It is interesting to note that few agencies appear to have in place any mechanism for assessing whether their initiatives are achieving their desired results with respect to these dimensions.

The second most common response from agencies describing the means by which they assess the effectiveness of their diversity initiatives was that they include diversity objectives in performance appraisal criteria for at least some of their employees. This approach was not fully explained by the respondents, but it appears to mean that if employees have performed agreed-upon diversity-related activities, the outcomes they were expected to achieve have been realized. In other words, it is a measure of whether a process took place, rather than focusing on the achievement of any specific outcomes. A supervisor may have ensured that all of his or her employees were provided diversity awareness training, but that does not mean that a desirable attitudinal or behavioral change was achieved. In fact, only ten agencies reported that they are monitoring employee attitudes through climate surveys. This suggests that few yet recognize the importance of perceptions in achieving an inclusive environment (see Chapters 6 and 7).

Resource Commitment.   For a diversity initiative to be successful, sufficient resources must be provided. At a minimum, staff time and a budget are required to develop specific programs designed to create additional opportunities for employees who may have been denied them in the past (Morrison 1992; Norton and Fox 1997; Thomas and Gabarro 1999; Cox 1994; Chambers and Riccucci 1997; Clayton and Crosby 1992; Fernandez 1999; Wilson 1997; Dobbs 1996; Chicago Area Partnerships 1996). As shown in Table 8.2, only about one-third of agencies reported that they have a specific, identifiable budget for their diversity initiatives. Only about one-quarter of agencies indicated that there is a person whose full-time job consists of day-to-day operational responsibility for the diversity initiative. There appears to be a greater willingness to devote part-time staff resources to the initiatives. Three-quarters of agencies reported that there are employees other than a full-time coordinator who perform significant duties related to the initiative. These include such activities as serving on a diversity council or conducting training. Most of those performing these duties are doing so fewer than twenty hours per week.

Although many advocate mentorship programs as a means for providing greater advancement opportunities (Morrison 1992; Fernandez 1999; Cox 1994; Payne 1998; Thomas and Gabarro 1999; Wilson 1997; Chicago Area Partnerships 1996; Dugan et al. 1993), only about one-third of agencies indicated that their initiatives include formal mentorship programs or even an informal mentorship program. A greater proportion of agencies (47 percent) offer internship programs as part of their initiatives. Again, this may be nothing new. Internships are a way of recruiting people (often students) to work in the agency part-time with the idea that they may be offered a full-time job upon completing their education. As such, they have long been in agencies' arsenals of affirmative employment tools.

Diversity Dimensions.   There is some debate in the literature as to how broadly diversity strategies should be focused. Some authors advocate a very broad approach that highlights all the ways people are different, including background, education, and personality (Thomas 1990, 1996; Norton and Fox 1997; Fernandez 1999; Wilson 1997). Others warn that such a sweeping definition of diversity may divert attention from the continuing exclusion of women and people of color in organizations (Morrison 1992; Caudron and Hayes 1997).

The NPR survey asked agencies to provide their definitions of diversity. Some of these focused on the traditional categories, that is, those characteristics where discrimination has been proscribed by law.[3] A typical definition provided by an agency in this category was: "Diversity means inclusion—hiring, developing, promoting, and retaining employees of all races, ethnic groups, religions, and ages; people with disabilities, men and women." Most agencies' definitions were broader, however. Some adopted a definition modeled on the one promoted by R. Roosevelt Thomas (1996): "Diversity is the mix of differences and similarities at all organizational levels." Still others came up with their own, all-encompassing definitions. For example: "Diversity is the mosaic of people who bring a variety of backgrounds, styles, perspectives, values and beliefs—as assets to the groups and organizations with which they interact."

In addition to asking agencies how they define diversity, the NPR survey provided agencies with a list of seventeen possible dimensions that are often addressed in diversity programs. These include the traditional categories (based on legal prohibitions) as well as other ways in which people's backgrounds often differ from one another. The percentage of agencies indicating that their initiatives address each aspect is presented in Table 8.3. Most agencies that have diversity initiatives include the traditional dimensions such as gender, race/color, and ethnicity/national origin. Most also appear to subscribe to the notion that diversity should address other differences as well. More than three-quarters of agency respondents indicated that their diversity programs include at least one dimension not covered by anti-discrimination laws. The average number of dimensions addressed by federal survey respondents was 9.6.

Thus, it should be clear that many federal agencies have followed the lead of private sector companies and consultants. They, too, have recognized the need for diversity initiatives that extend beyond the reach of traditional EEO and affirmative employment programs. More than three-quarters of the federal agencies and subagencies that the NPR surveyed reported that they had, or were about to adopt, a diversity initiative. Moreover, most of these agencies have given the initiative a broader scope than those encompassed by more traditional EEO/affirmative employment programs. Most agencies conduct training, hold employees accountable for achieving stated objectives, and devote at least some staff time to the initiative. In over half of agencies, the agency head has issued a diversity statement. The survey also revealed that agencies vary in the number of demographic dimensions their initiatives are designed to address, with most including at least one dimension beyond the traditional bases on which discrimination is specifically proscribed by law.

On average, federal agencies are making a considerable investment in their diversity initiatives. They are making a financial investment in the form of staff and other resources that directly support those initiatives. But they are making a political investment as well. As noted in the discussion of training earlier in this chapter, agencies run the risk that a diversity pro-

TABLE 8.3   Proportion of Agencies Specifically Addressing Diversity Dimensions in Their Diversity Initiatives (Percent)

Dimension	Percent of Agencies
Traditional Dimensions	
Age	77.4
Disability	83.1
Ethnicity/national origin	87.9
Gender	86.3
Race/color	91.9
Religion	70.2
Sexual orientation	66.1
Nontraditional Dimensions	
Communication style	48.4
Economic status	34.7
Education	47.6
Family status (e.g., single parent, elder-care provider)	45.2
First language	28.2
Geographic origin (e.g., East, West, Midwest, South)	35.5
Military experience/veteran status	40.3
Organizational role/level (e.g., managerial, clerical)	54.0
Work experience (e.g., routine, repetitive, creative)	31.5
Work style (e.g., individualistic, collaborative)	31.5
Total agencies with diversity initiatives	124

SOURCE: National Partnership for Reinventing Government (NPR), *Diversity Task Force Survey*, 1999.

gram that is not carefully designed to avoid stepping on toes will be reviled in the popular press. It may also draw the attention of Congress. It is therefore self-evident that an assessment should be made as to whether these initiatives have been effective in fostering an inclusive environment. Making that assessment, however, is not an easy task, as the next section of this chapter will demonstrate.

Assessing the Effectiveness of Federal Diversity Initiatives

Do the strategies federal agencies have undertaken reduce or eliminate the kinds of barriers to the full inclusion of women and people of color described in this book? As noted above, only about half of agencies report that they measure the effectiveness of their diversity initiatives. In many cases, they do so only by tracking the representation of various groups by grade level and occupation, or through inclusion of one or more diversity objectives in employees' performance appraisal plans.

The preceding chapters demonstrated a variety of ways in which barriers to inclusion can be detected. The chapter on the glass ceiling, for example, used survey data to identify whether the advancement of women and people of color was limited after controlling for differences in qualifications and work-related experiences. It also supplemented that analysis, in the case of women, with comments made by focus group participants. These comments helped provide a more complete understanding of what the barriers to the advancement of women look like.

We used another form of data—employment records from the government's employment database—to identify the disparity in the rates at which some people of color are subject to disciplinary action and to rule out some possible explanations for that disparity. In Chapter 6, we used survey data to evaluate employees' perceptions of discrimination, the circumstances under which such perceptions are most likely to occur, and the impact of such perceptions on career-related decisions. These are only some of the potential empirical measures agencies can use to identify barriers to the achievement of a representative bureaucracy. They are also baseline measures that can be used to assess whether diversity initiatives are successful in eliminating disparities that appear to be based on race/ethnicity or gender or on perceptions of unequal treatment.

Many diversity efforts have a much broader focus than increasing the representation of women and people of color or improving the environment in which they work. For example, some proclaim that the goal of their initiative is to "celebrate the uniqueness of each individual." But even with an objective as sweeping as that, one would expect to see greater opportunities for people of color, women, and other "nontraditional" employees than existed before the diversity initiative was established. Therefore it is appropriate to ask, how have the groups of interest in this book fared in the agencies that have undertaken diversity initiatives?

The advantage of having information about 137 federal agencies and subagencies regarding their initiatives is that two forms of assessment can be made. One is whether these initiatives have increased opportunities for people of color and women over time. The other is whether agencies that *have* undertaken certain types of initiatives have had greater success in creating such opportunities than those who *have not* undertaken those initiatives. Such an assessment requires having data by which to measure "success" in creating a more inclusive environment.

Ideally, a measure of agencies' success in achieving the goals envisioned by the theory of representative bureaucracy would include multiple measures, including rates at which various employment-related actions (e.g., promotion, discipline) are taken and measures of experiences (e.g., sexual harassment), attitudes, and perceptions. However, this inventory of data is not readily available at the subagency level. This chapter uses some data that are available to illustrate how an evaluation of whether specific diversity strategies are successful can be performed. Three proxies, albeit imperfect, for "success," are used.

The first proxy is the change in the representation of people of color between September 1993 and March 1999. This measure is designed to identify the extent to which agencies' diversity initiatives have been successful in creating more opportunities for the advancement of people of color. The year 1993 was chosen because it was at that time that a large number of senior executives retired, opening up the opportunity to promote more people of color and women into these positions if an agency had an interest in doing so. The numbers necessary to compute this measure were available for 109 of the agencies responding to the NPR survey. The numbers ranged from a net decrease in minority representation in the SES of 25 percentage points to a net increase of 33 percentage points. The mean increase was 4.8 points, and the median 4.1. This is about equal to the overall government-wide increase in minority representation in the SES from 1993 to 1999, which was 5.0 percent.

The second measure is simply the current representation (as of March 1999) of people of color in the SES of each agency. This measure is considered because there may well be agencies who show no *increase* in representation simply because the representation of people of color was already high in 1993, leaving little room for improvement. These data were available for 113 of the 137 agencies that responded to the NPR survey. The proportion of the SES represented by people of color ranged from 0 to 100 percent, the latter reflecting an agency that has a minority-oriented mission. The mean is 16.1 percent, and the median 11.1 percent. This is slightly higher than the representation of people of color in the SES government-wide, which was 14 percent in 1999.

The third proxy is arguably more important than the other two. It measures the attitudinal climate within agencies. In 1998, the National Performance Review administered a short attitudinal survey to a government-wide sample representative of forty-eight agencies and subagencies. It included only a single question related to diversity. The survey asked respondents to state their level of agreement or disagreement with the statement: "In my organization, differences among individuals (for example, gender, race, national origin, religion, age, cultural background, disability) are respected and valued."

The organizational units responding to the organizational assessment survey that we have been discussing in this chapter did not necessarily match the units by which responses to the attitudinal survey were aggregated. For example, many different components of the Department of Transportation (DOT) responded separately to the organizational assessment survey. The attitudinal survey was only administered to samples representative of the FAA, and "all other DOT employees." Hence, the only match between the two datasets that could be made for the Department of Transportation was for the FAA. Altogether, there were twenty-eight agencies with matched data that could be included in the analysis. The range of responses was very limited among these twenty-eight agencies. They ranged from 50.7 of employees agreeing with the statement to 66.0 in agreement, with a mean of 60.0 percent, and a median of 59.2 percent.

To assess the effectiveness of various components of the diversity initiatives, simple additive indices were computed summing the variables representing four dimensions: training, top leadership commitment and communication, accountability, and resource commitment (see Table 8.4). It was expected that these measures would be positively correlated with each of the three proxies for success.

As it turns out, there is little correlation between agency diversity initiatives, as measured by the four dimensions, and the three proxies for success (see Table 8.5). Only one correlation reaches statistical significance at the .10 level, and that is between top management commitment and communication and positive responses to the NPR attitude survey. These findings suggest that diversity initiatives have had little if any effect on improving the climate for diversity in agencies. It is certainly possible that many of such efforts are little more than "smoke and mirrors" with insufficient resources and authority to make an impact on the organizational culture.

However, this conclusion would be premature. First, the three measures are crude, and clearly more comprehensive ones are needed. The attitudinal question, in particular, suffers because there was little range in the responses among agencies. A better attitudinal measure would be a scale comprising responses to several questions, such as those used in Chapter 6. Moreover, not finding a correlation doesn't mean there is no relationship between agencies' diversity practices and the measures of success used—it just means there is not a linear relationship.

At this point, it seems useful to engage in a more exploratory analysis to detect patterns and raise questions that could be explored in more depth once better data become available. For this purpose, three cohorts of agencies are selected from among those that responded to the NPR organizational assessment survey, and for which data on representation and increase in representation are also available.

The first cohort includes the ten agencies with the highest representation of people of color within their SES ranks and those that have shown the greatest percentage point increase in SES representation between 1993 and 1999 (see Table 8.6). The second cohort consists of the ten agencies that are in the median range with respect to minority representation in the SES and percentage point increase in SES representation. The third cohort includes the ten agencies in the lowest range of the same two categories. Where an

TABLE 8.4   Items Making Up Indices

Index scores represent the sum of the following activities reported as part of organizations' diversity initiatives

Training (alpha = .83)
- Training is part of the organization's diversity initiative.
- The organization
    Conducts diversity training
    Has specific objectives for training
    Communicates those objectives for training
    Evaluates effectiveness of diversity training provided to
      employees.

Communication (alpha = .80)
- Components of diversity initiatives include
    Diversity statement by department/agency head
    Initiative implementation plan
    Incorporation of diversity into department/agency vision or
      mission statement
    Diversity policy, directive, administrative order, etc.
    Communication media (e.g., newsletter, intranet)
    Accomplishment or status report
- The diversity initiative is linked to strategic plan.

Accountability (alpha = .72)
- The organization uses measures (e.g., productivity, performance) to
  assess the effectiveness of its diversity initiative(s) in achieving
  stated objectives.
- Employees are held accountable for taking appropriate actions to
  achieve the objectives of the diversity initiative(s).
- The diversity initiative includes an accomplishment or status report.
- The diversity initiative is linked to the organization's annual
  performance plan.
- Awards and incentives are a component of the diversity initiative.
- The organization evaluates the effectiveness of diversity training
  provided to employees.

Resources (alpha = .77)
- Components of diversity initiatives include
    Diversity incorporated into department/agency vision or
      mission statement
    Diversity statement by department/agency head
    Diversity initiative implementation plan
    Diversity policy, directive, administrative order, etc.
    Formal mentoring program

(continues)

(continued)

        Informal mentoring program
        Internship program
        Awards and incentives.
- Other than one individual who has primary responsibility for diversity, there are other employees who perform significant duties directly related to diversity initiative (e.g., members of diversity council, diversity trainers).
- There is a specific identifiable amount designated in the organization's budget for diversity initiative(s).

TABLE 8.5   Relationship Between Diversity Initiative Components and Measures of Success (Correlation Coefficients, n)

	Representation of People of Color in SES 1999	Increase in Representation in SES 1993–1999	Percent Positive to Diversity Question
Training	−.128 (79)	−.157 (76)	.036 (25)
Top management commitment and communication	−.111 (104)	−.113 (100)	.324* (27)
Resource commitment	−.067 (93)	−.078 (89)	.234 (26)
Accountability	.000 (90)	−.024 (86)	.221 (26)

*p<.10
SOURCE: National Partnership for Reinventing Government (NPR), *Diversity Task Force Survey*, 1999.

agency would have been represented in two groups (e.g., highest proportion of minority representation and highest increase in minority representation), we substituted the next agency in line (e.g., the one with the next highest proportion of people of color in the SES) in one category.

    This examination is purely exploratory—it is certainly not the intention to generalize from these thirty agencies to the population of all federal agencies. Nevertheless, it does raise questions and pose some hypotheses that are important to investigate when considering or evaluating the effectiveness of diversity efforts.

TABLE 8.6   Characteristics of High, Median, and Low Agencies

Approximate Number in SES in Agency*	Minority Representation in SES 1999 (Percent)	Percentage Point Change in Minority Representation in SES 1993–1999	Approximate Number of Employees in Agency, 1999*	Minority Representation in Workforce, 1999 (Percent)	Do You Plan To Develop, or Have a Diversity Initiative?
Cohort 1: High agencies					
Highest representation					
5	100.0	0.0	100	81.7	Have one
20	100.0	0.0	11,000	78.0	Plan to
20	95.2	-0.2	6,000	89.4	Have one
5	60.0	10.0	100	39.8	Have one
40	55.0	-5.5	2,500	61.6	Have one
20	40.9	13.6	3,500	44.0	Have one
10	36.4	19.7	500	54.7	Have one
Highest increase					
5	33.3	33.3	1000	36.6	Have one
5	33.3	33.3	16,000	26.9	Don't have
10	25.0	25.0	2,000	45.6	Have one
15	41.2	24.5	1,500	47.3	Plan to
10	44.4	24.4	200	33.9	Plan to
30	28.6	20.5	2,000	20.3	Have one
50	28.6	21.8	3,500	21.7	Have one
Cohort 2: Median Agencies					
Median representation					
30	10.7	7.4	4,000	26.6	Have one
35	11.1	11.1	300	22.3	Have one

(continues)

(continued)

	Approximate Number in SES in Agency*	Minority Representation in SES 1999 (Percent)	Percentage Point Change in Minority Representation in SES 1993–1999	Approximate Number of Employees in Agency, 1999*	Minority Representation in Workforce, 1999 (Percent)	Do You Plan To Develop, or Have a Diversity Initiative?
	30	11.5	-6.6	15,500	21.0	Have one
	10	11.1	**	600	25.0	Have one
	20	11.1	4.4	800	20.3	Have one
Median increase						
	150	8.8	4.4	11,500	18.6.	Have one
	30	6.5	4.5	8,000	11.0	Have one
	100	10.3	3.4	12,000	15.3	Have one
	250	15.4	3.9	105,000	35.4	Have one
	100	7.6	4.1	3,000	22.8	Have one
Cohort 3: Low agencies						
Lowest representation	20	0.0	-6.9	6,000	24.4	Don't have
	20	0.0	-6.3	4,000	20.6	Have one
	10	0.0	0.0	1,500	50.9	Have one
	10	0.0	-11.1	1,700	19.2	Have one
	10	0.0	-9.1	1,700	12.2	Have one
	40	2.6	-1.2	6,500	17.0	Have one
Lowest increase	5	0.0	-25.0	300	25.7	Have one
	10	0.0	-11.1	4,000	21.1	Have one
	10	14.3	-10.7	2,000	8.4	Have one
	10	0.0	-10.0	400	30.3	Have one
	5	0.0	9.1	600	18.4	Have one

SOURCE: U.S. Office of Personnel Management, Central Personnel Data File (columns 1–5); NPR *Diversity Task Force Survey*, 1999 (column 6).
* Approximate numbers given to avoid identifying agencies. ** Data not available for 1993.

As shown in Table 8.6, most of the agencies in all three cohorts have a diversity initiative underway. The three agencies in which people of color constitute all, or nearly all, of the SES (and the majority of the workforce) are agencies that have a minority focus to their mission. That may explain why one of them has not instituted a diversity initiative yet. It is less clear why three agencies in the highest *increase* category do not have initiatives yet. This casts doubt on the importance of having a diversity initiative for achieving greater representation of people of color in high-level career positions.

In Table 8.7, comparisons are made among the three cohorts, excluding those that do not have diversity initiatives underway. With respect to the scope of their initiatives, there does not appear to be much of a difference among the three categories of agencies. Most say that their initiatives are broader than traditional equal employment opportunity/affirmative employment programs.

However, agencies in the highest cohort tend to have initiatives that address fewer dimensions than those in the other two cohorts. For example, high agencies are less likely to include differences with respect to age, education, geographic origin, military/veteran status, religion, and sexual orientation than the other two groups. Are these programs more focused on traditional EEO groups because their leadership includes a higher proportion of senior executives of color? Or is it that tight focus which has been responsible for achieving above-average representation in the SES?

Agencies in the median cohort report the greatest number of dimensions. They also have, on average, the greatest number of specific strategies or components (see Table 8.2 for examples of components). Median agencies are more likely to have established a diversity council, created diversity awareness material, and set up formal and informal mentoring and internship programs than the other agencies represented in Table 8.7.

Table 8.7 also presents the average score of each of the three groups on the indices representing training, top management commitment and communication, resources, and accountability (see Table 8.4 for examples of survey items constituting each index). The three cohorts appear to be similar with respect to the provision of diversity training. Most conduct diversity training for all employees and devote similar amounts of attention and resources to the provision of diversity training. Diversity training appears to have become a standard for agencies in the federal government; most agencies have it regardless of the extent to which other resources are devoted to fostering inclusion.

The median and high agencies have similar scores on the commitment/communication index, while the low agency cohort has a lower score. Diversity is less likely to be included in low agencies' mission statements or strategic plans. Agencies that have greater representation of people of color

TABLE 8.7   Number of High, Median, and Low Agencies Undertaking Various
Diversity-Related Actions

	Lowest	Median	Highest
Scope of Initiative			
Primarily encompasses EEO/AEP	2	2	3
Broader than EEO/AEP	7	7	6
Other	1	1	1
Average number of dimensions	9.5	11.1	6.0
Average number of components	3.9	8.2	4.4
Training			
Diversity training given for all employees	8	6	7
Average score on training index	6.0	5.7	5.9
Communication			
Diversity included in mission statement	3	6	5
Diversity linked to strategic plan	4	7	6
Average score on communication index	2.5	4.7	4.3
Resources			
Individual with primary responsibility			
Yes—full-time	1	5	3
Yes—part-time	5	3	7
No	4	1	0
Specific budget for initiative			
Yes	1	4	3
No	8	6	6
Average score on resource index	4.8	8.2	6.6
Accountability			
Use measures to assess effectiveness			
Yes	2	6	6
No	8	3	4
Diversity element in performance plan of			
Senior executives	5	7	7
Supervisors/managers/team leaders	6	6	7
Nonsupervisors	0	3	0
Average score on accountability index	4.0	5.6	5.2

NOTE: See Figure 8.4 for items in diversity indicies.
SOURCE: National Partnership for Reinventing Government (NPR), *Diversity Task Force Survey*, 1999.

may not be more likely to have a diversity initiative than ones with low representation, but they do appear more willing to make it a more visible part of agency communication from the top.

That low agencies have given less emphasis to their diversity initiatives is also clear with respect to resources and accountability. Although it seems to be very common and easy for agencies to undertake a diversity initiative and to provide training, devoting resources in the form of a budget and staff requires a different level of commitment. Low agencies are less likely to have an individual with primary responsibility for the diversity initiative, on either a part-time or full-time basis. Low agencies are also less likely to have a specific budget designated for their diversity initiatives. They are also less likely to have measures in place to assess the effectiveness of their initiatives.

Approximately the same number of agencies in each cohort are holding their supervisors, managers, and senior executives accountable for diversity objectives through their performance appraisal plans. It is not uncommon for top agency officials to mandate that a diversity element be included in all supervisors' (or, less frequently, employees') performance appraisal plans. For example, the FAA requires that the performance plans of all supervisors and managers include the element: "Create and maintain a productive and hospitable work force that mirrors the Nation's diversity." Such an element would be only one among many included in performance appraisal plans, so it is not clear how much importance it would be given at any particular agency. For that reason, it is also unlikely that supervisors' actions with respect to diversity would have any direct impact on their pay.

This exploratory examination suggests that there may indeed be a relationship between the extent of minority representation and increase in minority representation and the efforts devoted to diversity. What we cannot establish yet is whether the relationship is one of cause and effect. Do the agencies with poorer or declining minority representation at the top tend to devote fewer resources to diversity because there is less appreciation for its importance? Or is the lack of resources the reason for the poor and/or declining minority representation? Conversely, to what extent, if any, can an increase in minority representation in the SES be attributed to any or all of the diversity activities undertaken by an agency? Although we can track the increase or decrease in representation in agencies over time, the NPR survey did not ask agencies how long their diversity initiatives have been in place. This exploratory analysis has suggested that a more comprehensive, comparative analysis among agencies would be a worthwhile and important undertaking.

Conclusion

Since the publication of *Workforce 2000* and *Civil Service 2000* in the late 1980s, an entire industry has developed offering advice for ensuring that employers are making the most of their increasingly diverse workforces. Federal agencies have not been an exception. Most have recognized that it is important to undertake some kind of structured effort to lower barriers to the inclusion of people of color and women, although the scope of and resources devoted to these initiatives vary greatly. Agencies' recognition of the importance of creating a more inclusive climate for diversity is a positive step toward achieving a truly representative bureaucracy.

The majority of federal agencies have accepted the notion, promoted by R. Roosevelt Thomas and others, that managing diversity efforts should be broader in scope than traditional EEO/AEP programs. Most have also concurred with the concept that such efforts should highlight all of the ways people are different, including geographic origins, education, and work experiences, rather than solely addressing gender and race/ethnicity. Whether opportunities for women and people of color are indeed improved within the context of this approach is an open question. Exploratory analysis undertaken here suggests that those agencies with a more focused approach tend to have more success with people of color entering the ranks of the senior executive service.

Many federal agencies have adopted approaches endorsed by diversity consultants and/or benchmarking reports addressing diversity in other sectors. The most popular practice appears to be the provision of diversity training. The objectives for such training, however, vary widely from decreasing the incidents of sexual harassment to the more amorphous hope that people will "value diversity." Most agencies recognize the importance of evaluating the training to ensure it does meet specified objectives. Evaluation tends to take the form of gauging participants' reactions to it, rather than a more comprehensive approach that would look for changes in understanding, behavior, and results.

Some, but by no means the majority, of agencies with diversity initiatives are backing up their commitment with significant resources. These include the full-time appointment of individuals to oversee the day-to-day operation of the effort and the specification of a distinct budget for the initiatives. Those agencies with low representation appear less inclined to support their initiatives with these resources or to make an effort to assess the effectiveness of their diversity programs. Most of those that do such assessments appear to address only one dimension, representation by grade level. That is certainly an important parameter to monitor, but multiple measures would add validity.

In attempting to show the value of assessing the success of diversity initiatives from a comparative standpoint, this chapter has raised more questions than it has answered. We hope that researchers will go on to gather the kind of data needed to assess the worth of initiatives, both within particular agencies and across government. The financial and political capital invested in these initiatives certainly warrants our best efforts to do so. Initiatives that fail or create a backlash may tarnish the government's image as a model employer. Successful initiatives have the added benefit of lowering or eliminating barriers to achieving a representative and inclusive bureaucracy.

Notes

1. A recent report by the General Accounting Office (GAO) conveys different numbers. According to GAO, 17,696 complaints were filed in 1991, and that number climbed to nearly 30,000 by 1997 (General Accounting Office 1999). Although GAO also reports that there are problems with these numbers, it does not dispute that the number of complaints has increased significantly.

2. Subagencies are components of larger agencies and departments. Such departments and agencies were given an opportunity to identify which of their components should be surveyed separately. For example, subagencies include the U.S. Army Pacific Command within the Department of the Army, the Kennedy Space Center in NASA, and the U.S. Coast Guard within the Department of Transportation. In this section, the more generic term *agency* is used to refer to all of the agencies and agency components surveyed by the NPR Task Force.

3. Title VII of the Civil Rights Act prohibits discrimination based on race, color, religion, sex, or national origin. Discrimination based on disability and on age is proscribed by Section 501 of the Rehabilitation Act of 1973 and Section 15 of the Age Discrimination in Employment Act, respectively. Discrimination based on sexual orientation has not been outlawed by statute, but Executive Order 13087, issued by President Clinton in May 1998, prohibits it in the federal government.

9

Emerging Dimensions

It required consensus, trust. We had it on our team. Social distinctions and
grade and pay distinctions and "experts" disappear under the stars.

Frank Hissong, geosciences analyst with the Bureau of Land Management,
on the value of the team approach in an interview about
culture change in the federal government, July 1997

In this book I have examined the extent to which six potential barriers may
be standing in the way of achieving a representative bureaucracy by limiting the authority and inclusion of women and people of color in their federal jobs.[1] In doing so, I intended to add a missing piece to the literature
that focuses on passive representation, or the number of men of color and
women at various levels in the bureaucracy. Their presence in these jobs is
necessary but not sufficient to assure the achievement of a representative
bureaucracy. This is because even if women and people of color can be
found in those jobs, they may not have the opportunity to play significant
roles in the policy-making process in ways that benefit their communities.
For that reason, research looking for linkages between passive and active
representation, while important, is premature.

The preceding chapters summarized findings from previous research that
suggest the ways in which these barriers limit the participation of women
and people of color. The workplace dynamics described here can diminish
the prospects for advancement or contribute to the likelihood that those
who confront them will leave their jobs. Each chapter proposed means by
which potential barriers could be identified and measured empirically.
Empirical measurements are necessary to identify potential disparities and
assess whether agencies are making progress toward achieving a representative workforce. In many cases we found evidence that such barriers have

adverse consequences. Each chapter presented suggestions for dismantling these barriers.

Despite all of that detail and specificity, it seems appropriate to tie them together in some form of common strategy. Viewing these barriers in concert presents some larger issues to comprehend. Thus, we turn to a brief summary of lessons learned by the findings in the previous chapters. These represent the challenges that those interested in creating a truly representative bureaucracy must face today. The chapter will conclude by proposing some emerging dimensions. These include challenges that are likely to present themselves over the next five years. These are submitted in recognition of the necessity for organizations to prepare themselves to meet the evolving demands presented by an ever-changing external environment.

Summing Up: Lessons Learned

The Importance of Leadership

There are many kinds of leadership, and each affects opportunities for women and people of color in different ways. A president's views on the merits of programs designed to increase the representation of people of color and women can be alarming to those civil servants who believe such views will limit their career prospects. As it turns out, representation in career and noncareer senior executive positions in the federal government has fluctuated with the changes in presidential administrations in the way anticipated by their rhetoric, although this does not seem to be the case with the rank and file workforce.

The attitudes of the individual supervisors who make the hiring and promotion decisions that ultimately affect overall representation in government are also important. It appears that their views have some bearing on whether they actively try to recruit from groups underrepresented in their work units. What matters more than their attitudes, however, is their own race/ethnicity. A case in point is that it seems that the most effective method for eliminating the persistent underrepresentation of Latinos in federal agencies would be to ensure adequate Latino representation in the supervisory ranks.

Leadership also matters in that attention can be drawn to inequality in a way that penetrates national consciousness. *The Wall Street Journal* wrote of the glass ceiling limiting the advancement of women and people of color, a proposition that was later confirmed by the Department of Labor following its own pilot study of several corporations. This in turn propelled members of Congress and other federal agencies to devote attention to determining whether a glass ceiling was evident in the federal government. This attention to the issue brought it a legitimacy that other forms of inequality have not had. The importance of leadership, then, is not just about the authority wielded by individuals, but the synergistic effect created by spotlights in many arenas.

The Power of Perceptions

One of the most powerful propagators of inequality in the workplace is the perspectives and beliefs of those who work in them. What people believe, independent of what may be "objectively" occurring in the world around them, can significantly affect their own and others' work experiences. For example, stereotypes can strongly influence expectations of others and the means by which their potential and actual performance is evaluated. A glaring example is the stereotype of women as more committed to their families than their careers. This perception is at least part of the glass ceiling hindering women's advancement. Another example is the stereotype of Asian Pacific Americans as "not management material," which has limited their promotions into supervisory jobs. Still another powerful example is the tendency of Euro-Americans to judge more harshly the performance of their subordinates of color, which likely contributes to the disproportionately high rate of disciplinary actions taken against African Americans.

Also contributing to disproportionate discipline rates is a tendency for some people of color to discount feedback and engage in self-limiting behavior. This is often a product of subjective discrimination, or the perception that members of one's racial/ethnic group are not treated fairly in the organization. It is clear that significant proportions of women and people of color believe their opportunities are limited. Although such perceptions do not appear to deter women from seeking advancement, they do contribute to the likelihood that they will leave their organizations. Unfortunately, the well-intended development of family-friendly programs can also reinforce stereotypes, as when those who take advantage of such programs are assumed to be family- rather than career-oriented.

Another important finding is the mismatch in perceptions between men and women, people of color and Euro-Americans. Men and Euro-Americans have a much more optimistic view of how women and people of color are treated in their organizations than do people of color and women. That mismatch in perceptions has consequences for how people work together. Communication can be problematic between Euro-American supervisors and their employees of color, perhaps also contributing to the disparity in discipline rates. Even though men and women now define more behaviors as sexual harassment than they did a decade ago, the divide between men's and women's perspectives has not narrowed. That divergence means that women, already reluctant to report or even acknowledge that they've been harassed, may find their male superiors unwilling to accept that harassment has occurred. In such a situation, the harassment is likely to continue. Perceptions are not only powerful in themselves, but can set in motion self-perpetuating cycles that limit opportunities in increasingly indiscernible ways.

The Inadequacy of EEO Grievance Processes

Although they are an important and often successful form of redress for people who believe they have been discriminated against or harassed, EEO complaint processes are clearly inadequate for achieving a discrimination-free work environment. Such systems require the aggrieved individual to step forward, initiate a complaint, and then prove discrimination or harassment has occurred. But the subtle and complex ways in which race/ethnicity and gender affect opportunities for women and people of color these days make discrimination difficult to prove.

For example, suppose an African American is not selected for a promotion because he appears to be less qualified than a competitor. Suppose he seems to be less qualified because his competitor had more significant work assignments (facilitated by a powerful mentor), including opportunities for temporary promotions or details. In that case his complaint is unlikely to prevail. The fact that as an African American he was less likely to gain those credential-building experiences will not be considered.

Similarly, if women or people of color do not believe they are being discriminated against (or harassed) because of the natural reluctance to identify specific victims and villains, they will not file complaints. The lack of a uniformly agreed-upon definition of sexual harassment adds another impediment to the complaint resolution process. A woman may not be sure that what she experienced would meet the legal definition of harassment, even though it caused her much grief and anguish. Further disincentives to use the process are the fear that nothing will be done or that one will face retaliation.

Another predicament is supervisors' fears of becoming embroiled in the EEO complaint process, which may cause them to handle difficult situations with employees of color more formally than they would otherwise. That, in turn, can escalate the discord between them. It is important to pay attention to the unintended consequences of processes intended to assure equal treatment.

The Need for Empirical Measures

Instead of relying solely on EEO complaint processes to ensure equal treatment, it is clear that other forms of empirical assessment are needed. Attitude surveys should be used to determine the extent to which there are perceptions of discrimination. Rates of promotion, discipline, turnover, and other personnel actions should be examined to identify any disproportionate impact by race/ethnicity or gender. Once such imbalances are identified, further empirical investigation should look for underlying causes. Meanwhile, those "hard" data should be used to correct any misperceptions about the advantages or disadvantages faced by any group. For example, the presidents' perspectives on the importance of a diverse workforce have not had much impact on rank-and-file hiring and promotion rates. And yet many federal employees have been enraged by this perception and have devoted resources to visible protests and lawsuits.

At the same time, one must recognize the limitations of empirical assessment. The analyses undertaken in this book were only able to explain a small portion of the variance in perceptions, rates of promotion, etc. An unequivocal explanation for the disproportionate rate of disciplinary actions taken against people of color proved to be particularly elusive. Many of the more nebulous factors that can facilitate or deter work-related opportunities, such as stereotypes, misperceptions, self-fulfilling prophesies, attitudes, and assumptions, are nearly impossible to measure. Still, these issues are not going to go away. If anything, the challenges associated with achieving a representative bureaucracy are going to become more intricate. The final section of this chapter describes some of the emerging dimensions that make that so.

Emerging Dimensions

Penetrating the Circle: The Leadership Dimension

This book's opening chapter noted that Bill Clinton took office in 1993 promising to create a government that "looks like America," and appointed more women and people of color to his cabinet than any previous president (Shull 1993). Many of his appointees took his message to heart and reinforced the importance of diversity in the hiring and promotion decisions made by their subordinate managers—enough to incur the umbrage of many Euro-American men (Causey 1994; Goshko 1994; Larson 1993; Laurent 1996). Clinton nominated the most diverse group of federal judicial candidates ever. He made a much-publicized speech in support of affirmative action programs (albeit with the qualification that they be "mended") and opposed Proposition 209, a California ballot proposition designed to end affirmative action in that state. Clinton established the President's Initiative on Race, appointing an advisory board that held much-publicized meetings across the country.

And yet, such an exemplary record is not immune from criticism. A cover story in a December 1999 edition of *USA Today* rebuked the president for falling short of his promise in one important respect: His "inner circle" of advisers consists entirely of Euro-American men. When pressed on this issue by the *USA Today* reporter, Clinton was dumbfounded. He asked her to list the positions she was referring to and then responded defensively: "You might be interested to know there were a couple of people of color I tried to get to do those jobs that preferred other jobs in the administration. . . . All I can tell you is I have never not tried to recruit minorities for any job that was open in the White House" (Hall 1999, 2A).

In his book *Not All Black and White* (1996), former presidential advisor Christopher Edley offers some reasons for this apparent paradox—an impressively diverse cabinet and a homogenous circle of inner advisors. It is the cabinet-level positions that are very public and obvious to those keeping track of demographic balance (whom Clinton referred to at one time as the "bean counters"). Without the scrutiny created by the bean counters and reinforced by visible confirmation hearings, says Edley, even those who are well intentioned tend to fall back on habit. Those who are doing the recruiting tend to rely on such mechanisms for identifying candidates as making use of personal networks, calling on old friends, and bowing to the demands of powerful sponsors. Just as in private industry, these mechanisms tend to perpetuate the status quo and work against drawing in nonmainstream individuals (Edley 1996).

The point of this story is not to criticize Clinton's failing in this respect—he has done more than his recent predecessors to ensure women and people of color are well represented in some critical positions. Rather, it is to suggest that one cannot be satisfied that a representative government is in place until one has peeled back *all* of the layers of the onion. As Edley notes, "the lesson is that even for those most committed to inclusion, it requires unstinting and perhaps exhausting effort" (Edley 1996, 184).

For government leaders to be credible in their commitment to representativeness and equal employment opportunity, all levels must be diverse—from street level bureaucrats to members of boards and commissions to the president's closest advisors. Researchers who have studied the relationship between active and passive representation have largely focused on street level bureaucrats who are in positions to make decisions that directly affect the public. But representation at all levels is important, not only because it can affect the policy decisions that are made, but also because it sends a message about whose views are considered to be most important. This was aptly reinforced by the *USA Today* article, which noted, "There's a sense among critics and some supporters of the president that some critical decisions might have been made differently if there had been more diversity in the Oval Office when key advisors had gathered with the president" (Hall 1999, 1A).

The Heat of the Media: The Organizational Image Dimension

The tale of Clinton's inner circle helps to highlight the role that the media can play in putting pressure on decision makers who say they are committed to diversity to make good on their promise at all levels. For some time, the media have been quick to put before public view any inappropriate gender- or race-related remarks made by public figures. But the media are now more than prepared to make the entire organization the story.

A case in point is Texaco Oil Company. In the fall of 1996, the company was in the process of dealing with a discrimination suit filed by six African American employees when it was shaken by the release of a tape to *The New York Times*. That tape allegedly revealed racist comments by company executives, as well as their efforts to conceal company documents. As a result a "publicity firestorm" erupted that led to calls for boycotts and front page stories debating what executives had actually said on the tape (Schwartz and Gibb 1999).

According to Schwartz and Gibb (1999), Texaco chose to respond positively and aggressively to the incident, rather than by handling it with a short-term fix that would merely diffuse the media spotlight. The company paid a $115 million settlement to its employees of color, along with a one-time salary increase and $30 million for programs designed to advance the diversity climate in the company (Schwartz and Gibb 1999). The moral of this story is that any organization that is not assertively working to eliminate prejudice and discrimination is highly vulnerable to an incident like this one, which will attract the heat of the media and do considerable damage to an organization's reputation.

Federal agencies are just as vulnerable to these accusations. Witness the long battle by African Americans to force the U.S. Department of Agriculture (USDA) to admit it discriminated against them in lending decisions. Recently, the department settled what is perhaps the largest recovery in a civil rights case, agreeing to pay African American farmers $2 billion (Scott 1999). As if that were not enough, discrimination complaints filed by USDA employees have also made headlines. One story begins: "The [USDA] is grappling with a flood of discrimination complaints from minority and female employees who describe the agency as a hotbed of racial bias and harassment" (Fletcher 1999, A1). As that article goes on to note, many other federal agencies face class action discrimination complaints as well, a "troubling reality because for years federal employment was seen as a sure route to the middle class for women and minorities, particularly African Americans" (Fletcher 1999, A1).

These incidents make it clear that discrimination is more than a legal issue; it often presents a media challenge as well. When the complaints make the headlines, the organization is forced to respond to contain the damage to its image and the morale and performance of its employees, regardless of whether the complainants prevail in the long run. An organization that is not consciously and aggressively pursuing efforts to identify real and potential sources of bias is leaving itself vulnerable to this form of defensive management.

Elusive Bias: The Legal Dimension

Another emerging issue represents the converse of the circumstances faced by Texaco and the USDA, and that is proving discrimination. Recently, the San Francisco Unified School District found itself in the position of having to show that discriminatory practices—the basis for a 1983 settlement agreement with the NAACP—persist. At stake was nearly $37 million in state and federal funds that the district qualified for to further desegregation in the schools (Asimov 1999a).

There has been considerable concern recently that many of the nation's school districts are headed toward resegregation (Jones-Wilson 1990; "Racial Segregation in Education" 1994; Yeakey 1993). There is also evidence to suggest that even where students of color do remain in the same schools as Euro-Americans, they encounter "second generation education discrimination." This refers to the notion that students of color are isolated from Euro-Americans and receive poorer educations through the disproportionate use of academic grouping and discipline (Meier and Stewart 1991).

It is not unlikely, then, that some form of elusive bias exists in the San Francisco schools as elsewhere in the country. Data from the California Department of Education for the academic year 1997–1998 show that Latinos represent 19 percent of students in San Francisco high schools, but 28 percent of dropouts. African Americans represent 14 percent of students but 21 percent of dropouts. And yet San Francisco school districts have undoubtedly made progress in ending the extensive segregation that prompted the NAACP lawsuit more than a decade ago.

But rather than celebrating this progress, school officials were put in the position of having to document bias to continue to receive needed funds. As this book has made clear, documenting the elusive bias that pervades institutions today is extremely difficult. In fact, the district was unable to persuade the district court judge overseeing the case that race was needed as one of several criteria for assigning students to campuses. The judge ordered them to eliminate consideration of race. Without that criterion, the district cannot comply with federal and state requirements for special funds for programs to increase the achievement of students of color (Asimov 1999b).

The moral of that story is that as bias becomes more elusive, it becomes more difficult to "prove," even when the problem seems obvious and there is a working solution in progress. And yet there is clearly a need to continue to work toward narrowing persistent inequities among racial/ethnic groups, whether those inequities are the direct result of discrimination or not. In this case, what was at stake were funds designed to improve the performance of Latino and African American students who are clearly lagging behind other students. The law, which requires proof of discrimination before governments can consider race, has not kept up with the evolving nature of discrimination or the complex causes of unequal opportunities.

Changing Work Groups: The Structural Dimension

In the private sector, increased competition in a global economy, escalating customer demands, and accelerating advances in technology are just some of the pressures that are compelling companies to transform their organizational structures (Bowman and Kogut 1995; Nadler, Gerstein, and Shaw 1992; Mohrman, Galbraith and Lawler 1998). At the same time, public institutions, facing declining confidence in government and citizens' simultaneous demands for higher quality services and lower taxes, are seeking ways to become leaner, more decentralized, flexible, and innovative. Considerable literature addresses the ways in which organizations should transform themselves to meet these requirements. This discussion focuses on one: the transition to team-based work structures.

There are many reasons that organizations are transitioning to teams. The speed of change in the external environment and the growing complexity of problems facing organizations mean that an individual's expertise or authority is no longer sufficient to devise innovative solutions (Mohrman, Galbraith, and Lawler 1998; Schrage 1990). Rather, it is teams that have the capacity to produce the innovative thinking that results from a combination of different specialties and knowledge.

Research suggests that diversity has a significant impact on team performance (Rogelberg and Rumery 1996; Watson, Johnson, and Merritt 1998). Some of this literature suggests positive results, finding that ethnically diverse teams are more creative than homogenous ones (Rogelberg and Rumery 1996; Jackson, May, and Whitney 1995). But other researchers' findings are not so optimistic. For example, the "similarity-attraction paradigm" suggests that individuals are more attracted to people like themselves. That means that a more diverse group is more likely to be less cohesive and to have a more negative climate (Mayo, Meindl, and Pastor 1996). Cohesiveness in turn affects job satisfaction, absenteeism, attrition, and performance (Jackson, Stone, and Alvarez 1993; Jackson et al. 1991).

Some contend, however, that the establishment of diverse, cross-functional teams *fosters* rather than *impedes* the inclusion of people of color and women in organizations. Social identity theory proposes that people's self-identification is determined, at least in part, by their membership in groups (Riordan and Shore 1997). Two of the groups with which people naturally identify are their racial or ethnic group and their gender. Irvine and Baker (1995) argue that the development of cross-functional teams has the potential to create *new* identity groups for people so that their connection with their racial, ethnic, or gender group becomes less important. This is in part because, according to social contact theory, increased contact among dissimilar groups can help to break down stereotypes and generate greater attraction.

Cox (1994) suggests that reducing inter-group conflict is a reason that many organizations are shifting to team-based work structures. Properly structured teams can eliminate power imbalances systematically related to gender or race/ethnicity. Fernandez (1999) takes a different approach, but ends up in the same place. He begins by making the case for transitioning to teams and then asserts that for teams to be successful, team members must have mutual respect. If organizations are going to reap the benefits of high-performance teams, they simply must overcome discrimination and stereotypes.

There is one small bit of evidence to bring to bear on this controversy. In its 1996 "Merit Principles Survey," administered to a government-wide sample of federal employees, MSPB asked respondents to state their level of agreement or disagreement with the statement: "A spirit of cooperation and teamwork exists in my immediate work unit." The survey also included several questions related to the diversity climate in respondents' organizations. To examine the potential relationship between teamwork and the climate for diversity, we created two groups based on their responses to the statement about cooperation and teamwork. Those who agreed or strongly agreed are classified as being in team-oriented organizations and those who disagreed or strongly disagreed are classified as being in a non-team-oriented organization (leaving out those who neither agreed nor disagreed). Figure 9.1 shows the differences in their responses to several diversity related items included on the same survey.

The differences are remarkable. Fifty-two percent of people of color in team-oriented organizations agreed that people of their race are treated with respect, compared to only 27 percent in non-team-oriented organizations. Sixty-two percent of Euro-Americans in non-team-oriented organizations agreed that affirmative action has put minorities in positions for which they are unqualified, compared to just 49 percent of Euro-Americans in team-oriented organizations. Thirty-six percent of people of color in non-team-oriented organizations, but only 19 percent of people of color in

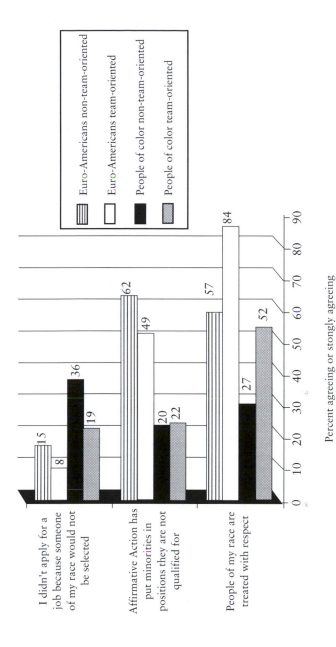

Percent agreeing or stongly agreeing

Figure 9.1. Perspectives of People of Color and Euro-Americans in Team-Oriented and Non-Team-Oriented Organizations

SOURCE: U.S. Merit Systems Protection Board, *Merit Principles Survey*, 1996.

team-oriented organizations reported they did not apply for a job because they assumed someone of their race would not be selected.

Granted, a statement describing a "spirit of teamwork and cooperation" is not the best means for operationalizing the structures of the organizations in which employees work. Further research will be necessary to assess whether transitioning to team-based work arrangements does, in fact, create a better climate for diversity. Nevertheless, the findings presented in Figure 9.1 are encouraging.

Representative Bureaucracy as a Core Value: The Cultural Dimension

The "emerging dimensions" described here are meant to be examples of new challenges and opportunities facing organizations as they resolve those presented in the preceding chapters. But the ultimate goal for any organization should be to reach the point where the understanding of the need for a truly representative bureaucracy is integrated into all of the core functions of that organization. It would simply be understood that diversity at all levels is needed. It would be remarkable if the workforce, upper management, job applicants, suppliers, contractors, and anyone else the agency works with are not diverse. Moreover, for that diversity to serve its intended purposes, stereotypes, bias, and discrimination would not be tolerated. There would be widespread recognition that traditional assumptions and practices based on outdated notions of what work, workers, and workplaces should look like would only limit agencies' performance and responsiveness. Ideally, these concepts should be so ingrained in the organization's culture that diversity programs and coordinators and offices are no longer needed.

A preliminary step toward that goal, however, would be ensuring that diversity objectives do appear across the organizational spectrum and are integrated into every component. The United States Postal Service (USPS) was criticized recently in a study conducted by the Aguirre International consulting firm. The firm noted that diversity efforts had separate reporting structures that "mitigate against integrating diversity into overall management and training processes. . . . As a result, diversity is seen as an *add-on*, especially since there are no consequences for managers who fail to address diversity issues" (Aguirre International 1997, iv).

Following the Aguirre report, the USPS took steps to improve its diversity program. For example, all executives are now held accountable for developing and meeting specific diversity indicators. Changes in the workforce in terms of accessions, promotions, and participation in key supervisory and management training programs are reported to each officer for review and action, where necessary. The USPS also sponsors programs to increase opportunities for businesses owned by women and people of color to do business with the Postal Service.

Other federal agencies have also taken steps toward more fully integrating diversity objectives into their day-to-day work. The U.S. Coast Guard has developed a diversity "roadmap" to orchestrate a five-year infusion of activities designed to hammer home the importance of diversity. One activity links diversity to its Leadership Training in such a way as to make it clear that advancement opportunities will only be available to those who embrace the agency's diversity goals.

Some agencies, such as the National Institutes of Health (NIH), have appointed "catalysts" who act as change agents. At NIH, catalysts participate in strategic planning and evaluate progress toward meeting specific diversity objectives. In the National Oceanic and Atmospheric Administration (NOAA), the growing network of catalysts attend an intensive one-week course and then are responsible for raising the awareness of diversity issues throughout the day-to-day work of the agency. They are often invisible, bringing up the diversity implications of routine decisions. For example, if a committee reviewing applicants for promotion were to suggest that a woman may not be able to carry out all the duties associated with the job because of her parental responsibilities (see Chapter 4), the diversity consultant would question this assumption. The consultants serve two-year terms and then are replaced, but the diversity consciousness in them remains, and they continue to raise awareness after their terms have ended.

In addition, NOAA has a process called "Survey Feedback Action" (SFA) in which all of the agency's 12,000 employees are asked to complete an anonymous climate survey. The first administration of the survey took place in 1998 and provides a baseline to measure change. Aggregate responses to the survey for each work group are reported to that group for discussion. Each work group (of at least six people) is required to meet within two weeks after receiving the work group report. The work group, with the assistance of a trained facilitator, is asked to come up with three to five actionable items to solve problems identified by the survey results. The survey will be re-administered in 2001.

These are just some examples of steps federal agencies are taking to integrate diversity awareness into their organizational culture. The goal is to raise awareness that many stereotypes, assumptions, and traditional ways of doing business are preventing people of color and women from being full and equal participants in the work of their organizations. These represent important first steps to take on a road that, with enough time and effort, will ultimately lead to a truly representative bureaucracy.

The essence of government requires that the means be as important as the ends, because it is those means that foster legitimacy, effective policy making, political inclusion, and a role as a model employer. Looking like America requires more than just creating an image—even if the reflection were fairly accurate in terms of who is included. It is about leadership and consciousness, working relationships and trust. It is about a culture that supports, indeed enables, government to function in its role in solving public problems and in demonstrating that true representativeness can be realized.

Note

1. Although some might argue that some of the survey data here are several years old and may no longer reflect the perspectives of federal employees, there is evidence that such attitudes are slow to change. John Palguta, an executive with MSPB, noted in a recent publication that the proportion of African American federal employees who believe that members of their race are subject to blatant discrimination (55 percent) did not decline between 1993 and 2000. Moreover, the divide in perspectives between African Americans and Euro-Americans has not narrowed (Palguta 2000).

Appendices

APPENDIX 1   Coding for Items Included in Tables 3.2 and 3.3

Support for representative workforce (dependent variable)	Addition of responses to 1st and 2nd items in Table 3.1 where 1 = strongly disagree and 5 = strongly agree (range 2–10)
Person of color	Euro-American = 0, Person of color = 1
Gender	Male = 0, Female = 1
Supervisor of color	Euro-American = 0, Person of color = 1
Supervises primarily people of color	Supervises primarily people of color = 1; supervises primarily Euro-Americans or equally Euro-Americans and people of color = 0
Supervises primarily women	Supervises primarily men or equally men and women = 1, 1; supervises primarily women; supervises primarily men or equally men and women = 0
Supervisor's gender	Male = 1, Female = 2
Professional/administrative	Work supervised is primarily administrative/professional/scientific = 1; work supervised is primarily manual, clerical, technical = 0
Education	Five categories from some high school to graduate or professional degree
Tenure as supervisor	Six categories from less than one year to more than twenty years
Pay grade SES GS 13–15	SES = 1; else = 0 GS 13–15 = 1; else = 0
Supervisory level Executive	Executive in charge of an agency organization or major program = 1; else = 0
Manager	Manager of a program component or staff office = 1; else = 0
Second-level	Second-level supervisor with two or more similar work units = 1; else = 0

(continues)

(continued)

Knows how representative work unit is	See Table 3.1
Tried to recruit Latinos	Was actively involved in recruiting Latinos or actively considered Latino applicants in last three years = 1; else = 0
Latino	Latino = 1; else = 0

APPENDIX 2   Coding for Variables Included in Tables 4.2, 4.3, 4.6, 4.7 and 4.8

Tables 4.2, 4.3

Item	Coding
Current grade (dependent variable)	GS grade coded from 1 to 16 (for SES)
Education	1 through 9 representing less than high school through doctorate
Federal experience	Years of civilian federal government experience in categories from less than one year to more than thirty years
Other work experience	Work in profession outside the government in categories from less than one year to more than thirty years
Average hours of work	Number of hours worked each week, on average, in categories from less than forty to more than sixty
Average days of travel	Average number of days per month of travel in categories from five or less to more than twenty
Work location	Dummy variables representing headquarters = 1, else = 0; regional office = 1, else = 0; field office = 1, else = 0
Relocations	Number of times relocated geographically since employed with government in categories from none to five or more times
Leaves of absence	Number of leaves of absence taken during government service from none to four or more
Mentor	1 = has or had; 0 has not had
Spouse	1 = had spouse/partner during federal career; 0 = has not had
Young children	1 = had elementary school-aged children or younger living with during career; 0 = has not had
Gender	1 = male; 2 = female

(continues)

(continued)

Tables 4.6–4.8

Current Grade (dependent variable)	GS grade coded from 1 to 16 (for SES)
Education	1 through 9 representing less than high school through doctorate
Federal service	Total years of service
Average hours of uncompensated overtime	Total average hours of overtime
Travel	Average number of weeks per year in categories from none to more than four
Geographic relocations	Number of geographic relocations in categories from none to more than four
Leave of at least six weeks	Did not = 0; did = 1
Downgrade	Did not = 0; did = 1
Lateral transfers	In categories from none to five or more times
Temporary promotion/detail	No = 0; yes = 1
Had mentor	Had not had = 0; has had = 1
Gender	1 = male; 2 = female
Race/ethnicity variables	African American, identified race as African American = 1; else = 0 (same for other race/ethnicities)
Race/ethnicity and gender variables	African American man, identified race as African American, sex as male = 1; else = 0 (same for other combinations)
Supervisor (dependent variable)	Nonsupervisor = 0; supervisor = 1

APPENDIX 3   Coding for Items Included in Tables 6.2, 6.5, and 6.7

Table 6.2

Item	Coding
Group subjective discrimination (dependent variable)	Sum of responses to items in Table 6.1 recoded where necessary so score of five perceives most disparate treatment
Personal subjective discrimination (dependent variable)	Sum of responses to two items, one asking effect of gender on career advancement (scale helped a lot to largely hindered) and one asking effect of gender on chances of being selected for promotion (scale from very positive to very negative)
Denied promotion	Was not denied promotion in last five years = 1; was denied = 2
Denied training	Was not denied developmental opportunity in last five years = 1; was denied = 2
Female mentor	Have or had female mentor = 1; has not had female mentor = 0
Male mentor	Have or had male mentor = 1; has not had male mentor = 0
Work with more men than women	Work with all men or more men than women = 1; work with more women than men or equal numbers = 0
Supervisory status	Nonsupervisor = 1; first-line supervisor = 2; second or higher level = 3
Federal experience	In categories from less than one year to more than thirty
Educational attainment	In categories from less than high school to doctorate
Woman of color	Person of color = 1; Euro-American = 0
Age	In categories from under twenty to sixty-five or older
Has spouse or partner	Has had spouse/partner = 1; has not had = 0

Table 6.5

Group subjective discrimination	Sum of responses to items in Table 6.3, recoded where necessary so higher score means greater perceptions of disparate treatment

(continued)

Personal subjective discrimination	Sum of responses to items in Table 6.4, recoded where necessary so higher score means greater perceptions of disparate treatment
Denied promotion	Denied competitive promotion in last three years = 1; not denied promotion = 0
Cash awards	Number received in last three years in categories from none to more than three
Has mentor	Has or had mentor = 1; else = 0
Federal experience	Total number of years of federal, civilian experience
Educational attainment	In categories from less than high school to doctorate
Supervisory status	Nonsupervisor = 1; first-line supervisor = 2; second or higher level = 3
Age	In categories from under twenty to sixty-five or older
Gender	Male = 1; female = 2
African American	Race/ethnicity is African American = 1; else = 0

Additional items in Table 6.7

Size of agency	Total number in white collar workforce in 1991/1000
Works at headquarters	Works at headquarters = 1; else = 0
Works at field office	Works in field office = 1; else = 0
Current grade level	1 to 16 (representing SES)
Has children	Has children = 1; does not = 0

APPENDIX 4 Coding and Wording for Items Included in Tables 7.1 to 7.6

Complete wording for items used in Table 7.1 and 7.2

We would like to know what you would think if the following happened to you or to someone else at work. *Please mark one response for each question.*

Response choices: 5 point scale from definitely yes to definitely not

1. Uninvited letters, telephone calls, or materials of a sexual nature
    a) If supervisor did this, would you consider this sexual harassment?
    b) If another worker did this, would you consider this sexual harassment?

2. Uninvited and deliberate touching, leaning over, cornering or pinching
    (a and b as above)

3. Uninvited sexually suggestive looks or gestures
    (a and b as above)

4. Uninvited pressure for sexual favors
    (a and b as above)

5. Uninvited pressure for dates
    (a and b as above)

6. Uninvited sexual teasing, jokes, remarks or questions
    (a and b as above)

Complete wording for items used in Table 7.3

How often have you received any of the following uninvited and unwanted sexual attention *during the last 24 months* from someone where you work(ed) in the Federal Government? *Mark one response for each attention.*

a. Actual or attempted rape or assault (response choices: never, once, more than once)

Response choices for b - h: never, once, once a month or less, 2–4 times a month, once a week or more

b. Unwanted pressure for sexual favors
c. Unwanted, deliberate touching, leaning over, cornering, or pinching
d. Unwanted sexual looks or gestures
e. Unwanted letters, telephone calls, or materials of a sexual nature
f. Unwanted pressure for dates
g. Unwanted sexual teasing, jokes, remarks or questions
h. Stalking (unwanted following or intrusion into your personal life)

Complete wording for Items in Table 7.4

What action(s) did you take in response to this unwanted sexual attention?
(Respondent asked to check actions taken)

a. I ignored the behavior or did nothing
b. I avoided the person(s)
c. I asked/told the person to stop
d. I threatened to tell or told others
e. I reported the behavior to a supervisor or other official(s) such as an EEO counselor
f. I made a joke of the behavior
g. I went along with the behavior
h. I changed jobs

Did you take any formal actions? (response choices: no or yes)

Coding for Items Included in Tables 7.5 and 7.6

External response (dependent variable)	Took at least one of the actions listed under "external" in Table 7.4
Experienced level 2 harassment	Experienced at least one of behaviors listed as "level 2" in Table 7.2 = 1; else = 0
Experienced level 3 harassment	Experienced at least one of behaviors listed as "level 3" in Table 7.2 = 1; else = 0
Harasser was supervisor	Person who sexually bothered you was immediate supervisor or higher level supervisor = 1; else = 0
Frequence of harassment	Five categories from once to every day
Number of behaviors considered to be harassment	Total number of items listed in Table 7.2 marked "definitely" sexual harassment
Aware of formal complaint channels	Yes = 1; no or aren't any = 0
Proportion of women worked with	Five categories from all men to all women, at time of incident
Young	Age was forty-four or younger at time of incident = 1, age was forty-five or older = 0
Educational attainment	Seven categories from less than high school to graduate or professional degree (at time of incident)
Married	Marital status at time of incident is married = 1; else = 0

References

Adams, James P., Jr., and William W. Dressler. 1988. "Perceptions of Injustice in a Black Community: Dimensions and Variation." *Human Relations* 41 (10): 753–767.

Aguirre International. 1997. *It's Good Business: A Study of Diversity in the United States Postal Service*. Bethesda, MD: Aguirre International.

Alderfer, Clayton P., Charleen J. Alderfer, Leota Tucker, and Robert Tucker. 1980. "Diagnosing Race Relations in Management." *Journal of Applied Behavioral Science* 16 (1): 135–167.

Alvarez, Rodolfo. 1979. "Institutional Discrimination in Organizations and Environment." In Rodolfo Alvarez and Kenneth G. Lutterman, eds., *Discrimination in Organizations*. San Francisco: Jossey-Bass.

Alvarez, Rodolfo, and Kenneth G. Lutterman. 1979. *Discrimination in Organizations*. San Francisco: Jossey-Bass.

American Psychological Association. 1991. "Amicus Curiae Brief in the Supreme Court Case *Price Waterhouse v. Ann B. Hopkins.*" Reprinted in *American Psychologist* 46 (10): 1061–1070.

Aronson, Joshua A., Diane M. Quinn, and Steven J. Spencer. 1998. "Stereotype Threat and the Academic Underperformance of Minorities and Women." In Janet K. Swim and Charles Stangor, eds., *Prejudice: The Target's Perspective*. San Diego: Academic Press.

Arvey, Richard D., and Marcie A. Cavanaugh. 1995. "Using Surveys to Assess the Prevalence of Sexual Harassment: Some Methodological Problems." *Journal of Social Issues* 51 (1): 39–52.

Asante, Molefi, and Alice Davis. 1985. "Black and White Communication: Analyzing Work Place Encounters." *Journal of Black Studies* 16 (September): 77–93.

Asian Americans for Community Involvement. 1993. *Qualified, But . . . : A Report on Glass Ceiling Issues Facing Asian Americans in Silicon Valley*. San Jose, CA: Asian Americans for Community Involvement.

Asimov, Nanette. 1999a. "S.F. Schools Offer 'Race-Neutral' Option." *San Francisco Chronicle*. February 2: A13.

_____. 1999b. "S.F. Schools Can't Use Race in Admissions." *San Francisco Chronicle*. December 18.

"Averting Career Damage from Family Policies." 1992. *The Wall Street Journal*. June 24.

Ball, Gail A., Linda K. Trevino, and Henry P. Sims, Jr. 1994. "Just and Unjust Punishment: Influences on Subordinate Performance and Citizenship." *Academy of Management Journal* 37 (April): 299–322.

Banaszak, Lee Ann, and Eric Plutzer. 1993. "Contextual Determinants of Feminist Attitudes: National and Subnational Influences in Western Europe." *American Political Science Review* 87 (March): 147–157.

Bargh, John A., Mark Chen, and Lara Burrows. 1996. "Automaticity of Social Behavior: Direct Effects of Trait Construct." *Journal of Personality and Social Psychology* 71 (2, August): 230–244.

Barr, Stephen. 1993. "Minority Workers Discharged at Higher Rate Than Whites." *The Washington Post*. December 15, A21.

Baugh, S. Gayle. 1997. "On the Persistence of Sexual Harassment in the Workplace." *Journal of Business Ethics* 16: 899.

Bayes, Jane. 1991. "Women in Public Administration in the United States." *Women and Politics* 11 (4): 85–109.

_____. 1995. "Evaluating the Effectiveness of Affirmative Action Policies in Top Federal Administrative Positions for Women and Minorities 1968–1994." Paper presented to the annual meeting of the Western Political Science Association, Portland, OR. March.

Bell, Ella L., and Stella M. Nkomo. 1994. "Barriers to the Work Place Advancement Experienced by African Americans." Paper prepared for the Federal Glass Ceiling Commission., U.S. Department of Labor. March.

Bendick, Mark, Jr., Charles W. Jackson, and Victor A. Reinoso. 1994. "Measuring Employment Discrimination Through Controlled Experiments." *Review of Black Political Economy* 23 (Summer): 25–48.

Biskupic, Joan. 1991. "Bush Signs Anti-job Bias Bill Amid Furor Over Preferences." *Congressional Quarterly* 49 (November 23): 3463.

Bledsoe, Timothy, and Mary Herring. 1990. "Victims of Circumstances: Women in Pursuit of Political Office." *American Political Science Review* 84 (March): 213–223.

Blum, Linda M. 1990. *Between Feminism and Labor*. Berkeley: University of California Press.

Borjas, George J. 1978. "Discrimination in HEW: Is the Doctor Sick or Are the Patients Healthy?" *Journal of Law and Economics* 21 (April): 97–110.

Bowen, William G., and Derek Bok. 1998. *The Shape of the River*. Princeton, NJ: Princeton University Press.

Bowman, Edward, and Bruce Kogut, eds. 1995. *Redesigning the Firm*. New York: Oxford University Press.

Braddock, Jomills H., II, and James M. McPartland. 1987. "How Minorities Continue to Be Excluded from Equal Employment Opportunities: Research on Labor Market and Institutional Barriers." *Journal of Social Issues* 43 (1): 5–39.

Brett, Jeanne M., and Linda K. Stroh. 1999. "Women in Management: How Far Have We Come and What Needs to Be Done as We Approach 2000?" *Journal of Management Inquiry* 8 (4, December): 392–398.

Bridger, Chet. 1994. "Dorn Denies Job Bias Against White Men." *The Federal Times*. October 10.

Brown, Ryan P., and Robert A. Josephs. 1999. "Burden of Proof: Stereotype Relevance and Gender Differences in Math Performance." *Journal of Personality and Social Psychology* 76 (2, February): 246–257.

Bruce, Willa, and Christine Reed. 1994. "Preparing Supervisors for the Future Work Force: The Dual-Income Couple and the Work-Family Dichotomy." *Public Administration Review* 54 (1, January/February): 36–43.

Bryant, Carleton R. 1991. "Recession, Racism Double Trouble for Black Americans." *The Washington Times*. January 9: A1, A6.

Bullock, Charles S., and Joseph Stewart, Jr. 1979. "Incidence and Correlates of Second-Generation Discrimination." In Marian L. Palley and Michael B. Preston, eds., *Race, Sex, and Policy Problems*. Lexington, MA: Lexington Books.

Burns, Sarah E. 1995. "Issues in Workplace Sexual Harassment Law and Related Social Science Research." *Journal of Social Issues* 51 (1, Spring): 193–208.

Burstein, Paul. 1992. "Affirmative Action, Jobs, and American Democracy: What Has Happened to the Quest for Equal Opportunity?" *Law and Society Review* 26: 901–922.

_____. 1998. *Discrimination, Jobs and Politics*. Chicago: University of Chicago Press.

Burstein, Paul, and Kathleen Monaghan. 1986. "Equal Employment Opportunity and the Mobilization of the Law." *Law and Society Review* 20 (3): 355–388.

Butler, Dore, and Florence L. Geis. 1990. "Nonverbal Affect Responses to Male and Female Leaders: Implications for Leadership Evaluations." *Journal of Personality and Social Psychology* 58 (January): 48–59.

Canady, Charles T. 1995. *Opening Statement for the Hearing on H.R. 2128 before the Subcommittee on the Constitution, Judiciary Committee, U.S. House of Representatives*. 104th Cong., 1st sess., December 7.

Cannings, Kathleen, and Claude Montmarquette. 1991. "Managerial Momentum: A Simultaneous Model the Career Progress of Male and Female Managers." *Industrial and Labor Relations Review* 44: 212–228.

Carmines, Edward G., and James A. Stimson. 1989. *Issue Evolution: Race and the Transformation of American Politics*. Princeton, NJ: Princeton University Press.

Carnoy, Martin. 1994. *Faded Dreams: The Politics and Economics of Race in America*. New York: Cambridge University Press.

Carrell, Michael R., and Everett E. Mann. 1995. "Defining Workforce Diversity in Public Sector Organizations." *Public Personnel Management* 24 (1): 99–111.

Catalyst. 1992. *On the Line: Women's Career Advancement*. New York: Catalyst.

Caudron, Shari, and Cassandra Hayes. 1997. "Are Diversity Programs Benefiting African Americans?" *Black Enterprise*. February: 121–124.

Causey, Mike. 1994. "Defense Adds Hiring Rule." *The Washington Post*. September 13: B2.

Center for Women in Government. 1991/1992. "Women Face Barriers in Top Management." *Women in the Public Service* 2 (Winter): 1.

_____. 1992. "Women Still Stuck in Low-Level Jobs." *Women in the Public Service* 3 (Fall): 1.

Chambers, Tamu, and Norma Riccucci. 1997. "Models of Excellence in Workplace Diversity." In Carolyn Ban and Norma Riccucci, eds., *Public Personnel Management: Current Concerns, Future Challenges*. New York: Longman.

Chicago Area Partnerships (CAPS). 1996. *Pathways and Progress: Corporate Best Practices to Shatter the Glass Ceiling.* Chicago: Chicago Area Partnerships.

Clayton, Susan D., and Faye J. Crosby. 1992. *Justice, Gender, and Affirmative Action.* Ann Arbor: University of Michigan Press.

Cohn, D'Vera. 1995. "Ambivalence in Maryland Echoes Across the Nation." *The Washington Post.* October 11: A1, A12.

Cole, Leonard A. 1976. *Blacks in Power: A Comparative Study of Black and White Elected Officials.* Princeton, NJ: Princeton University Press.

Coleman, Lerita M., Les Jussim, and Jerry L. Isaac. 1991. "Black Students' Reactions to Feedback Conveyed by White and Black Teachers." *Journal of Applied Social Psychology* 2 (6): 460–481.

Collins, Sharon M. 1983. "The Making of the Black Middle Class." *Social Problems* 30 (4, April): 369–382.

Cose, Ellis. 1993. *The Rage of the Privileged Class.* New York: HarperCollins.

Cox, Taylor Jr. 1994. *Cultural Diversity in Organizations.* San Francisco: Berrett-Koehler.

Crocker, Jennifer, and Brenda Major. 1989. "Social Stigma and Self-Esteem: The Self-Protective Properties of Stigma." *Psychological Review* 96 (October): 608–630.

Crocker, Jennifer, and Kathleen M. McGraw. 1984. "What's Good for the Goose Is Not Good for the Gander." *American Behavioral Scientist* 27 (January/February): 357–369.

Crocker, Jennifer, Kristin Voelkl, Maria Testa, and Brenda Major. 1991. "Social Stigma: The Affective Consequences of Attributional Ambiguity." *Journal of Personality and Social Psychology* 60 (2): 218–228.

Crosby, Faye. 1982. *Relative Deprivation and Working Women.* New York: Oxford University Press.

———. 1984. "The Denial of Personal Discrimination." *American Behavioral Scientist* 27 (3, January): 371–386.

Crosby, Faye, et al. 1986. "Cognitive Biases in the Perception of Discrimination: The Importance of Format." *Sex Roles* 14: 637–646.

Crosby, Faye, Susan Clayton, Olaf Alsnis, and Kathryn Hemker. 1986. "Cognitive Biases in the Perception of Discrimination: The Importance of Format." *Sex Roles* 14 (11–12): 637–646.

Crum, John, and Katherine C. Naff. 1997. "Looking Like America: The Continuing Importance of Affirmative Action in Federal Employment." *Public Productivity and Management Review* 20 (3): 272–287.

Dailey, Robert C., and Delaney J. Kirk. 1992. "Distributive and Procedural Justice as Antecedents of Job Satisfaction and Intent to Turnover." *Human Relations* 45 (3): 305–317.

Daley, Dennis. 1984. "Political and Occupational Barriers to the Implementation of Affirmative Action: Administrative, Executive, and Legislative Attitudes Toward Representative Bureaucracy." *Review of Public Personnel Administration* 4 (Summer): 4–15.

Daniel, Lisa. 1999. "Feds and Families." *Government Executive* 31 (4, April): 41–46.

Davis, Charles E., and Jonathan P. West. 1984. "Implementing Public Programs: Equal Employment Opportunity, Affirmative Action, and Administrative Policy Options." *Review of Public Personnel Administration* 4 (Summer): 16–30.

Davis, Nancy J., and Robert V. Robinson. 1991. "Men's and Women's Consciousness of Gender Inequality: Austria, West Germany, Great Britain and the United States." *American Sociological Review* 56 (February): 72–84.

Devine, Patricia G. 1989. "Stereotypes and Prejudice: Their Automatic and Controlled Components." *Journal of Personality and Social Psychology* 56 (1): 5–18.

Digh, Patricia. 1997. "Well-Managed Employee Networks and Business Value." *HR Magazine*. August: 67–72.

Dobbs, Matti. 1996. "Managing Diversity: Lessons from the Private Sector." *Public Personnel Management* 25 (3): 351–367.

Dometrius, Nelson C., and Lee Sigelman. 1984. "Assessing Progress Toward Affirmative Action Goals in State and Local Government: A New Benchmark." *Public Administration Review* 44 (May/June): 241–246.

Dougherty, Thomas, Daniel B. Turban, Diane England Olson, Peggy D. Dwyer, and Melody W. Lapreze. 1996. "Factors Affecting Perceptions of Workplace Sexual Harassment." *Journal of Organizational Behavior* 17 (5 September): 489–501.

Dowd, Maureen. 1991. "Bush Appoints More Women, But Most of Top Aides Are Men." *The New York Times*. May 20: A1.

Dreher, George G., and Ronald A. Ash. 1990. "A Study of Mentoring Among Men and Women in Managerial, Professional, and Technical Positions." *Journal of Applied Psychology* 5: 539–546.

Dugan, Beverly A., et al. 1993. *The Glass Ceiling: Potential Causes and Possible Solutions*. Alexandria, VA: Human Resources Research Organization. July.

Duleep, Harriet O., and Seth Sanders. 1992. "Discrimination at the Top: American-Born Asian and White Men." *Industrial Relations* 31 (3, Fall): 416–432.

Dunivan, Karen O. 1988. "Gender and Perceptions of the Job Environment in the U.S. Air Force." *Armed Forces and Society* 15 (1): 71–91.

Durst, Samantha. 1999. "Assessing the Effect of Family Friendly Programs on Public Organizations." *Review of Public Personnel Administration* 16 (3, Summer): 19–33.

Duxbury, Linda E., and Christopher A. Higgins. 1991. "Gender Differences in Work-Family Conflict." *Journal of Applied Psychology* 76 (1): 60–74.

Dye, Thomas R., and James Renick. 1981. "Political Power City Jobs: Determinants of Minority Employment." *Social Science Quarterly* 62 (September): 475–486.

Eastland, Terry. 1994. "Discrimination in the Name of Diversity." *The Wall Street Journal*. November 2: A15.

Eberhardt, Bruce J., Steven B. Moser, and David McFadden. 1999. "Sexual Harassment in Small Government Units: An Investigation of Policies and Attitudes." *Public Personnel Management* 28 (3, Winter): 351–364.

Edley, Christopher Jr. 1996. *Not All Black and White*. New York: Hill and Wang.

Edsall, Thomas Byrne, and Mary D. Edsall. 1992. *Chain Reaction: The Impact of Race, Rights, and Taxes on American Politics*. New York: W. W. Norton and Company.

Edwards, Jack E., Marie D. Thomas, and Regina L. Burch. 1992. "Hispanic Representation in the Federal Government." In Stephen B. Knouse, Paul Rosenfeld, and Amy L. Culbertson, eds., *Hispanics in the Workplace*. Newbury Park, CA: Sage Publications.

Egan, Timothy. 1993. "Teaching Tolerance in Workplaces: A Seattle Program Illustrates Limits." *The New York Times*. October 4: A18.

Eisinger, Peter K. 1982. "Black Employment in Municipal Jobs: The Impact of Black Political Power." *American Political Science Review* 76 (June): 380–392.

Ewoh, Andrew I. E., and Euel Elliott. 1998. "Affirmative Action and Reaction in the 1990s." *Review of Public Personnel Administration* (17): 38–51.

Eyler, Janet, Valerie J. Cook, and Leslie E. Ward. 1983. "Resegregation: Segregation within Desegregated Schools." In Christine H. Rossell and Willis D. Hawley, eds., *The Consequences of School Desegregation*. Philadelphia: Temple University Press.

Ezra, Marni, and Melissa Deckman. 1996. "Balancing Work and Family Responsibilities: Flextime and Childcare in the Federal Government." *Public Administration Review* 56 (2, March/April): 174–179.

Feagin, Joe R., and Melvin P. Sikes. 1994. *Living with Racism: The Black Middle-Class Experience*. Boston: Beacon Press.

Federal Glass Ceiling Commission. 1995a. *A Solid Investment: Making Full Use of the Nation's Human Capital, Recommendations of the Federal Glass Ceiling Commission*. Washington, DC: Federal Glass Ceiling Commission. November.

_____. 1995b. *Good for Business: Making Full Use of the Nation's Human Capital*. Washington, DC: Federal Glass Ceiling Commission. March

Fernandez, John P. 1981. *Racism and Sexism in Corporate Life* Lexington, MA: D.C. Heath and Company.

_____. 1991. *Managing a Diverse Workforce*. Lexington, MA: Lexington Books.

_____. 1999. *Race, Gender and Rhetoric*. New York: McGraw-Hill.

Fernandez, Sandy Michelle. 1993. "Does Uncle Sam Want You?" *Hispanic* (August): 52, 54.

Ferris, Frank. 1992. "Intraorganizational Cultural Conflict." Ph.D. diss., University of Southern California Washington Public Affairs Center, Washington, DC.

Fine, Marlene G. 1995. *Building Successful Multicultural Organizations*. Westport, CT: Quorum Books.

Fine, Marlene G., Fern L. Johnson, and M. Sallyanne Ryan. 1990. "Cultural Diversity in the Workplace." *Public Personnel Management* 19 (Fall): 305–319.

Fine, T. S. 1992. "The Impact of Issue Framing on Public Opinion: Toward Affirmative Action Programs." *Social Science Journal* 29: 323–334.

Fiske, Susan T., and Peter Glick. 1995. "Ambivalence and Stereotypes Cause Sexual Harassment: A Theory with Implications for Organizational Change." *Journal of Social Issues* 51 (1): 97–115.

Fiske, Susan T., et al. 1991. "Social Research on Trial: Use of Sex Stereotyping Research in *Price Waterhouse v. Watkins*." *American Psychologist* 46 (10): 1049–1060.

Fitzgerald, Louise F. 1990. "Sexual Harassment: The Definition and Measurement of a Construct." In Michele A. Paludi, ed., *Ivory Power: Sexual Harassment on Campus*. Albany: State University of New York Press.

Fitzgerald, Louise F., Suzanne Swan, and Karla Fischer. 1995. "Why Didn't She Just Report Him? The Psychological and Legal Implications of Women's Responses to Sexual Harassment." *Journal of Social Issues* 51 (1): 117–138.

Flagg, Barbara J. 1995. "Fashioning a Title VII Remedy for Transparently White Subjective Decision Making." *Yale Law Journal* 104: 2009–2051.

Fletcher, Michael A. 1999. "Worker Bias Lawsuits Flood Agriculture Dept." *The Washington Post.* April 20: A01

Ford, Carol A., and Francisco J. Donis. 1996. "The Relationship Between Age and Gender in Workers' Attitudes Toward Sexual Harassment." *Journal of Psychology* 130 (6, November): 627–633.

Foreman, Christopher H. 1988. *Signals from the Hill.* New Haven, CT: Yale University Press.

Franklin, James C. 1997. "Industry Output and Employment Projections to 2006." *Monthly Labor Review* 120: 39–57.

Friedman, Raymond A., and David Krackhardt. 1997. "Social Capital and Career Mobility: A Structural Theory of Lower Returns to Education for Asian Employees." *Journal of Applied Behavioral Science* 33 (3, September): 316–334.

"From Action to Outreach." 1985. *The Economist* 294 (January 5): 16–17.

Fuertes, Monica. 1999. "Adverse Action." *Government Executive,* January: 53–56.

Gallese, Liz Roman. 1991. "Why Women Aren't Making It to the Top." *Across the Board,* April: 19–22.

Galloway, George B. 1951. "The Operation of the Legislative Reorganization Act of 1946." *American Political Science Review* 45 (March): 41–68.

Gallup, George Jr., and Larry Hugick. 1990. "Racial Tolerance Grows, Progress on Racial Equality Less Evident." *Gallup Poll Monthly* 297 (June): 23–25.

Gardenswartz, Lee, and Anita Rowe. 1993. *Managing Diversity: A Complete Desk Reference and Planning Guide.* New York: Irwin.

Garfield, Leslie Y. 1996. "Squaring Affirmative Action Admissions Policies with Federal Judicial Guidelines." *Journal of College and University Law* 22 (4): 895–934.

Gillespie, Dair L., and Ann Leffler. 1987. "The Politics of Research Methodology in Claims-Making Activities." *Social Problems* 24 (5, December): 490–501.

Glazer, Sarah. 1996. "Crackdown on Sexual Harassment." *CQ Researcher* 6 (27, July 19): 627–640.

Gleckman, Howard, Tim Smart, Paula Dwyer, Troy Segal, and Joseph Weber. 1991. "Race in the Workplace: Is Affirmative Action Working?" *Business Week* 3221 (July 8): 50–63.

Goodman, Allan E. 1993. *The Dilemma Endures.* Washington, DC: Georgetown University.

Goodnow, Frank J. 1900. *Politics and Administration.* New York: Russell and Russell.

Gormley, William T. 1989. *Taming the Bureaucracy: Muscles, Prayers, and Other Strategies.* Princeton, NJ: Princeton University Press.

Goshko, John M. 1994. "Foreign Service's Painful Passage to Looking More Like America." *The Washington Post.* April 21: A29.

Grabosky, Peter N., and David H. Rosenbloom. 1975. "Racial and Ethnic Integration in the Federal Service." *Social Science Quarterly* 56 (1, June): 71–84.

Grady, Denise. 1999. "Racial Discrepancy is Reported in Surgery for Lung Cancer." *The New York Times.* October 14: A24.

Grandjean, Burke D. 1981. "History and Career in a Bureaucratic Labor Market." *American Journal of Sociology* 86 (March): 1057–1092.

Graves, Laura M., and Gary N. Powell. 1994. "Effects of Sex-Based Preferential Selection and Discrimination in Job Attitudes." *Human Relations* 47 (2): 133–157.

Greenhaus, Jeffrey H., and Saroj Parasuraman. 1993. "Job Performance Attributions and Career Advancement Prospects: An Examination of Gender and Race Effects." *Organizational Behavior and Human Decision Processes* 55: 273–297.

Greenhaus, Jeffrey H., Saroj Parasuraman, and Wayne Wormley. 1990. "Effects of Race on Organizational Experiences, Job Performance Evaluations, and Career Outcomes." *Academy of Management Journal* 33 (1, March): 64–86.

Greve, Frank. 1993a. "Minorities Hit Hard by Federal Firings." *Pioneer Press.* December 14.

_____. 1993b. "Federal Government Dismisses Minorities Most Often." *New York Daily News.* December 14.

_____. 1994a. "Study Says Race Plays a Key Role in Fed Firings." *Sunday Patriot News.* October 23.

_____. 1994b. "Anger and Bias Are Revealed by U.S. Workers." *The Times-Picayune.* October 30.

Gruber, James E. 1992. "A Typology of Personal and Environmental Sexual Harassment: Research and Policy Implications for the 1990s." *Sex Roles* 26 (11/12): 447–464.

Gruber, James E., and Lars Bjorn. 1988. "Routes to a Feminist Orientation Among Women Autoworkers." *Gender and Society* 2 (4): 496–509.

Guajardo, Salomon A. 1996. "Representative Bureaucracy: An Estimation of the Reliability and Validity of the Nachmias-Rosenbloom MV Index." *Public Administration Review* 56 (5, September/October): 467–486.

Gulick, Luther. 1937. "Notes on the Theory of Organization." In Luther Gulick and L. Urwick, eds., *Papers on the Science of Administration.* New York: Institute of Public Administration.

Gurin, Patricia. 1985. "Women's Gender Consciousness." *Public Opinion Quarterly* 49: 143–163.

Gutek, Barbara A. 1989. "Sexuality in the Workplace: Key Issues in Social Research and Organizational Practice." In Jeff Hearn, Deborah L. Sheppard, Pete Tancred-Sheriff, and Gibson Burrell, eds., *Sexuality in Organizations.* London: Sage Publications.

Guy, Mary E. 1992. "Summing Up What We Know." In Mary E. Guy, ed., *Women and Men of the States.* Armonk, NY: M.E. Sharpe.

_____. 1993. "Three Steps Forward, Two Steps Backward: The Status of Women's Integration into Public Management." *Public Administration Review* 53 (4, July/August): 285–291.

_____. 1994. "Organizational Architecture: Gender and Women's Careers." *Review of Public Personnel Administration* 14: 77–90.

_____. 1997. "Gender Issues in the Workplace." In Philip J. Cooper and Chester A. Newland, eds., *Handbook of Public Law and Administration.* San Francisco: Jossey-Bass.

Hacker, Andrew. 1992. *Two Nations: Black and White, Separate, Hostile and Unequal.* New York: Charles Scribner's Sons.

Hajdin, Mane. 1997. "Why the Fight Against Sexual Harassment Is Misguided." In Linda LeMoncheck and Mane Hajdin, eds., *Sexual Harassment: A Debate.* Lanham, MD: Rowman and Littlefield Publishers.

Hale, Mary M. 1992. "Mentoring." In Mary E. Guy, ed., *Women and Men of the States.* New York: Greenwood Press.

Hale, Mary M., and Rita Mae Kelly. 1989. *Gender, Bureaucracy, and Democracy: Careers and Equal Opportunity in the Public Sector.* New York: Greenwood Press.

Hall, Mimi. 1999. "White House's Missing Voices." *USA Today.* December 9: 1A–2A.

Halloran, Richard. 1988. "Navy Is Studying Bias in Promotions." *The New York Times.* July 24: 14.

Hamner, W. Clay, Jay S. Kim, Lloyd Baird, and William J. Bigoness. 1974. "Race and Sex as Determinants of Ratings by Potential Employers in a Simulated Work-Sampling Task." *Journal of Applied Psychology* 59 (6, October): 705–711.

Harmon, Gloria, Walter Vaughn, and Martin F. Cromwell. 1987. *Review of Disciplinary Actions in State Service.* Sacramento: State Personnel Board. June 2.

Harris, Christy. 1994. "Black Agents Suit Could Grow." *The Federal Times.* August 8.

_____. 1995. "Culture Shock: Is Diversity Training Really Curbing Bias?" *The Federal Times.* January 23.

Heilman, Madeline E. 1983. "Sex Bias in Work Settings: The Lack of Fit Model." In L. L. Cummings and Barry M. Staw, eds., *Research in Organizational Behavior*, vol. 5. Greenwich, CT: JAI Press.

_____. 1994. "Affirmative Action: Some Unintended Consequences for Working Women." In Barry M. Staw and L. L. Cummings, eds., *Research in Organizational Behavior*, vol. 16. Greenwich, CT: JAI Press.

Heilman, Madeline E., C. J. Block, and J. A. Lucas. 1992. "Presumed Incompetent? Stigmatization and Affirmative Action Efforts." *Journal of Applied Psychology* 77: 536–544.

Heilman, Madeline E., Michael C. Simon, and David P. Repper. 1987. "Intentionally Favored, Unintentionally Harmed? Impact of Sex-Based Preferential Selection on Self-Perceptions and Self-Evaluations." *Journal of Applied Psychology* 72 (1): 62–68.

Heim, Robert. 1997. "Study of Factors Relating to the Likelihood of Promotion in the Federal White-Collar Work Force. U.S. Office of Personnel Management." Unpublished manuscript. June.

Hellriegel, Don, and Larry Short. 1972. "Equal Employment Opportunity in the Federal Government: A Comparative Analysis." *Public Administration Review* 32: 851–858.

Henderson, L. J. 1979. *Administrative Advocacy: Black Administrators in Urban Bureaucracy.* Palo Alto, CA: R&E Research Associates.

Herbert, Adam W. 1974. "The Minority Administrator: Problems, Prospects, and Challenges." *Public Administration Review* 34 (6, November/December): 556–564.

Hindera, John J. 1993a. "Representative Bureaucracy: Further Evidence of Active Representation in the EEOC District Office." *Journal of Public Administration Research and Theory* 3 (4, October): 415–442.

_____. 1993b. "Representative Bureaucracy: Imprimis Evidence of Active Representation in the EEOC District Offices." *Social Science Quarterly* 74: 95–108.

Hindera, John J., and Cheryl D. Young. 1994. "Gypsies in the Palace: A Comprehensive Theory of Active Representative Bureaucracy." Paper presented to the annual meeting of the American Political Science Association, New York. September 1–4.

_____. 1998. "Representative Bureaucracy: The Theoretical Implications of Statistical Interaction." *Political Research Quarterly* 51 (3, September): 655–671.

Hochschild, Jennifer L. 1995. *Facing Up to the American Dream*. Princeton, NJ: Princeton University Press.

Hoffman, Eric. 1985. "The Effect of Race-Ratio Composition on the Frequency of Organizational Communication." *Social Psychology Quarterly* 48 (March): 17–26.

Holland, Jesse J. 1997. "Black Employees Allege Racial Bias at Forest Service." *The Washington Post*. January 2: A15.

Hopkins, Anne H. 1980. "Perceptions of Employment Discrimination in the Public Sector." *Public Administration Review* 40 (2, March/April): 131–137.

Hotelling, Kathy. 1991. "Sexual Harassment: A Problem Shielded by Silence." *Journal of Counseling and Development* 69 (July/August): 497–501.

Huckle, Patricia. 1983. "A Decade's Difference: Mid-level Managers and Affirmative Action." *Public Personnel Management* 12 (Fall): 249–257.

Hudson, J. Blaine, and Bonetta M. Hines-Hudson. 1996. "Improving Race Relations in a Public Service Agency: A Model Workshop Series." *Public Personnel Management* 25 (1): 1–12.

_____. 1999. "A Study of Contemporary Racial Attitudes of Whites and African Americans." *Western Journal of Black Studies* 23 (1, Spring): 22–34.

Hull, Jon D. 1994. "Do Teachers Punish According to Race?" *Time*. April 4: 30–31.

Hymowitz, Carol, and Timothy D. Schellhardt. 1986. "The Glass Ceiling." *The Wall Street Journal*. March 24: 1D, 4D–5D.

Hyneman, Charles S. 1950. *Bureaucracy in a Democracy*. New York: Harper & Brothers.

Ilgen, Daniel R., and Youtz, Margaret A. 1986. "Factors Affecting the Evaluation and Development of Minorities in Organizations." In Kendrith M. Rowland and Gerald R. Ferris, eds., *Research in Personnel and Human Resources Management*, vol 4. Greenwich, CT: JAI Press.

Irvine, Diane, and G. Ross Baker. 1995. "The Impact of Cross-Functional Teamwork on Workforce Integration." *International Journal of Conflict Management* 6 (2): 171–191.

Jacobson, Cardell K. 1983. "Black Support for Affirmative Action Programs." *Phylon* 44 (4): 299–311.

Jackson, Susan E., Veronica K. Stone, and Eden B. Alvarez. 1993. "Socialization Amidst Diversity: The Impact of Demographics on Work Team Old-timers and Newcomers." In L. L. Cummings and Barry M. Staw, eds., *Research in Organizational Behavior*, vol. 15. Greenwich, CT: JAI Press, pp. 45–109.

Jackson, Susan E., Karen E. May, and Kristina Whitney. 1995. "Understanding the Dynamics of Diversity on Decision-Making Teams." In Richard A. Guzzo et al., eds., *Team Effectiveness and Decision Making in Organizations*. San Francisco: Jossey-Bass.

Jackson, Susan E., et al. 1991. "Some Differences Make a Difference: Individual Dissimilarity and Heterogeneity as Correlates of Recruitment, Promotions and Turnover." *Journal of Applied Psychology* 76 (5, October): 675–689.

James, K., C. Lovato, and R. Cropanzano. 1994. "Correlational and Known-Group Comparison Validation of a Workplace Prejudice/Discrimination Inventory." *Journal of Applied Psychology* 24: 1573–1592.

James, Keith, Willie Wolf, Chris Lovato, and Steve Byers. Undated. "Barriers to Workplace Advancement Experienced by Native Americans." Paper prepared for the Federal Glass Ceiling Commission, U.S. Department of Labor, Washington, DC.

Jennings, Veronica T. 1993. "Blacks Describe How Bias Hurt Their Careers at NIH." *The Washington Post*. August 10: A1.

Johnson, Cathy M., and Georgia Duerst-Lahti. 1992. "Public Work, Private Lives." In Mary E. Guy, ed., *Women and Men of the States*. Armonk, NY: M. E. Sharpe.

Johnston, William B., and Arnold E. Packer. 1987. *Workforce 2000: Work and Workers for the 21st Century*. Indianapolis: Hudson Institute.

Johnston, William B., et al. 1988. *Civil Service 2000*. Washington, DC: U.S. Office of Personnel Management.

Jones, Tricia S., Martin S. Remland, and Claire C. Brunner. 1987. "Effects of Employment Relationship on Response of Recipient and Sex of Rater on Perceptions of Sexual Harassment." *Perceptual and Motor Skills* 65: 55–63.

Jones-Wilson, Faustine C. 1990. "Race, Realities, and American Education: Two Sides of the Coin." *Journal of Negro Education* 59 (2): 119–128.

Jordan, Katrina. 1998. "Diversity Training in the Workplace Today: A Status Report." *Journal of Career Planning and Employment*, Fall: 48–51, 61–64.

Judiesch, Michael K., and Karen S Lyness. 1999. "Left Behind? The Impact of Leaves of Absence on Managers' Career Success." *Academy of Management Journal* 42 (6, December): 641–651.

Judy, Richard W., and Carol D'Amico. 1997. *Workforce 2020*. Indianapolis: Hudson Institute.

Kanter, Rosabeth Moss. 1977. *Men and Women of the Corporation*. New York: Basic Books.

Kaplan, Sally J. 1991. "Consequences of Sexual Harassment in the Workplace." *Affilia* 6 (3, Fall): 50–65.

Katz Pinzler, Isabelle. 1997. "The Future of Equal Opportunity Policy in the Public Sector." Address to the Brookings Institution Seminar on Federal Civil Service and Labor Management Reform, Washington, DC. May 14.

Kaufman, Leslie. 1994. "Painfully Aware." *Government Executive* 26: 16–22.

_____. 1999. "Some Companies Derail the 'Burnout' Track." *The New York Times*. May 4: A1, C8.

Kellough, J. Edward. 1989. "The 1978 Civil Service Reform and Federal Equal Employment Opportunity." *American Review of Public Administration* 19: 313–324.

_____. 1990. "Integration in the Public Workplace: Determinants of Minority and Female Employment in Federal Agencies." *Public Administration Review* 50: 557–566.

_____. 1992. "Affirmative Action in Government Employment." *Annals of the American Academy of Political Science* 523: 117–130.

Kellough, J. E., and Susan Ann Kay. 1986. "Affirmative Action in the Federal Bureaucracy: An Impact Assessment." *Review of Public Personnel Administration* 6: 1–13.

Kellough, J. Edward, and Will Osuna. 1995. "Cross-Agency Comparisons of Quit Rates in the Federal Service." *Review of Public Personnel Administration* 25 (4, Fall): 58–68.

Kellough, J. E., and David H. Rosenbloom. 1992. "Representative Bureaucracy and the EEOC: Did the Civil Service Reform Act Make a Difference?" In Patricia Ingraham and David Rosenbloom, eds., *The Promise and Paradox of Civil Service Reform.* Pittsburgh: University of Pittsburgh Press.

Kelly, Rita Mae. 1995. "Offensive Men, Defensive Women: Sexual Harassment, Leadership, and Management." In Georgia Duerst-Lahti and Rita Mae Kelly, eds., *Gender Power, Leadership and Governance.* Ann Arbor: University of Michigan Press.

Kelly, Rita Mae, and Phoebe Stambaugh. 1992. "Sexual Harassment in the States." In Mary E. Guy, ed., *Women and Men of the States.* Armonk, NY: M. E. Sharpe.

Kelly, Rita Mae, Mary E. Guy, Jane Bayes, and Cathy Johnson. 1991. "Public Managers in the States: A Comparison of Career Advancement by Sex." *Public Administration Review* 51 (5, September/October): 402–412.

Kennelly, Ivy. 1999. "'That Single-Mother Element': How White Employers Typify Black Women." *Gender and Society* 13 (2, April): 168–192.

Kilborn, Peter T. 1999. "Bias Worsens for Minorities Buying Homes." *The New York Times.* September 16: A15.

Kim, Pan Suk, and Gregory B. Lewis. 1994. "Asian Americans in the Public Service: Success, Diversity, and Discrimination." *Public Administration Review* 54 (3, May/June): 285–290.

King, Desmond. 1995. *Separate and Unequal.* Oxford: Clarendon Press.

Kingsley, J. Donald. 1944. *Representative Bureaucracy: An Interpretation of the British Civil Service.* Yellow Springs, OH: The Antioch Press.

Kirkpatrick, Donald L. 1998. *Evaluating Training Programs: The Four Levels.* 2nd ed. San Francisco: Berrett-Koehler.

Kirschenman, Joleen, and Kathryn M. Neckerman. 1991. "'We'd Love to Hire Them, But . . .': The Meaning of Race for Employers." In Christopher Jenks and Paul E. Peterson, eds., *The Urban Underclass.* Washington, DC: The Brookings Institution.

Kluegel, James R., and Eliot R. Smith. 1983. "Affirmative Action Attitudes: Effects of Self-interest, Racial Affect and Stratification Beliefs on Whites' Views." *Social Forces* 61 (March): 796–822.

Konrad, Alison M., and Barbara A. Gutek. 1986. "Impact of Work Experiences on Attitudes Toward Sexual Harassment." *Administrative Science Quarterly* 31: 422–438.

Koss, Mary P. 1990. "Changed Lives: The Psychological Impact of Sexual Harassment." In Michele A. Paludi, ed., *Ivory Power: Sexual Harassment on Campus*. Albany: State University of New York Press.

Kraiger, Kurt, and J. Kevin Ford. 1985. "A Meta-Analysis of Ratee Race Effects in Performance Ratings." *Journal of Applied Psychology* 70 (February): 56–65.

Kranz, Harry. 1974. "Are Merit and Equity Compatible?" *Public Administration Review* 34 (September/October): 434–441.

Kravitz, David A., and Judith Platania. 1993. "Attitudes and Beliefs About Affirmative Action." *Journal of Applied Psychology* 78 (6): 928–938.

Krislov, Samuel. 1967. *The Negro in Federal Employment*. Minneapolis: University of Minnesota Press.

_____. 1974. *Representative Bureaucracy*. Englewood Cliffs, NJ: Prentice-Hall.

Krislov, Samuel, and David H. Rosenbloom. 1981. *Representative Bureaucracy and the American Political System*. New York: Praeger Publishers.

Larson, Arthur D. 1973. "Representative Bureaucracy and Administrative Responsibility: A Reassessment." *Midwest Review of Public Administration* 7 (April): 79–89.

Larson, Ruth. 1993. "Agriculture Agency Queried on Memo Indicating Quotas." *The Washington Times*. November 24: A–8.

_____. 1994a. "FAA to Pay for Trauma of Groping Gantlets." *The Washington Times*. September 23.

_____. 1994b. "FAA Men Charge 'Tailhook II.'" *The Washington Times*. September 8.

_____. 1995. "FAA Puts Diversity Above Qualifications." *The Washington Times*. August 16.

Larwood, Laurie, Eugene Szwajkowski, and Suzanna Rose. 1988. "Sex and Race Discrimination Resulting from Manager-Client Relationships: Applying Rational Bias Theory of Managerial Discrimination." *Sex Roles* 18 (1-2): 9–29.

Laurent, Anne. 1996. "The Great Divide." *Government Executive* 28: 12–22.

Lawn-Day, Gayle A., and Steven Ballard. 1996. "Speaking Out: Perceptions of Women Managers in the Civil Service." *Review of Public Personnel Administration* 16 (1, Winter): 41–53.

Lee, Robert D., Jr., and Paul S. Greenlaw. 1995. "The Legal Evolution of Sexual Harassment." *Public Administration Review* 55 (4, July/August): 357–363.

_____. 1996. "The Complexities of Human Behavior." *Review of Public Personnel Administration* 16 (4, Fall): 15–28.

Lee, S. J. 1995. *Testimony on the "Equal Opportunity Act of 1995" before the Subcommittee on the Constitution, Committee on the Judiciary, U.S. House of Representatives*. 104th Cong., 1st sess., December 7.

LeMonchek, Linda. 1997. "Taunted and Tormented or Savvy and Seductive." In Linda LeMoncheck and Mane Hajdin, eds., *Sexual Harassment: A Debate*. Lanham, MD: Rowman and Littlefield Publishers.

Leonard, Jonathan S. 1994. "Use of Enforcement Techniques in Eliminating Glass Ceiling Barriers." Report prepared for the Federal Glass Ceiling Commission. April.

Levine, Charles H. 1974. "Beyond the Sound and Fury of Targets." *Public Administration Review* 34 (May/June): 240–241.

Levitan, David M. 1946. "The Responsibility of Administrative Officials in a Democratic Society." *Political Science Quarterly* 61 (December): 562–598.

Lewin, Tamar. 1994. "Men Whose Wives Work Earn Less, Studies Show." *The New York Times*. October 12: A1.

Lewis, Diane. 1993. "Some Women Find Themselves Penalized for Having Babies, Outside Interests." *The Washington Post*. August 8: H2.

Lewis, Gregory B. 1986a. "Equal Employment Opportunity and the Early Career in Federal Employment." *Review of Public Personnel Administration* 6 (Summer): 1–18.

_____. 1986b. "Race, Sex and Supervisory Authority in Federal White-Collar Employment." *Public Administration Review* 46 (January/February): 25–30.

_____. 1986c. "Gender and Promotions: Promotion Chances of White Men and Women in Federal White-Collar Employment." *Journal of Human Resources* 21: 406–419.

_____. 1987. "Changing Patterns of Sexual Discrimination in Federal Employment." *Review of Public Personnel Administration* 7: 1–13.

_____. 1988. "Progress Toward Racial and Sexual Equality in the Federal Civil Service?" *Public Administration Review* 48 (May/June): 700–707.

_____. 1992. "Men and Women Toward the Top: Backgrounds, Careers, and Potential of Federal Middle Managers." *Public Personnel Management* 21 (4, Winter): 473–485.

_____. 1995. "Federal Pay Inside and Outside the Beltway: Why Do Federal Employees Earn More in Headquarters?" *Review of Public Personnel Administration* 25 (Fall): 37–57.

_____. 1997. "Race, Sex and Performance Ratings in the Federal Service." *Public Administration Review* 57 (6, November/December): 479–489.

_____. 1998. "Continuing Progress Toward Racial and Gender Pay Equality in the Federal Service." *Review of Public Personnel Administration* 17 (2, Spring): 23–40.

Lewis, Gregory B., and Pan Suk Kim. 1997. "Asian Americans in the Federal Service: Education, Occupational Choice, and Perceptions of Discrimination: A Reply." *Public Administration Review* 57 (3, May/June): 267–269.

Lindenberg, Karen E., and Laura A. Reese. 1995. "Sexual Harassment Policy Implementation Issues: Learning from a Public Higher Education Case Study." *Review of Public Personnel Administration* 15 (1, Winter): 84–97.

Lipset, S. M., and W. Schneider. 1978. "The Bakke Decision: How Would It Be Decided at the Bar of Public Opinion?" *Public Opinion* 1: 38–44.

Long, James E. 1976. "Employment Discrimination in the Federal Sector." *Journal of Human Resources* 17 (Winter): 86–97.

Long, Norton E. 1952. "Bureaucracy and Constitutionalism." *American Political Science Review* 46 (September): 808–818.

Loury, Glenn C. 1992. "Incentive Effects of Affirmative Action." *Annals of the American Academy* 523 (September): 19–29.

Love, Alice A. 1999. "Black Men Allege Bias at SSA." *The Washington Post*. April 20: A21.

Lynch, Frederick R. 1997. *The Diversity Machine*. New York: The Free Press.

Major, B., J. Feinstein, and J. Crocker. 1994. "Attributional Ambiguity and Affirmative Action." *Basic and Applied Social Psychology* 15: 113–141.

Major, Brenda, and Toni Schmader. 1998. "Coping with Stigma Through Psychological Disengagement." In Janet K. Swim and Charles Stangor, eds., *Prejudice: The Targets Perspective*. San Diego: Academic Press.

Maluso, Diane. 1995. "Shaking Hands with a Clenched Fist: Interpersonal Racism." In Bernice Lott and Diane Maluso, eds., *The Social Psychology of Interpersonal Racism*. New York: The Guildord Press.

Mamman, Aminu. 1996. "A Diverse Employee in a Changing Workplace." *Organization Studies* 17 (3, Summer): 449–478.

Markham, William T., Patrick O. Macken, Charles M. Bonjean, and Judy Corder. 1983. "A Note on Sex, Geographic Mobility and Career Advancement." *Social Forces* 61 (4, June): 1138–1146.

Mathews, Audrey. 1998. "Diversity: A Principle of Human Resource Management." *Public Personnel Management* 27 (2): 175–186.

Maume, David J., Jr. 1999. "Glass Ceilings and Glass Escalators." *Work and Occupations* 26 (4, November): 483–509.

Mauricio Gaston Institute for Latino Community Development and Public Policy. 1994. "Barriers to the Employment and Work-Place Advancement of Latinos." Paper prepared for the Federal Glass Ceiling Commission, U.S. Department of Labor. August.

Mayo, Margarita C., James R. Meindl, and Juan-Carlos Pastor. 1996. "The Cost of Leading Diversity: Effects of Group Diversity on Leaders' Perceptions." In Marian N. Ruderman, Martha W. Hughes-James, and Susan E. Jackson, eds., *Selected Research on Work Team Diversity*. Washington, DC: American Psychological Association.

Meier, Kenneth J. 1975. "Representative Bureaucracy: An Empirical Assessment." *American Political Science Review* 69 (2, June): 526–542.

_____. 1984. "Teachers, Students and Discrimination: The Policy Impact of Black Representation," *Journal of Politics* 46 (1): 252–263.

_____. 1993a. "Latinos and Representative Bureaucracy: Testing the Thompson and Henderson Hypotheses." *Journal of Public Administration Research and Theory* 3 (4): 393–414.

_____.1993b. "Latinos and Representative Bureaucracy." *Journal of Public Administration Research and Theory* 3 (4): 393–414.

Meier, Kenneth J., and Robert E. England. 1984. "Black Representation and Educational Policy: Are They Related?" *American Political Science Review* 78 (June): 392–403.

Meier, Kenneth J., and Lloyd G. Nigro. 1976. "Representative Bureaucracy and Policy Preferences: A Study in the Attitudes of Federal Executives." *Public Administration Review* 36 (July/August): 458–469.

Meier, Kenneth J., and Kevin B. Smith. 1994. "Representative Democracy and Representative Bureaucracy: Examining the Top-Down and Bottom-Up Linkages." *Social Science Quarterly* 75 (4, December): 790–803.

Meier, Kenneth J., and Joseph Stewart Jr. 1991. *The Politics of Hispanic Education*. Albany: State University of New York Press.

Meier, Kenneth J., Joseph Stewart Jr., and Robert E. England. 1989. *Race, Class, and Education: The Politics of Second-Generation Discrimination*. Madison: University of Wisconsin Press.

Merida, Kevin. 1995. "Study Finds Little Evidence of Reverse Discrimination." *The Washington Post*. March 31: AO2.

Meyerson, Debra E., and Joyce K Fletcher. 2000. "A Modest Manifesto for Shattering the Glass Ceiling." *Harvard Business Review* 78 (1, January/ February): 126–136.

Mills, Nicolaus. 1994. "Introduction: To Look Like America." In Nicolaus Mills, ed., *Debating Affirmative Action*. New York: Delta.

Milward, H. Brinton, and Cheryl Swanson. 1979. "Organizational Response to Environmental Pressures: the Policy of Affirmative Action." *Administration and Society* 11: 123–143.

Mishel, Lawrence, and Ruy A. Teixera. 1991. *The Myth of the Coming Labor Shortage: Jobs, Skills, and Incomes of America's Workforce 2000*. Washington, DC: Economic Policy Institute.

Mohrman, Susan A., Jay A. Galbraith, and Edward E. Lawler III. 1998. *Tomorrow's Organization*. San Francisco: Jossey-Bass.

Moore, Gwen. 1992. "Gender and Informal Networks in State Government." *Social Science Quarterly* 73 (1, March): 46–61.

Morin, Richard. 1995. "A Distorted Image of Minorities." *The Washington Post*. October 8: A1, A27–28.

Morrison, Ann M. 1992. *The New Leaders: Guidelines on Leadership Diversity in America*. San Francisco: Jossey-Bass.

Morrison, Ann M., and M. A. von Glinow. 1990. "Women and Minorities in Management." *American Psychologist* 45 (2): 200–208.

Morrison, Ann M., Randall P. White, and Ellen vanVelsor. 1987. *Breaking the Glass Ceiling*. Reading, MA: Addison-Wesley.

Morrow, Paul C., James C. McElroy, and Catharine M. Phillips. 1994. "Sexual Harassment Behaviors and Work Related Perceptions and Attitudes." *Journal of Vocational Behavior* 45 (3, December): 295–309.

Mosher, Frederick C. 1968. *Democracy and the Public Service*. New York: Oxford University Press.

_____. 1982. *Democracy and the Public Service*. 2nd ed. New York: Oxford University Press.

Moskos, Charles C., and John Sibley Butler. 1996. *All That We Can Be: Black Leadership and Racial Integration in the Army*. New York: Basic Books.

Moynahan, Brigid. 1993. "Creating Harassment-Free Work Zones." *Training and Development* 47 (5): 67–70.

Murray, Sylvester, Larry D. Terry, Charles A. Washington, and Lawrence F. Keller. 1994. "The Role Demands and Dilemmas of Minority Public Administrators: The Herbert Thesis Revisited." *Public Administration Review* 54 (5, September/ October): 409–417.

Murrell, Audrey J., Josephine E. Olson, and Irene Hanson Frieze. 1995. "Sexual Harassment and Gender Discrimination: A Longitudinal Study of Women Managers." *Journal of Social Issues* 51 (1, Spring): 139–149.

Nachmias, David, and David H. Rosenbloom. 1973. "Measuring Bureaucratic Representation and Integration." *Public Administration Review* 33 (November/ December): 590–596.

Nacoste, Rupert W., and Beth Hummels. 1994. "Affirmative Action and the Behavior of Decision Makers." *Journal of Applied Social Psychology* 24 (7): 595–613.

Nadler, David A., Marc S. Gerstein, and Robert B. Shaw. 1992. *Organizational Architecture: Designs for Changing Organizations*. San Francisco: Jossey Bass.

Naff, Katherine C. 1994. "Through the Glass Ceiling: Prospects for the Advancement of Women in the Federal Government." *Public Administration Review* 54 (November/December): 507–514.

_____. 1995. "Perceptions of Discrimination: Moving Beyond the Numbers of Representative Bureaucracy." *Policy Studies Journal* 23 (3): 483–498.

Naff, Katherine C., and Sue Thomas. 1994. "The Glass Ceiling Revisited: Determinants of Federal Job Advancement." *Policy Studies Review* 23 (Autumn/Winter): 249–269.

National Aeronautics and Space Administration (NASA). 1994. *Equal Opportunity and Diversity Management Plan*. Washington, DC: NASA. May 1.

National EEO Task Force Report. 1991. Washington, DC: National Treasury Employees Union and U.S. Internal Revenue Service. April.

National EEO Task Force Report. 1993. Washington, DC: National Treasury Employees Union and U.S. Internal Revenue Service. April.

National Institutes of Health. Undated. "Managing Diversity, Equal Employment Opportunity and Affirmative Action." http://www1.od.nih.gov.ohrm/oeo/wdi/wdieeaad.htm.

National Performance Review. 1993. *From Red Tape to Results: Creating a Government That Works Better and Costs Less*. Washington, DC: Office of the Vice President. September 7.

Newell, Sue. 1992. "The Myth and Destructiveness of Equal Opportunities." *Personnel Review* 21 (4): 37–47.

Newlin, Eliza. 1991. "Doing What Feds Say, Not What Feds Do." *National Journal* 25 (June 22): 1570–1572.

Newman, Meredith A. 1993. "Career Advancement: Does Gender Make a Difference?" *American Review of Public Administration* 23 (4, December): 361–384.

Newman, Meredith A., and Kay Matthews. 1999. "Federal Family-Friendly Workplace Policies." *Review of Public Personnel Administration* 16 (3, Summer): 34–48.

Norton, J. Renae, and Ronald E. Fox. 1997. *The Change Equation: Capitalizing on Diversity for Effective Organizational Change*. Washington, DC: American Psychological Association.

Office of the Vice President. 1993. *Reinventing Human Resource Management: Accompanying Report of the National Performance Review*. Washington, DC: Office of the Vice President.

Ogul, Morris S. 1976. *Congress Oversees the Bureaucracy*. Pittsburgh: University of Pittsburgh Press.

Ospina, Sonia. 1996. *Illusions of Opportunity: Employee Expectations and Workplace Inequality*. Ithaca, NY: Cornell University Press.

Pachon, Henry P. 1988. "Hispanic Underrepresentation in the Federal Bureaucracy: The Missing Link in the Policy Process." In F. Chris Garcia, ed., *Latinos and the Political System*. Notre Dame, IN: University of Notre Dame Press.

Page, Paul. 1994. "African-Americans in Executive Branch Agencies." *Review of Public Personnel Administration* 19 (Winter): 24–51.

Palguta, John M. 2000. "Director's Perspective: The Real Challenge in Workforce Diversity." *Issues of Merit*. June: 1–2.

Patterson, Orlando. 1997. *The Ordeal of Integration: Progress and Resentment in America's "Racial" Class.* Washington, DC: Counterpoint.

Paulin, Elizabeth A., and Jennifer M. Mellor. 1996. "Gender, Race, and Promotions Within a Private Sector Firm." *Industrial Relations* 35 (2, April): 276–295.

Payne, Richard J. 1998. *Getting Beyond Race: The Changing American Culture.* Boulder, CO: Westview Press.

Perman, Florence. 1988. "The Players and Problems in the EEO Enforcement Process: A Status Report." *Public Administration Review* 48: 827–833.

Peterson, Randall S. 1994. "The Role of Values in Predicting Fairness Judgments and Support of Affirmative Action." *Journal of Social Issues* 50 (Winter): 95–115.

Pettigrew, Thomas F. 1979. "Racial Change and Social Policy." *American Academy of Political and Social Science* 441 (January): 114–131.

Pettigrew, Thomas F., and Joanne Martin. 1987. "Shaping the Organizational Context for Black American Inclusion." *Journal of Social Issues* 43 (1): 41–78.

Pierce, Greg. 1993. "Federal Minority Workers Fired at Much Higher Rates Than Whites." *The Washington Times.* December 21.

Pitkin, Hannah. 1969. *Representation.* New York: Atherton Press.

Plous, S., and Tyrone Williams. 1995. "Racial Stereotypes from the Days of American Slavery: A Continuing Legacy." *Journal of Applied Social Psychology* 25 (9, May 1–15): 795–817.

Pomerleau, Raymond. 1994. "A Desideratum for Managing the Diverse Workplace." *Review of Public Personnel Administration* 19 (Winter): 85–100.

Powell, Gary N., and D. Anthony Butterfield. 1994. "Investigating the 'Glass Ceiling' Phenomenon: An Empirical Study of Actual Promotions to Top Management." *Academy of Management Journal* 37 (1): 68–86.

Price, Don K. 1946. "Legislative-Executive Relations." In Fritz Morstein Marx, ed., *Elements of Public Administration.* New York: Prentice-Hall.

"Racial Disparity Found in Firings of U.S. Workers." 1993. *Arizona Republic.* December 15.

"Racial Disparity Seen in Firings of Federal Workers." 1993. *Dallas Morning News.* December 14.

"Racial Segregation in Education as an Art Form." 1994. *Journal of Blacks in Higher Education* 3 (Spring): 14–15.

Ransford, H. Edward, and Jon Miller. 1983. "Race, Sex and Feminist Outlooks." *American Sociological Review* 48 (February): 46–59.

"Records Show Federal Firing Bias." 1993. *Philadelphia Inquirer.* December 14: A12.

Reese, Laura A., and Karen E. Lindenberg. 1997. "'Victimhood' and the Implementation of Sexual Harassment Policy." *Review of Public Personnel Administration* 17 (1, Winter): 37–57.

———. 1999. *Implementing Sexual Harassment Policy: Challenges for the Public Sector Workplace.* Thousand Oaks, CA: Sage Publications.

Rehfuss, John A. 1986. "A Representative Bureaucracy? Women and Minority Executives in California Career Service." *Public Administration Review* 46 (September/October): 454–460.

Riger, Stephanie. 1991. "Gender Dilemmas in Sexual Harassment Policies and Procedures." *American Psychologist* 46 (5): 497–505.

Riordan, Christine M., and Lynn M. Shore. 1997. "Demographic Diversity and Employee Attitudes: An Empirical Examination of Relational Demography Within Work Units." *Journal of Applied Psychology* 82 (3): 342–358.

Rivenbark, Leigh. 1994a. "Bias Alive at NIH, Employees Claim." *Federal Times*. November 28.

_____.1994b. "More Bias Charges at Justice." *Federal Times*. May 9.

_____. 1994c. "Blacks Say Racism Common." *Federal Times*. November 7.

Robinson, Edward, and Jonathan Hickman. 1999. "The Diversity Elite." *Fortune*. July 19: 62.

Robinson, Robert K., Billie M. Allen, and Yohannan T. Abraham. 1992. "Affirmative Action Plans in the 1990s: A Double-Edged Sword?" *Public Personnel Management* 21 (Summer): 261–272.

Rogelberg, Steven G., and Steven M. Rumery. 1996. "Gender Diversity, Team Decision Quality, Time on Task, and Interpersonal Cohesion." *Small Group Research* 27 (1): 79–90.

Rosen, Benson, and Thomas H. Jerdee. 1974. "Sex Stereotyping in the Executive Suite." *Harvard Business Review* 52 (2, March/April): 45–58.

Rosenbaum, James E. 1979. "Career Paths and Advancement Opportunities." In Rodolfo Alvarez, Kenneth G. Lutterman, and Associates, eds., *Discrimination in Organizations*. San Francisco: Jossey-Bass.

Rosenbloom, David H. 1971. *Federal Service and the Constitution*. Ithaca, NY: Cornell University Press.

_____. 1975. "Implementing Equal Employment Opportunity Goals and Timetables in the Federal Service." *Midwest Review of Public Administration* 9 (2/3): 107–119.

_____. 1977. *Federal Equal Employment Opportunity: Politics and Public Personnel Administration*. New York: Praeger.

_____. 1981. "Federal Equal Employment Opportunity: Is the Polarization Worth the Preference?" *Southern Review of Public Administration* 5 (Spring): 63–72.

_____.1984a. "The Declining Salience of Affirmative Action in Federal Personnel Management." *Review of Public Personnel Administration* 4 (Summer): 31–40.

_____. 1984b. "What Have Policy Studies Told Us About Affirmative Action and Where Can We Go from Here?" *Policy Studies Review* 4: 43–48.

Rosenbloom, David H., and Jeanette G. Featherstonhaugh. 1977. "Passive and Active Representation in the Federal Civil Service: A Comparison of Blacks and Whites." *Social Science Quarterly* 57 (March): 873–882.

Rowe, Mary P. 1990. "Barriers to Equality: The Power of Subtle Discrimination to Maintain Unequal Opportunity." *Employee Responsibilities and Rights Journal* 3 (2): 153–163.

Rubaii-Barrett, Nadia, and Ann C. Beck. 1993. "Minorities in the Majority: Implications for Managing Cultural Diversity." *Public Personnel Management* 22 (Winter): 503–521.

Ruble, Thomas L., Renae Cohen, and Diane N. Ruble. 1984. "Sex Stereotypes: Occupational Barriers for Women." *American Behavioral Scientist* 27 (January/February): 339–356.

Russell Sage Foundation. 1999. "Major RSF Program Shows How Race Affects Job Prospects in U.S." http://www.russellsage.org/special_interest/race.htm.

Rutte, Christel G., and David M. Messick. 1995. "An Integrated Model of Perceived Unfairness in Organizations." *Social Justice Research* 8 (3): 239–261.

Sackett, Paul R., Cathy L. Z. DuBois, and Ann Wiggins Noe. 1991. "Tokenism in Performance Evaluation: The Effects of Work Group Representation on Male-Female and White-Black Differences in Performance Ratings." *Journal of Applied Psychology* 76 (2): 263–267.

Salzstein, Grace Hall. 1979. "Representative Bureaucracy and Bureaucratic Responsibility: Problems and Prospects." *Administration and Society* 10 (February): 465–475.

Sandroff, Ronni. 1992. "Sexual Harassment: The Inside Story." *Working Woman* 17 (June): 47–51.

Savage, David G., and Maura Dolan. 1995. "Clinton Vows He'll Fight to Regain Affirmative Action." *Los Angeles Times.* June 14: A1.

Sayre, Wallace S. 1965. *The Federal Government Service.* Englewood Cliffs, NJ: Prentice-Hall.

Scarborough, Rowan. 1994. "Navy Officers Balk at Pro-Gay Seminar." *The Washington Times.* September 4.

Scher, Seymour. 1963. "Conditions for Legislative Control." *Journal of Politics* 25 (August): 526–551.

Schmidt, John R. 1996. "Post-*Adarand* Guidance on Affirmative Action in Federal Employment." Washington, DC: U.S. Department of Justice. February 29.

Schneider, Kimberly T., Suzanne Swan, and Louise F. Fitzgerald. 1997. "Job-Related and Psychological Effects of Sexual Harassment in the Workplace: Empirical Evidence from Two Organizations." *Journal of Applied Psychology* 82 (3, June): 401–415.

Schrage, Michael. 1990. *No More Teams: Mastering the Dynamics of Creative Collaboration.* New York: Currency Doubleday.

Schwartz, Debra B. 1994. "An Examination of the Impact of the Family-Friendly Policies on the Glass Ceiling: Final Report." Paper prepared for the Glass Ceiling Commission, U.S. Department of Labor. January.

Schwartz, Felice N. 1989. "Management, Women and the New Facts of Life." *Harvard Business Review* 67: 65–76.

Schwartz, Peter, and Blair Gibb. 1999. *When Good Companies Do Bad Things.* New York: John Wiley.

Scott, James M., and Elizabeth A. Rexford. 1997. "Finding a Place for Women in the World of Diplomacy." *Review of Public Personnel Administration* 17 (2): 31–56.

Scott, Peter. 1999. "Black Farmers Settle Racial Bias Suit." *The Atlanta Constitution.* April 15: 4b.

Selden, Sally Coleman. 1997a. "Representative Bureaucracy: Examining the Linkage Between Passive and Active Representation in the Farmers Home Administration." *American Review of Public Administration* 27 (1, March): 22–42.

_____.1997b. *The Promise of Representative Bureaucracy.* Armonk, NY: M. E. Sharpe.

Sharpe, Rochelle. 1994. "Family Friendly Firms Don't Always Promote Females." *The Wall Street Journal.* March 29: B1, B5.

Sherman, Martin F., Robert J. Smith, and Nancy C. Sherman. 1983. "Racial and Gender Differences in Perceptions of Fairness: When Race Is Involved in a Job Promotion." *Perceptual and Motor Skills* 57: 719–728.

Shipler, David K. 1997. *A Country of Strangers: Blacks and Whites in America.* New York: Alfred A. Knopf.

Shull, Steven A. 1993. *A Kinder, Gentler Racism?* Armonk, NY: M. E. Sharpe.

Sigelman, Lee, and Susan Welch. 1991. *Black Americans' View of Racial Inequality.* Cambridge: Cambridge University Press.

Sisneros, Antonio. 1992. "Hispanics in the Senior Executive Service: Continuity and Change in the Decade 1980–1990." *Review of Public Personnel Administration* 12 (January/February): 5–25.

Slack, James D. 1987. "Affirmative Action and City Managers: Attitudes Toward Recruitment of Women." *Public Administration Review* 47 (March/April): 199–206.

Sniderman, Paul M., and Thomas Piazza. 1993. *The Scar of Race.* Cambridge, MA: Belknap Press.

Society for Human Resource Management/Commerce Clearing House, Inc. (SHRM/CCH). 1993. *1993 SHRM/CCH Survey.* Chicago: Commerce Clearing House.

Solomon, Denise Haunani, and Mary Lynn Miller Williams. 1997. "Perceptions of Social-Sexual Communication at Work: The Effects of Message, Situation and Observer Characteristics on Judgments of Sexual Harassment." *Journal of Applied Communication Research* 25 (3, August): 196–216.

Sorenson Aage B., and Sarah Fuerst. 1978. "Black-White Differences in the Occurrence of Job Shifts." *Sociology and Social Research* 62 (4): 537–567.

Spencer, Steven J., Claude M. Steele, and Diane M. Quinn. 1999. "Stereotype Threat and Women's Math Performance." *Journal of Experimental Social Psychology* 35 (2, January): 4–28.

Steele, Claude M. 1999. "Thin Ice: 'Stereotype Threat' and Black College Students." *The Atlantic Monthly* 284 (2, August): 44–54.

Steele, Claude M., and Joshua Aronson. 1995. "Stereotype Threat and the Intellectual Test Performance of African Americans." *Journal of Personality and Social Psychology* 69 (5, November): 797–811.

Steele, Shelby. 1990. *The Content of Our Character: A New Vision of Race in America.* New York: St. Martin's Press.

Stein, Lana. 1986. "Representative Local Government: Minorities in the Municipal Workforce." *Journal of Politics* 48 (August): 694–711.

Steinberg, R. J., L. Haignere, and C. Chertos. 1990. "Managerial Promotions in the Public Sector: The Impact of Eligibility Requirements on Women and Minorities." *Work and Occupations* 17: 284–301.

Stetson, Dorothy M. 1997. *Women's Rights in the USA.* 2nd ed. New York: Garland Publishing.

Storing, Herbert J. 1964. "Political Parties and the Bureaucracy." In Robert A. Goldwin, ed., *Political Parties, U.S.A.* Chicago: Rand McNally.

Stringer, Donna M., Helen Remick, Jan Salisbury, and Angela B. Ginorio. 1990. "The Power and Reasons Behind Sexual Harassment: An Employer's Guide to Solutions." *Public Personnel Management* 19 (1, Spring): 43–53.

Stroh, Linda K., Jeanne M. Brett, and Anne H. Reilly. 1992. "All the Right Stuff: A Comparison of Female and Male Managers' Career Progression." *Journal of Applied Psychology* 77 (3): 251–260.

Subramanian, V. 1967. "Representative Bureaucracy: A Reassessment." *American Political Science Review* 61 (December): 1010–1019.

Summers, Russell J. 1991. "Determinants of Judgments of and Responses to a Complaint of Sexual Harassment." *Sex Roles* 25 (7/8): 379–392.

Swim, Janet K., and Lauri L. Hyers. 1999. "Excuse Me—What Did You Just Say?!: Women's Public and Private Responses to Sexist Remarks." *Journal of Experimental and Social Psychology* 35 (January): 68–88.

Swim, Janet K., Laurie L. Cohen, and Lauri L. Hyers. 1998. "Experiencing Everyday Prejudice and Discrimination." In Janet K. Swim and Charles Stangor, eds., *Prejudice: The Target's Perspective*. San Diego: Academic Press.

Swoboda, Frank. 1994. "Labor Department Settles Lawsuit by Black Employees." *The Washington Post*. September 30: A27.

Tata, Jasmine. 1993. "The Structure and Phenomenon of Sexual Harassment: Impact of Category of Sexually Harassing Behavior, Gender and Hierarchical Level." *Journal of Applied Social Psychology* 23 (3): 199–211.

Taylor, Marylee C. 1994. "Impact of Affirmative Action on Beneficiary Groups: Evidence From the 1990 General Social Survey." *Basic and Applied Social Psychology* 15: 143–178.

Taylor, Maurice C., and Gerald A. Foster. 1986. "Bad Boys and School Suspensions: Public Policy Implications for Black Males." *Sociological Inquiry* 56 (4, Fall): 498–506.

Taylor, Patricia A. 1979. "Income Inequality in the Federal Civilian Government." *American Sociological Review* 44 (June): 468–479.

Terborg, James R. 1977. "Women in Management: A Research Review." *Journal of Applied Psychology* 62 (6): 647–664.

Thacker, Rebecca A. 1992. "Preventing Sexual Harassment in the Workplace." *Training and Development* 46 (2, February): 51–53.

Thacker, Rebecca A., and Stephen F. Gohmann. 1993. "Male/Female Differences in Perceptions and Effects of Hostile Environment Sexual Harassment: 'Reasonable' Assumptions?" *Public Personnel Management* 22 (3, Fall): 461–472.

Thernstrom, Stephan, and Abigail Thernstrom. 1997. *America in Black and White: One Nation, Indivisible*. New York: Simon & Schuster.

Thielemann, Gregory S., and Joseph Stewart Jr. 1996. "A Demand-Side Perspective on the Importance of Representative Bureaucracy: AIDS, Ethnicity, Gender, and Sexual Orientation." *Public Administration Review* 56 (2, March/April): 168–173.

Thomas, David A., and Clayton P. Alderfer. 1989. "The Influence of Race on Career Dynamics: Theory and Research on Minority Career Experiences." In Michael B. Arthur, Douglas T. Hall, and Barbara S. Lawrence, eds., *Handbook of Career Theory*. Cambridge: Cambridge University Press.

Thomas, David A., and Robin J. Ely. 1996. "Making Differences Matter: A New Paradigm for Managing Diversity." *Harvard Business Review* 74 (September/October): 79–90.

Thomas, David A., and John J. Gabarro. 1999. *Breaking Through: The Making of Minority Executives in Corporate America*. Boston: Harvard University Press.

Thomas, Jennifer C., and Paul Mohai. 1995. "Racial, Gender, and Professional Diversification in the Forest Service from 1983 to 1992." *Policy Studies Journal* 23 (Summer): 296–309.

Thomas, R. Roosevelt, Jr. 1990. "From Affirmative Action to Affirming Diversity." *Harvard Business Review* 68(2): 107–117.

_____. 1991. *Beyond Race and Gender: Unleashing the Power of Your Total Work Force by Managing Diversity.* New York: Amacom.

_____. 1996. *Redefining Diversity.* New York: Amacom.

_____. 1999. *Building a House for Diversity.* New York: Amacom.

Thompson, Frank J. 1976. "Minority Groups in Public Bureaucracies: Are Passive and Active Representation Linked?" *Administration and Society* 8 (August): 201–248.

Thornton, Arland, Duane F. Alwin, and Donald Camburn. 1983. "Causes and Consequences of Sex-Role Attitudes and Attitude Change." *American Sociological Review* 48 (April): 211–227.

Till, F. J. 1980. *Sexual Harassment: A Report on Sexual Harassment of Students.* Washington, DC: National Advisory Council on Women's Educational Programs.

Tomaskovic-Devey, Donald. 1994. "Race, Ethnic and Gender Earnings Inequality." Report prepared for the Glass Ceiling Commission, U.S. Department of Labor. January.

Trost, Cathy. 1990. "Women Managers Quit Not for Family But to Advance Their Corporate Climb." *The Wall Street Journal.* May 2.

Tsui, Anne S., and Charles A. O'Reilly III. 1989. "Beyond Simple Demographic Effects: The Importance of Relational Demography in Superior-Subordinate Dyads." *Academy of Management Journal* 32 (2): 402–423.

Turner, M. E., and A. R. Pratkanis. 1994. "Affirmative Action as Help: A Review of Recipient Reactions to Preferential Selection and Affirmative Action." *Basic and Applied Social Psychology* 15: 43–69.

"Two Minority Perspectives on Discrimination in the Federal Government." 1996. *Federal Human Resources Week* 3 (20, September 9): 312.

Ungar, Bernard L. 1991. *Federal Affirmative Action: Better EEOC Guidance and Agency Analysis of Underrepresentation Needed.* Statement before the Committee on Governmental Affairs, U.S. Senate, 102d Cong., 1st sess. May 16.

U.S. Bureau of the Census. 1996. *Statistical Abstract of the United States.* 116th ed. Washington, DC: U.S. Bureau of the Census.

_____. 1999. "Resident Population Estimates of the United States by Sex, Race, and Hispanic Origin: April 1, 1990 to October 1, 1999." http://www.census.gov/population/estimates/nation/intfile3–1.txt. November 29.

U.S. Civil Service Commission. 1973. *Biography of an Ideal.* Washington, DC: Civil Service Commission.

U.S. Department of Justice, Office of Legal Policy. 1987. *Redefining Discrimination: Disparate Impact and the Institutionalization of Affirmative Action.* Washington, DC: Government Printing Office.

U.S. Department of Labor. 1991a. *Directors Report Fiscal Year 1991.* Washington, DC: Office of Contract Compliance Programs, U.S. Department of Labor.

_____. 1991b. *Report on the Glass Ceiling Initiative.* Washington, DC: Office of Contract Compliance Programs, U.S. Department of Labor.

U.S. Equal Employment Opportunity Commission. 1980. "Discrimination Because of Sex Under Title VII of the Civil Rights Act of 1964, As Amended; Adoption of Final Interpretive Guidelines." 29 C.F.R. Part 1604. *Federal Register* 45: 219. November 10.

———. 1983. "Instructions for Preparing Multi-year Affirmative Action Plans for Minorities and Women, FY 82–FY 86." EEO-MD–707. Washington, DC: Equal Employment Opportunity Commission.

———. 1987. "Equal Employment Opportunity Management Directive." EEO-MD–714. Washington DC: Equal Employment Opportunity Commission.

———. 1997a. *Annual Report on the Employment of Minorities, Women and People With Disabilities in the Federal Government.* Washington, DC: U.S. Equal Employment Opportunity Commission.

———. 1997b. *Best Practices of Private Sector Employers.* Washington, DC: U.S. Equal Employment Opportunity Commission. December.

———. 1999a. "EEOC Chairwoman Announces Comprehensive Efforts to Improve Federal Government EEO Process." Press release. http://www.eeoc.gov/press/8–10–99.html. August 10.

———. 1999b. "Enforcement Guidance: Vicarious Employer Liability for Unlawful Harassment by Supervisors." http://www.eeoc.gov/docs/harassment.html. June 18.

———. Undated. "Equal Employment Opportunity and Affirmative Employment for Minorities, Women, and People with Disabilities." Unpublished paper.

U.S. General Accounting Office. 1991a. *Federal Workforce: Continuing Need for Federal Affirmative Employment.* GAO/GGD–92–27BR. Washington, DC: U.S. General Accounting Office.

———. 1991b. *Federal Affirmative Employment: Better EEOC Guidance and Agency Analysis of Underrepresentation Needed.* GAO-GGD–91–86. Washington, DC: U.S. General Accounting Office. May 10.

———. 1991c. *Federal Affirmative Employment: Status of Women and Minority Representation in the Federal Workforce.* GAO/T-GGD–92–2. Washington, DC: U.S. General Accounting Office. October 23.

———. 1992. *The Changing Workforce: Demographic Issues Facing the Federal Government.* GAO/GGD–92–38. Washington, DC: U.S. General Accounting Office. March.

———. 1993a. *Affirmative Employment: Assessing Progress of EEO Groups in Key Federal Jobs Can Be Improved.* GAO/GGD–93–65. Washington, DC: U.S. General Accounting Office. March.

———. 1993b. *Political Appointees: Ten-year Staffing Trends at 30 Agencies.* GAO/GGD–93–74FS. Washington DC: U.S. General Accounting Office.

———. 1994. *Equal Employment Opportunity: Displacement Rates, Unemployment Spells, and Reemployment Wages by Race.* GAO/HEHS–94–229FS. Washington, DC: U.S. General Accounting Office.

———. 1999. *Equal Employment Opportunity: Data Shortcomings Hinder Assessment of Conflicts in the Federal Workplace.* GAO/GGD–99–75. Washington, DC: U.S. General Accounting Office. May.

U.S. Merit Systems Protection Board. 1981. *Sexual Harassment in the Federal Workplace: Is It a Problem?* Washington, DC: U.S. Merit Systems Protection Board. March.

_____. 1988. *Sexual Harassment in the Federal Government: An Update.* Washington, DC: U.S. Merit Systems Protection Board. June.

_____. 1989. *First-line Supervisory Selection in the Federal Government.* Washington, DC: U.S. Merit Systems Protection Board. June.

_____. 1992. *A Question of Equity: Women and the Glass Ceiling in the Federal Government.* Washington, DC: U.S. Merit Systems Protection Board.

_____. 1993a. *Evolving Workforce Demographics: Federal Agency Action and Reaction.* Washington, DC: U.S. Merit Systems Protection Board.

_____. 1993b. *The Changing Face of the Federal Workforce: A Symposium on Diversity.* Washington, DC: U.S. Merit Systems Protection Board

_____. 1995. *Sexual Harassment in the Federal Workplace: Trends, Progress, Continuing Challenges.* Washington, DC: U.S. Merit Systems Protection Board. October.

_____. 1996. *Fair and Equitable Treatment: A Progress Report on Minority Employment in the Federal Government.* Washington, DC: U.S. Merit Systems Protection Board.

_____. 1997. *Achieving a Representative Federal Workforce: Addressing the Barriers to Hispanic Participation.* Washington, DC: U.S. Merit Systems Protection Board. September.

_____. 1999. *Federal Supervisors and Poor Performance.* Washington, DC: U.S. Merit Systems Protection Board.

U.S. Naval Air Warfare Center Weapons Division—China Lake. 1994. *The Glass Ceiling Seeking New Directions.* China Lake, CA: Naval Air Warfare Center Weapons Division.

U.S. Office of Personnel Management. 1979. "Policy Statement and Definition on Sexual Harassment." Memorandum to heads of departments and independent agencies December 12.

_____. 1994a. "The Status of the Senior Executive Service." Washington, DC: U.S. Office of Personnel Management.

_____. 1994b. *Annual Report to Congress, Federal Equal Opportunity Recruitment Program, October 1, 1994–September 30, 1995.* Washington, DC: U.S. Office of Personnel Management.

_____. 1995. *Minority/Nonminority Disparate Discharge Rates.* Washington, DC: U.S. Office of Personnel Management. April.

_____. 1997. *Federal Equal Opportunity Recruitment Program, October 1, 1996–September 30, 1997.* Washington, DC: U.S. Office of Personnel Management.

_____. 1999. *Hispanics in the Federal Government: A Statistical Profile.* Washington, DC: U.S. Office of Personnel Management. July.

Van Riper, Paul P. 1958. *History of the United States Civil Service.* Evanston, IL: Row, Peterson and Company.

Verba, S., and G. R. Orren. 1985. *Equality in America.* Cambridge, MA: Harvard University Press.

Vertz, Laura L. 1985. "Women, Occupational Advancement, and Mentoring: An Analysis of One Public Organization." *Public Administration Review* 45 (3, May/June): 415–423.

Vinciguerra, Jennifer L. 1994. "The Present State of Sexual Harassment Law." *Cleveland State Law Review* 42 (2): 301–337.

Walworth, Carla R., and Wendy Dunne DiChristina. 1994/1995. "The Long Road Back to Birmingham: Race-conscious Affirmative Action and Reverse Discrimination." *Employee Relations Law Journal* 20 (Winter): 407–419.

Warner, Rebecca L., Brent S. Steel, and Nicholas P. Lovrich. 1989. "Conditions Associated with the Advent of Representative Bureaucracy: The Case of Women in Policing." *Social Science Quarterly* 70 (September): 562–578.

Watson, Warren E., Lynn Johnson, and Deanna Merrit. 1998. "Team Orientation, Self-Orientation, and Diversity in Task Groups." *Group and Organization Management* 23 (2, June): 161–188.

Weber, Max. 1968. *Economy and Society*. New York: Bedminster Press.

Weiner, Tim. 1994. "The Nation: The Bias Suits Are Piling Up; The Men in the Gray Federal Bureaucracy." *The New York Times*, April 10: sec. 4, p. 4.

Welch, Susan, et al. 1998. "Black and White Perceptions of Racial Discrimination." Paper presented to the annual meeting of the Midwest Political Science Association, Chicago, IL. April 22–25.

Wick and Company. 1990. *Don't Blame the Baby: Why Women Leave Corporations*. Wilmington, DE: Wick and Company.

Wilcox, Clyde. 1991. "Support for Gender Equality in Western Europe." *European Journal of Political Research* 20: 127–147.

Williams, Christine L. 1992. "The Glass Escalator: Hidden Advantages for Men in 'Female' Professions." *Social Problems* 39 (August): 253–267.

Willoughby, W. F. 1927. *Principles of Public Administration*. Washington, DC: The Brookings Institution.

Wilson, Trevor. 1997. *Diversity at Work: The Business Case for Equity*. Toronto: John Wiley.

Wilson, Woodrow. 1887. "The Study of Administration." *Political Science Quarterly* 2 (June): 197–222.

Wise, Lois R. 1990. "Social Equity in Civil Service Systems." *Public Administration Review* 50 (September/October): 567–575.

Witt, L. Alan. 1990. "Equal Opportunity Perceptions and Job Attitudes." *Journal of Social Psychology* 13 (3): 431–433.

Wong, Samuel. 1994. *Neither Black nor White: A New American Dilemma*. Washington, DC: U.S. Department of Agriculture. September.

Woo, Deborah. 1994. "The Glass Ceiling and Asian Americans." Paper prepared for the Federal Glass Ceiling Commission, U.S. Department of Labor. July.

Wylie, Janet C. 1996. *Chances and Choices: How Women Can Succeed in Today's Knowledge-Based Businesses*. Vienna, VA: EBW Press.

Xin, Katherine R. 1997. "Asian American Managers: An Impression Gap?" *Journal of Applied Behavioral Science* 33 (3, September): 335–355.

Yeakey, Carol C. 1993. "The Social Consequences of Public Policy." *Journal of Negro Education* 62 (2, Spring): 125–143.

Zwerling, C., and H. Silver. 1992. "Race and Job Dismissals in a Federal Bureaucracy." *American Sociological Review* 57: 651–660.

Index